The Co

By the same author

Antique or Fake?
Cabinet Making for Beginners
Carpentry for Beginners
The Complete Book of Woodwork
English Period Furniture
Furniture Repairs
Making Toys in Wood
Period Furniture Designs
Practical Veneering
Staining and Polishing
Woodwork Joints
The Woodworker's Pocket Book
Woodworker's Question Box
Practical Woodcarving and Gilding
(with W. Wheeler)

The Complete Book of Woodwork

Charles H. Hayward

BELL & HYMAN LIMITED
London

Published by Bell & Hyman Limited, Denmark House,
37–39 Queen Elizabeth Street, London SE1 2QB

First published by Evans Brothers Limited in 1955

This edition completely revised and reset
Fourth printing 1978
Published in paperback 1983

Set in 9 on 10 point Univers by
Photoprint Plates Limited, Rayleigh, Essex
and printed in Great Britain by
Hazell Watson & Viney Ltd,
Aylesbury, Bucks

ISBN 0 7135 1422 1

Contents

Metrication

The changeover from Imperial to metric measurement has resulted in certain complications in the dimensions given in this book for both tools and designs. So far as tools are concerned it makes little difference because the exact length of a plane, saw, or whatever it may be does not affect its working. Generally we have given both metric and Imperial sizes but it will be realised that none of them will work out exactly. In the designs and their cutting lists we have kept to metric sizes as timber nowadays is nearly all sold to these dimensions. Those who prefer to work to Imperial sizes should use the following conversion table, or better still should use a flexible rule which has metric sizes at one edge and Imperial at the other. Remember, however, that the conversion will not work out exactly, but providing one keeps to one or the other throughout, there should not be any difficulty. Another useful detail to note is that in the timber trade 25mm. is taken as equalling 1in. Here again it is not exact, and in a large item there will be a marked divergence which should be allowed for.

Woodworkers' Conversion Tables

Imperial inches	Metric millimetres	Woodworkers' parlance (mm.)		Metric millimetres	Imperial inches	Woodworkers' parlance (in.)	
$\frac{1}{32}$	0·8	1	bare	1	0·039	$\frac{1}{16}$	bare
$\frac{1}{16}$	1·6	$1\frac{1}{2}$		2	0·078	$\frac{1}{16}$	full
$\frac{1}{8}$	3·2	3	full	3	0·118	$\frac{1}{8}$	bare
$\frac{3}{16}$	4·8	5	bare	4	0·157	$\frac{5}{32}$	
$\frac{1}{4}$	6·4	$6\frac{1}{2}$		5	0·196	$\frac{3}{16}$	full
$\frac{5}{16}$	7·9	8	bare	6	0·236	$\frac{1}{4}$	bare
$\frac{3}{8}$	9·5	$9\frac{1}{2}$		7	0·275	$\frac{1}{4}$	full
$\frac{7}{16}$	11·1	11	full	8	0·314	$\frac{5}{16}$	
$\frac{1}{2}$	12·7	$12\frac{1}{2}$	full	9	0·354	$\frac{3}{8}$	bare
$\frac{9}{16}$	14·3	$14\frac{1}{2}$	bare	10	0·393	$\frac{3}{8}$	full
$\frac{5}{8}$	15·9	16	bare	20	0·787	$\frac{13}{16}$	bare
$\frac{11}{16}$	17·5	$17\frac{1}{2}$		30	1·181	$1\frac{3}{16}$	
$\frac{3}{4}$	19·1	19	full	40	1·574	$1\frac{9}{16}$	full
$\frac{13}{16}$	20·6	$20\frac{1}{2}$		50	1·968	$1\frac{15}{16}$	full
$\frac{7}{8}$	22·2	22	full	60	2·362	$2\frac{3}{8}$	bare
$\frac{15}{16}$	23·8	24	bare	70	2·755	$2\frac{3}{4}$	
1	25·4	$25\frac{1}{2}$		80	3·148	$3\frac{1}{4}$	full
2	50·8	51	bare	90	3·542	$3\frac{9}{16}$	bare
3	76·2	76	full	100	3·936	$3\frac{15}{16}$	
4	101·4	$101\frac{1}{2}$		150	5·904	$5\frac{15}{16}$	bare
5	127·0	127		200	7·872	$7\frac{7}{8}$	
6	152·4	$152\frac{1}{2}$		300	11·808	$11\frac{13}{16}$	
7	177·5	178	bare	400	15·744	$15\frac{3}{4}$	
8	203·2	203	full	500	19·680	$19\frac{11}{16}$	
9	228·6	$228\frac{1}{2}$		600	23·616	$23\frac{5}{8}$	bare
10	254·0	254		700	27·552	$27\frac{9}{16}$	
11	279·5	$279\frac{1}{2}$		800	31·488	$31\frac{1}{2}$	
12	304·8	305	bare	900	35·424	$35\frac{7}{16}$	
18	457·2	457	full	1,000	39·360	$39\frac{3}{8}$	bare
24	609·6	$609\frac{1}{2}$					
36	914·4	$914\frac{1}{2}$					

Introduction

Woodwork is a subject with many branches, each of which calls for a book in itself if it is to be dealt with adequately. Many people, however, need a general book which includes information on all the branches of woodwork which the home craftsman is likely to tackle. So this book was written. It does not pretend to cover any particular subject as fully as a book which specializes in that branch, but it does give all basic information, and in this sense it should be the best all-round book for the comparative beginner in the subject.

More people are doing woodwork as a hobby to-day than at any other period, and it is one of the most heartening signs of this age when the temptation to accept things ready-made is almost irresistible. Just as it is so much easier to listen to the music of radio or gramophone than to produce it yourself, so it is simpler to accept the product of the machine which in an effortless way turns out uniform items with a speed and regularity equalled only by its lack of individuality and feeling for the material.

If we have more leisure to-day than ever before, there is so much more temptation to do nothing useful with it. Radio, television, motoring, and the cinema all have their place in the scheme of things, but only too often they claim far more than their share of our spare time, and leave little to show for themselves. Thus it is, one hails this renaissance of handwork with relief, for through it comes the realization of what honesty of construction stands for, and an appreciation of the value of good design. And it is in this that the chief hope for the future lies.

Chapter one

Tools   The Kit

The selection of tools depends to an extent upon the type of work generally to be done, but there is a fundamental range which is always needed. The choice of individual items may vary slightly with the stature and the age of the user, but the list given on pages 11–17 makes a good representative kit, and we have marked with an asterisk the items the beginner should start with. As he progresses the necessity for other tools will become obvious. He can obtain them as the need makes itself felt.

Do not buy a 'complete box of tools'. If you do you will be accepting what someone else thinks you ought to have, and you will have to take the whole without being able to exercise any judgement on the individual items. Quite likely, too, you will pay for some items which you will never use, or which may be unsuitable for you. The best plan is to go to a reliable tool dealer and tell him what you want, explaining that you do not want 'cheap' tools (in fact they are not cheap in the long run). A good, sound tool should last you a lifetime (some last several lifetimes), and, though you pay more for it in the first place, it will easily repay its cost. It may easily happen that in buying a poor quality tool you may be handicapping yourself from the start. A plane or square which is inaccurate; a chisel or screwdriver which is soft; a stone which is liable to become hard; any of these may cause endless and quite unnecessary trouble in the future.

The choice of tools on pages 11–17 has been made on the assumption that the reader is a comparative beginner, and as such is not likely to be considering at present the installation of any machines. Those who have had some experience will know that much back-aching work can be saved by having a small machine, and we therefore give in Chapter VI some advice on the choice and installation of suitable machines. Those who propose to install a machine could modify the kit of hand tools in accordance with the operations the machine can tackle.

It pays in the long run to buy tools by a reputable maker. Faults in poor quality tools such as inaccuracy, second grade metal or bad design soon make themselves felt.

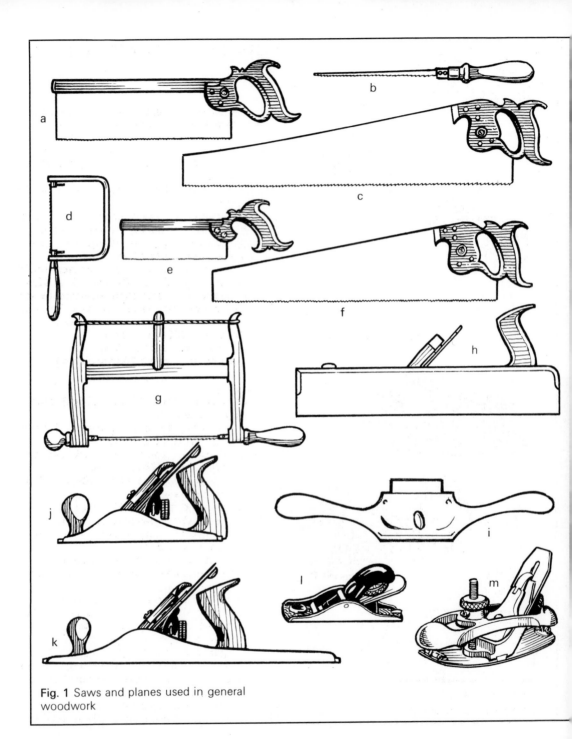

Fig. 1 Saws and planes used in general
woodwork

Fundamental Kit of Tools

Fig. 1 Special-purpose planes

Items marked with an asterisk are what we suggest the beginner should start off with.

Saws (Fig. 1)

*(C) Cross-cut saw, 610 or 660mm. (24 or 26in.), teeth 8 or 9 points.

(F) Panel saw, 500mm. (20in.), teeth 10–12 points.

*(A) Tenon saw, 350 or 400mm. (14 or 16in.), teeth 12 or 14 points, brass or iron back.

(E) Dovetail saw, 200mm. (8in.), teeth 18–22 points, brass or iron back.
(If you wish to limit your kit you could substitute a 230 or 250mm. (9 or 10in.) backsaw with teeth about 16 points for the tenon saw and the dovetail saw. The two saws are the better choice, however.)

(G) Bow saw, 300mm. (12in.).

(D) Coping saw, 150mm. (6in.).

(B) Keyhole saw, about 280mm. (11in.).

Planes (Fig. 1)

*(H) Jack plane, wood, 400mm. (16in.), 50mm. (2in.) cutter.

*(J) Smoothing plane, adjustable metal, 228mm. (9in.), 50mm. (2in.) cutter.

(K) Fore plane, adjustable metal, 457mm. (18in.), 60mm. ($2\frac{3}{8}$in.) cutter.

(Q) Toothing plane, wood, 50mm. (2in.) cutter, medium teeth.

(L) Block plane, 42mm. ($1\frac{5}{8}$in.) cutter.

(M) Compass plane, 44mm. ($1\frac{3}{4}$in.) cutter.

(R) Rebate plane, metal adjustable fillister, 38mm. ($1\frac{1}{2}$in.) cutter.

(P) Bullnose plane, 25mm. (1in.) cutter.

(N) Shoulder plane, 25mm. (1in.) or 31mm. ($1\frac{1}{4}$in.) cutter.

(I) Scraper plane, 70mm. ($2\frac{3}{4}$in.) blade.

(S) Plough plane, metal. Wide range available. Smallest works grooves, 4mm., 6mm., 12mm., also $\frac{1}{8}$in., $\frac{3}{16}$in., and $\frac{1}{4}$in. Larger sizes up to 12·7mm. ($\frac{1}{8}$in. to $\frac{9}{16}$in.) Also the combination which works beads in addition. Get the best you can afford, but even the smallest works well.

(O) Router, metal adjustable.

(T) Moulding planes. Obtain only as required.

Chisels and Gouges (Fig. 2)

(A)   Firmer chisels, *25mm. (1in.), 13mm. ($\frac{1}{2}$in.) *6mm. ($\frac{1}{4}$in.), 3mm. ($\frac{1}{8}$in.).

(B)   Bevelled-edge chisels, 31mm. (1$\frac{1}{4}$in.), *19mm. ($\frac{3}{4}$in.)

(C)   Sash mortise chisels, 6mm. ($\frac{1}{4}$in.), *8mm. ($\frac{5}{16}$in.), 10mm. ($\frac{3}{8}$in.).

(F)   Drawer lock chisel.

(D)   Firmer gouges   }   Obtain only
(E)   Scribing gouges   }   as needed.
      page 108.

Brace and Bits, etc. (Fig. 2)

(G)   Ratchet brace, 200mm. or 250mm. (8in. or 10in.) sweep.

(O)   Twist bits, *6mm. ($\frac{1}{4}$in.), *10mm. ($\frac{3}{8}$in), 12·5mm. ($\frac{1}{2}$in.), 19mm. ($\frac{3}{4}$in.)

*(J)   Drill bits, 3mm. to 6mm. ($\frac{1}{8}$in. to $\frac{1}{4}$in.). (Used mainly for screw holes) Alternatively, engineer's drills can be used.

(K)   Forstner bits. Obtain as needed.

(H, I) Countersinks, *snail and rose.

(M)   Centre bits, 12·5mm. ($\frac{1}{2}$in.), *19mm. ($\frac{3}{4}$in.), 25mm. (1in.).

(L)   Turnscrew bit.

(N)   Expansion bit.

*(P)   Bradawls. Birdcage maker's (square in section is preferable). Get two of varying sizes. Dowelling jig. Enables bits of various sizes to be used. Needs only one setting. See page 108.

Marking-out Tools (Fig. 2)

*(W)   Try square, 300mm (12in), preferably engineer's type with sliding blade.

(Q)   Try square, 600mm. (24in.), wood, home-made. Those having a steel roofing square will prefer this.

(X)   Mitre square, 300mm. (12in.).

(Y)   Adjustable or sliding bevel, 250mm. (10in.).

(Z)   Straight-edges, 450mm. (18in.) and 910mm. (3ft.) wood, home-made.

*(T)   Rule, metric, folding.

*(R)   Gauge, cutting.

(R)   Gauge, marking.

(S)   Gauge, mortise.

(U)   Dividers, 150mm. (6in.) with fine screw adjustment.

(V)   Parallel strips.

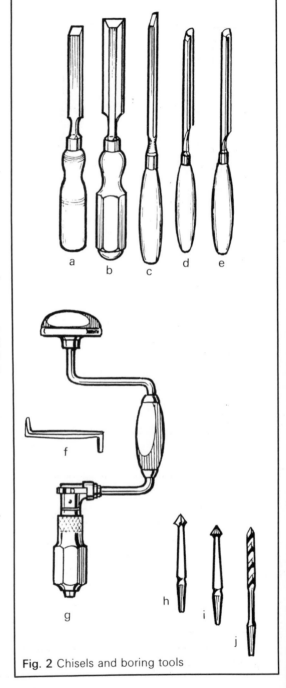

Fig. 2 Chisels and boring tools

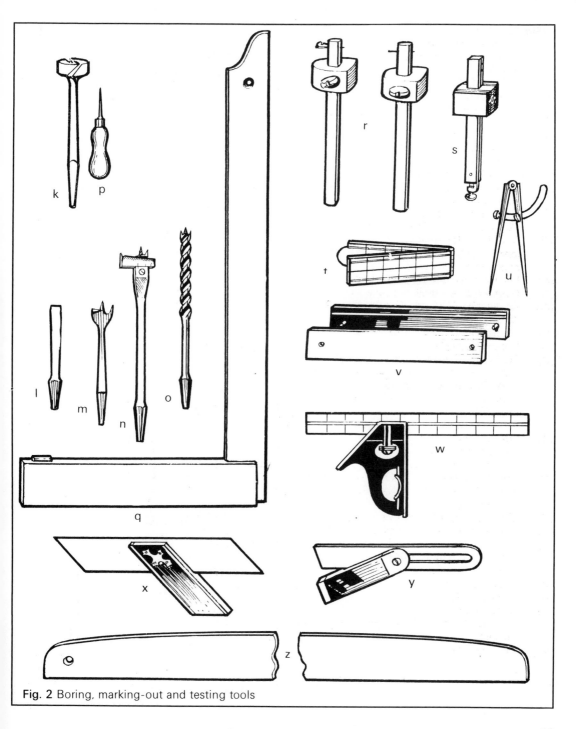

Fig. 2 Boring, marking-out and testing tools

General Tools (Fig. 3)

* (A) Hammer, Warrington or London pattern, about 8oz. Hammer, pattern maker's, about 3oz.
* (C) Mallet, about 150mm. (6in.) head.
* (B) Pincers, 200mm. (8in.).
* (D) Punches, hollow point. One for small panel pins, other larger.
  (E) Screwdrivers, *200mm. (8in.), cabinet type.
* (F, G) 120mm. (5in.) ratchet, and fine. You need screwdrivers for screws ranging from about 12's to about 2's.
  (I, J) Wood file, half-round, 180mm. (7in.) rat tail; 150mm. (6in.).
  (H) Wood rasp, half-round, 180mm. (7in.).
  (L) Spokeshave, *wood, about 60mm. (2$\frac{1}{4}$in.) cutter.
  (M) Spokeshave, metal, round-face, 50mm. (2in.) cutter.
  (N) Scraper, *cabinet, 125mm. (5in.). About 1·2mm. ($\frac{3}{64}$in.) thick.
  (O) Shaped cabinet scraper.
* (K) Oilstone, medium or fine grade, or combination fine-coarse, India, Carborundum, Unirundum, etc., 200 by 50mm. (8in by 2in.)
  (P) Oilstone slip, having two varying rounded edges.
* (R) Cork rubber, about 110mm. (4$\frac{1}{2}$in.)
  (S) Veneering hammer, home-made.
  (Q) Scratch-stock, home-made.
  (T) Shaper tool. Various patterns available; flat, half-round, circular.

Tools and metrication. Except in a few cases metrication scarcely affects tools. The exact length of a saw or plane, for instance, is not in any sense critical. Generally the Imperial sizes are maintained and the nearest metric equivalent stamped on them. Possible exceptions are certain grooving plane cutters which may have to be made to suit plywood made to metric thicknesses or chisels to suit fittings made in metric sizes.

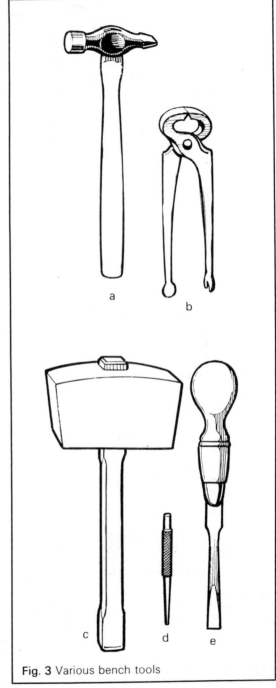

a b c d e

Fig. 3 Various bench tools

14

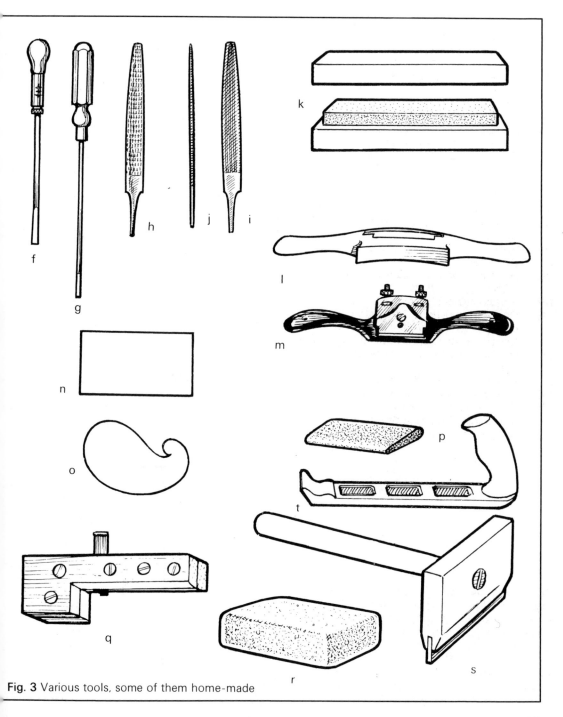

Fig. 3 Various tools, some of them home-made

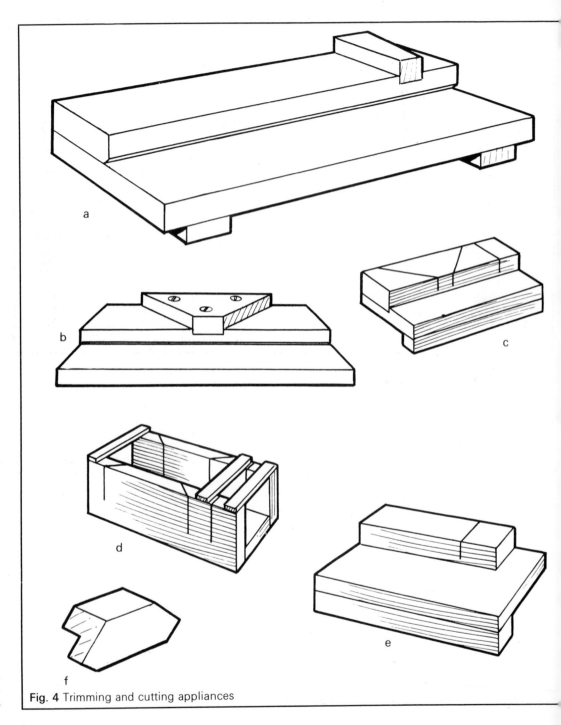

a

b

c

d

e

f

Fig. 4 Trimming and cutting appliances

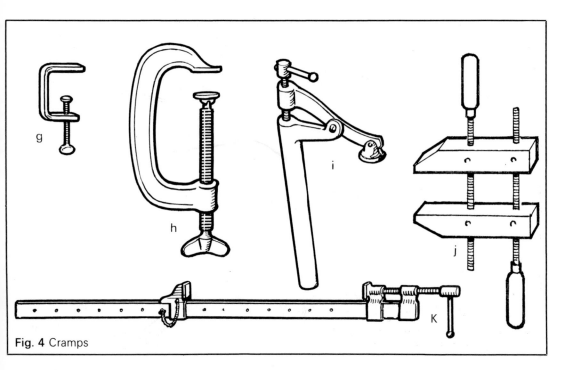

Fig. 4 Cramps

(A) Shooting board, about *600mm. (2ft.) and 1·5m. (5ft.), home-made.
(B) Mitre shooting board, about 450mm. (18in.)
*(C) Mitre block, about 220mm. (9in.), home-made.
(D) Mitre box, for mouldings up to 100mm. (4in.) home-made.
*(E) Bench hook, about 180mm. (7in.), home-made.
(F) Mitre template, home-made.

Cramps (Fig. 4)

(K) Sash cramps, metal, pair about 600mm. (2ft.), pair about 1·2m (4ft.)
*(J) Handscrews, pair about 200mm. (8in.) More as needed.
(H) G cramps. Alternatives to handscrews.
(G) Thumbscrews, 80–100mm. (3–4in.) About 6 at least.
(I) Bench holdfast.

CBOW—2**

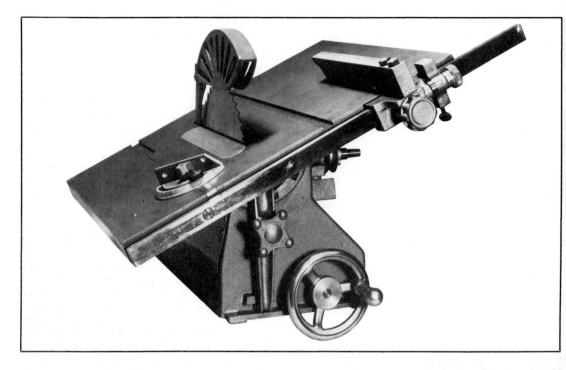

Fig. 5 Small bench circular saw with tilting table, ripping fence and mitre gauge. (photo: courtesy of Parry and Sons (Tools) Ltd.)

As soon as possible after obtaining your tools make yourself a container of some sort for them. It may be a simple box, cupboard, or be built into the bench. Remember to allow for expansion. You will undoubtedly buy more tools later, and it is as well to allow for what you envisage as your eventual kit.

Try to arrange things so that edge tools do not come into contact with each other; chisels and saws in racks, planes in compartments, and so on. It will save you a lot of time in the long run in that you will avoid gashed edges, etc. It is possible to obtain a special paper known as V.P.I. (Vapour Phase Inhibitor) which prevents rust. A sheet of this in the tool box, and renewed from time to time, will save much trouble in this connection.

Circular saw. Of the many machines available to the home craftsman the circular saw is the most generally useful. Apart from ripping, cross-cutting, and mitreing it can be used for grooving, rebating, and in some cases for moulding. Essential features of the machine are rise-and-fall saw or table, ripping fence, mitre gauge, crown guard, and preferably a canting table or saw.

An alternative to the above is the basic lathe with various attachments such as circular saw, band saw, disc sander, belt sander, mortiser, planer with thicknessing attachment. One of the advantages of this lathe machine is the small space it occupies, an obvious benefit in the small workshop. Additionally it is less costly than buying several separate machines. Those who have the space, however, and are not worried by cost will find that machines designed to do one type of work are more effective than one machine which has to be designed to do several jobs.

Chapter two

How to Maintain and Use Tools

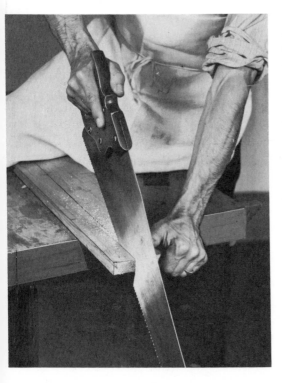

You can learn the chief points to note about using tools in this chapter, but, to quote an old adage, skill to do comes of doing.

Saws

Handsaw. This is used for cutting the larger pieces of wood. For instance, having marked out on a board the pieces you need, you cut them out with the handsaw. Choose a cross-cut saw as distinct from a rip-saw, because this can be used for cutting both with and across the grain. You can saw either with the wood laid on trestles or boxes, or on the bench, or held in the vice. It is just a matter of which is the most convenient.

Fig. 1 shows the method of sawing on trestles or boxes. Start the cut with the saw held at a low angle as in Fig. 2 because in this way you will be able to see whether the saw is in alignment with the line. This is most important because if you start wrong the saw will continue to go wrong, and in endeavouring to put it right you will probably err the other way. To start the cut hold the left hand over the end of the wood and raise the thumb so that the saw can bear against it as in Fig. 3. This steadies the blade and enables you to start it in the exact position. Once the cut has been started a short way the hand can be brought back and used to help steady the wood.

Move the saw up and down a few times so that the teeth find their way into the wood, and when a reasonable start has been made hold the saw so that it makes an angle about 45 deg. with the wood. It can then be worked in long, full, steady strokes. Forcing should never be necessary. If it cuts badly or slowly it needs sharpening. Apply light pressure on the down stroke to keep it up to its work. Note

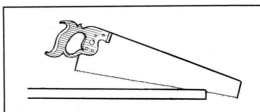

Fig. 2 (above) Start with the saw held at a low angle

Fig. 1 (left) Ripping a board with the handsaw

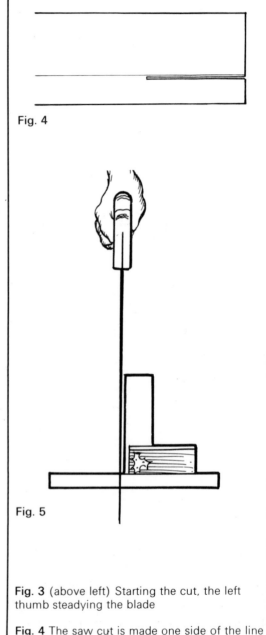

Fig. 4

Fig. 5

from Fig. 1 how the first finger of the right hand points along the blade. This is a great help in giving control.

Invariably the cut is made to one side of the line so that the plane can be used to trim the wood to the finished size. The idea is shown in Fig. 4. It is a help if the line is not hidden by the saw. Thus when practicable place the wood so that the saw cuts to the right of the line. Sometimes this cannot be done, but it is an advantage to have the line visible. Remember that the saw must always be on the waste side of the line.

It is clearly necessary to hold the saw upright. Undercutting may result in the wood being too small, and if the cut runs the other way a lot of unnecessary work in planing is involved. As a guide place a square of wood as in Fig. 5. You will not want to keep it there all the time, but it will give you an indication of whether the saw is upright. Try to get the feel of the position when it is upright, and look at your edge after sawing to see whether you err one way or the other. It is worth while taking trouble early on because it will save you a great deal of work in other operations.

Fig. 3 (above left) Starting the cut, the left thumb steadying the blade

Fig. 4 The saw cut is made one side of the line

Fig. 5 Guide to holding the saw upright

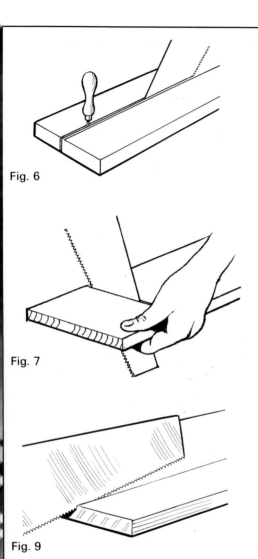

Fig. 6

Fig. 7

Fig. 9

Fig. 6 Preventing the wood binding on the saw

Fig. 7 Supporting overhand on completion of cut

Fig. 8 (above right) Overhand ripping on the bench

Fig. 9 Starting the cut for the overhand rip

It sometimes happens when you have a long cut to make that the kerf will tend to close so that the wood binds on the saw. A bradawl stuck to the kerf as in Fig. 6 will keep it open and prevent binding.

When cross-cutting a board never arrange the wood so that the cut is between the trestles. It will only cause the wood to bend as the cut progresses, and at best will cause the saw to bind. At worst the wood will snap off. Instead arrange the wood so that the piece to be sawn off overhangs at one end. The start of the cut is much as has already been described, but as the cut reaches its completion the left hand should be brought over so that the wood is supported as in Fig. 7. Otherwise it is liable to splinter off, especially when the overhanging piece is of any great size.

Another method of ripping is what is known as the overhand rip shown in Fig. 8. Many consider it less back-aching. The wood is cramped down on to the bench with the line to be sawn overhanging the edge. To start the cut a few strokes are made with the saw pointed upwards (Fig. 9). As soon as a short cut has been made the upright position is assumed, the saw grasped in both hands, and used for its full stroke. In some ways it is easier to tell when the saw is being held upright.

When the cut has to be along the middle of the board and it is inconvenient to fix it to the bench, you can lay the board on trestles and use the overhand rip, sitting astride the wood.

Comparatively short cuts or cuts in short wood are generally best made with the wood held in the vice as in Fig. 10. Do not give it more projection than is essential as otherwise it will chatter. To an extent it depends upon the thickness, but 22mm. ($\frac{7}{8}$in.) stuff, say, should project about 200mm. (8in.). As the saw approaches the bench top the wood is raised in the vice. Remember to see that no tools are lying on the bench top, otherwise the saw may foul them.

The back saw is used for the general cutting up of smaller pieces, cutting joints and so on. It is a matter for discretion whether the tenon saw or the dovetail saw is used. Sometimes it is convenient to hold the wood in the vice; sometimes the bench hook is better; occasionally it is desirable to fix the wood to the bench with a cramp.

Exact sizes are not important in a bench hook. The dimensions given in Fig. 11 can be taken as a general guide. Note, however, that the lower strip which bears against the edge of the bench is held with a dowel at the end where the saw operates. This is because the saw eventually scores a rut across the wood with continual use, and a screw would be liable to be bared and so blunt the saw. Screws or nails can be used for fixing at the other end.

Fig. 12 shows the bench hook in use. Note how the ball of the left hand presses on to the edge of the wood being sawn, so keeping it up to the back of the hook. The lower edging of the bench hook prevents movement due to thrust from the saw, but unless the wood is kept up to the back it is liable to shift at the return stroke. The thumb of the left hand is used to steady the saw when the cut is started, as shown. Begin by raising the saw handle slightly so that the far corner is sawn first, and gradually lower it as the cut proceeds. For work of great accuracy, as when sawing the shoulders of a tenon, make a few strokes in this way, then start at the front corner. It is a matter of just bringing the saw level, so joining the two cuts.

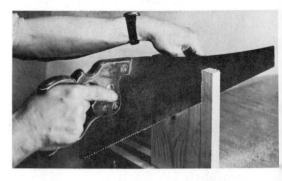

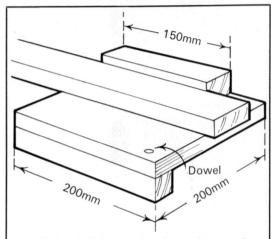

Fig. 10 (top) Using the handsaw, the wood held in a vice
Fig. 11 (above) The bench hook
Fig. 12 (opposite) The use of the bench hook when sawing. The left hand presses the wood hard up against the back of the hook to prevent it from moving backwards

Learning to cut square is of great importance. A useful help in this respect is to square the line round on to all four surfaces of a thick block. Cut down about 2mm. ($\frac{1}{8}$in.) on one surface, turn the wood once towards you so that this cut faces you and make a second cut also about 2mm. ($\frac{1}{8}$in.) deep on the surface now on top. Repeat this until you have sawn all four surfaces, then gradually deepen each cut in turn. In this way the saw tends to run into the cuts already made.

When an end must be sawn perfectly square, as

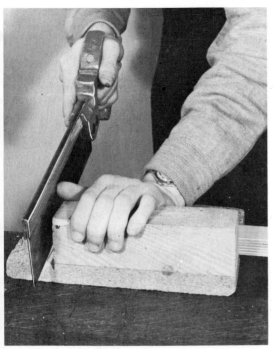

when dowelling or when sawing shoulders, it is a great help if the line is squared across with the chisel. By making a sloping cut against the line on the waste side a channel is formed in which the saw can run. This is shown in Fig. 4, page 107.

When the cut is being made with the wood held in the vice, make sure that the wood is level. Otherwise it will be awkward to saw to the line. On this score, when a cut has to be made at an angle it is a help to position the wood so that the cut is vertical. In this way it is only necessary to hold the saw upright. This idea is often useful when sawing dovetails, the wood being fixed at a slight angle so that the saw is used upright.

Never try to use the saw without supporting the wood in one of the ways mentioned. Wood which is not firmly held will shift about, making the sawing difficult, and may result in a buckled saw blade. If you turn to Fig. 13a and b you will see that a pivoted end support to the bench is suggested. This is excellent for holding wood whilst being sawn. Another and still simpler plan is to bore a 12·5mm. ($\frac{1}{2}$in.) hole through the bench top near the tail, and knock a length of dowel rod into it as at

(C). It can be tapped down flush when not in use. At all events avoid the bad practice of holding the wood against the bench stop when cutting right through. Eventually the saw scores a deep furrow, and when the stop is used for planing the wood is liable to tilt into the gash(see F).

For general sawing the bench hook is perfectly satisfactory, but when it is essential that the wood is held more rigidly you can use either the holdfast at (D) or the handscrew or cramp at (E). The former is extremely handy, but needs a fairly thick top to be effective as it relies upon the angularity of the post in the hole in the bench top to obtain its grip. If the top is thin you will have to thickness it on the underside locally. Of course, there must be clear space beneath. Some holdfasts have a metal socket for recessing into the bench top.

Saws for curves. For fairly large curves in, say, 22mm. ($\frac{7}{8}$in.) wood the most generally useful tool is the bow saw (see page 25). Its blade is held in tension by a tourniquet arrangement, and with its handles can be turned to cut in any direction. The advantage of the latter is that it enables a shape to be cut which is more or less parallel with an edge. It will be realized that when set square the saw can only cut in from an edge a distance equal to that of the blade from the cross bar. By turning the handles, however, the saw can cut along the wood parallel with the edge. It is important that the blade is not twisted.

Square sawing is clearly important, as otherwise a great deal of unnecessary cleaning up is involved —in fact it may easily happen that the wood is spoilt by being undercut. It is purely a matter of judgment and practice. The best plan is to test your work as you saw it, note whether you are tending to cut one way or the other, and endeavour to correct it in future cutting. You can tell within a little whether the blade is square with the work. Fig. 14 shows the bow saw in use.

When a cut is to be made internally in the wood, that is, not emerging at the edge, it is necessary to bore a hole in the wood big enough to allow the saw blade to be passed through. This is bored on the waste side of the line, of course. The blade is held by a rivet which is easily punched out.

Generally the wood is held in the vice and it is

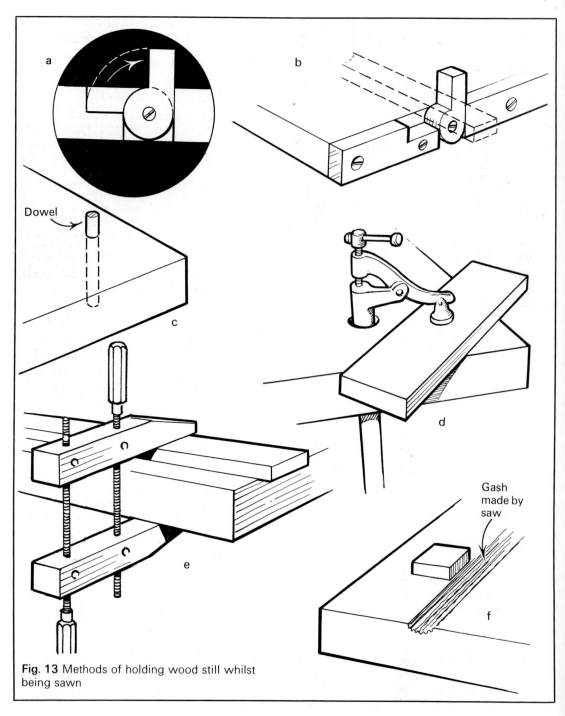

a

b

Dowel

c

d

e

Gash made by saw

f

Fig. 13 Methods of holding wood still whilst being sawn

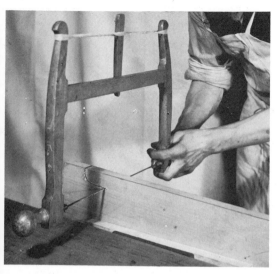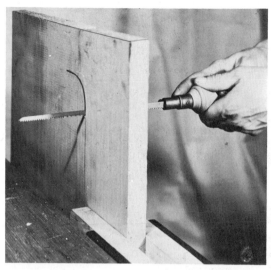

advisable to keep it as low as possible to avoid vibration. This may necessitate raising the wood once or twice, but it makes the sawing much easier. Grasp the handle with both hands and work in long strokes, gradually turning the saw so that it follows the curve.

Another saw which has similar uses but is for smaller work is the coping saw (p. 10). In this case the wood is frequently horizontal, and is fixed so that it overhangs the bench top. Avoid too great an overhang as this will cause chatter. Here upright cutting is essential. For a start you can hold a small square near the blade as a guide, but soon you should be able to do without it. Tension in this case is secured by turning the handle.

Used in this way the teeth of the saw point towards the handle. Sometimes, however, it is more convenient to hold the wood upright in the vice, and in this case it is better to point the teeth away from the handle so that the rag from the saw is at the back of the wood. Really thin wood is cut with the fretsaw, and a special table with a V cut at the projecting end is used.

Sometimes an internal cut has to be made at a distance from the edge too far for the bow saw to reach. You then have to use the keyhole saw. It is not a very efficient tool, however, as the blade has to rely upon its stiffness to keep it from buckling. The rule then is to give the blade the minimum

projection consistent with a reasonable stroke. Fortunately not many cuts of this kind occur in woodwork, and the chief use of the saw is in sawing the side of keyholes when fitting locks. You could, of course, use a bow saw if necessary, but it would involve taking out the rivet and threading the blade through the hole to make two short cuts. Fig. 15 shows the saw in use for a larger curve. Note that both hands grasp the handle.

Generally it is not advisable for the beginner to sharpen his own saws, as he will probably file the teeth unevenly, and a professional saw sharpener would charge more to put right the damage than the money saved. If you do decide to make the attempt, start on the saw with the largest teeth.

You will realize that, in addition to filing, the teeth have to be set—that is bent outwards alternately right and left. This is an essential feature of a saw in that it makes a kerf slightly wider than the thickness of its blade. Without it the saw would bind in the wood. The sharpener will give just the amount which experience has shown to be necessary. Excessive set is to be avoided since it means that you are removing wood unnecessarily (and so working harder than you need with no advantage).

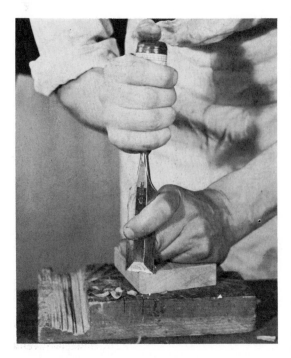

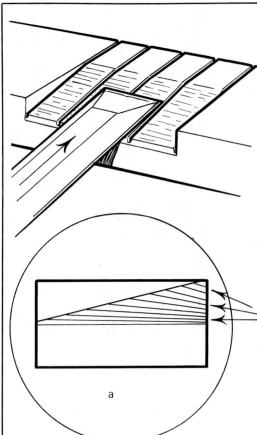

Chisels and Gouges

Apart from chisels made for special jobs, there are three general kinds: firmer, bevelled-edge, and mortise. Of these the first (A, Fig. 2, p. 12) is the bench tool for general purposes. It is robustly made so that it will stand up to the work involved in chopping dovetails and other joints, yet can if necessary be used for finer work such as paring. The latter, however, is better done with a lighter chisel kept specially for the job, the bevelled-edge chisel shown at (B, Fig. 2, p. 12). Mortising, which calls for heavy blows with the mallet, and for a certain amount of levering over, needs the specially made chisel (C, Fig. 2, p. 12). Two kinds are available, the heavy mortise chisel, and the lighter sash mortise which is strong enough for most work without being so cumbersome.

Paring. A typical operation, that of paring a groove, is shown in Fig. 18. The left hand can either be held as shown, or the fingers can be brought up over the top leaving the thumb below. In all cases, no matter what the operation, both

Fig. 16 (left) Cutting down the corner of wood with the chisel

Fig. 17 (above) Stages in chiselling the groove

hands are behind the cutting edge. In a job of this kind the sides of the groove are sawn first, and one or two intermediate, shallower cuts are made to break up the grain. The chisel is then taken in at a slight angle as in Fig. 17, the handle being struck either with the palm of the hand or the mallet. The waste is removed down to about the diagonal. Then, reversing the wood, work from the other side as at A. Finish off as in Fig. 18, using the chisel with a slicing action if possible. This not only eases the cut, but shows more clearly the high parts which need reducing.

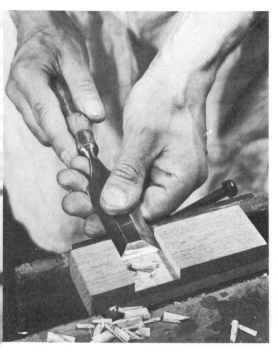

Fig. 16 shows another typical paring operation. The wood must be held on a flat surface, as any unevenness may cause the lower edge to split out.

Fig. 18 (left) Paring groove with bevelled-edge chisel
Fig. 19 (above) Chopping a mortise

Mortising. Fig. 19 shows a door stile being mortised, and there are several points to note. Firstly the worker stands at the end of the wood, because it is then obvious whether the chisel leans to the right or left (it is clearly important that the mortise is upright). Secondly the wood is cramped down over a solid part of the bench, generally the leg. Also a thumbscrew is put on at the end to prevent any tendency for the wood to split. It is usual to leave about 25mm. (1in.) of wood beyond the mortise to minimise this risk, but even so the thumbscrew is advisable. When several stiles are being mortised they can be cramped together side by side. To lighten the work much of the waste can be removed by boring a series of holes with a twist bit slightly narrower than the mortise width.

The first cut is made at about the centre of the mortise and is shallow only. The next, about 3mm. ($\frac{1}{8}$in.) from the first, is deeper, and so until within about 1mm. ($\frac{1}{16}$in.) of the end when much of the waste can be levered away. A slightly narrower

chisel is useful for this. Work up to the other end in the same way, levering away the waste as you proceed. The depth, of course, has already been decided, and it is useful to stick a piece of paper to the chisel as a depth guide. When the mortise has been cleared in this way the final cuts can be taken on the lines at each end. This cleans up the dubbed-over ends caused by the levering.

Drawer lock chisel. This, shown at (F, Fig. 2, p. 12) is intended for use in the restricted space of a drawer. It is also useful when chopping the recess into which the bolt shoots in the drawer rail. Fig. 21 shows how it can be struck with the side of the hammer. It will be realized that it would be practically impossible to chop down with the ordinary chisel.

Sharpening the chisel. This procedure is much the same as when sharpening a plane iron. The usual grinding angle is about 25 deg., whereas sharpening on the oilstone is in the region of 30

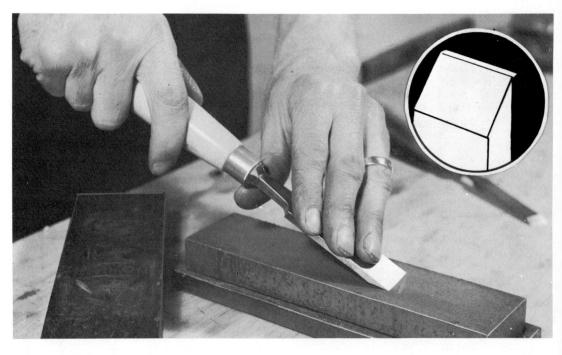

Fig. 20 (above) Sharpening the chisel on the oilstone

Fig. 21 (below) How the drawer lock chisel is used in a confined space

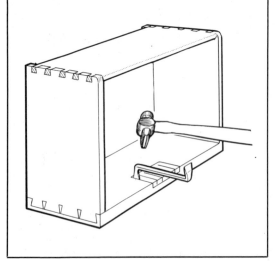

deg., except in the case of mortise chisels and those reserved for chopping which are better sharpened at nearer 35 deg. as this gives a stronger edge. Fig. 20 shows the sharpening operation. The burr is turned back on the stone (again as in the plane cutter), and it is vital that it is held flat as otherwise it will be impossible to pare with it properly. The burr is got rid of finally by stropping.

Gouges. These are not widely used, but are required sometimes for forming a hollow or recess. Carving tools are dealt with more fully in the chapter on carving. The firmer gouge has the bevel at the outside, and is for general work. To sharpen it hold it at right angles with the stone with the bevel flat. Raise the handle a trifle so that just the edge touches, and work back and forth with a rocking movement until a burr is turned up at the inside. To turn this back use the oilstone slip at the inside, keeping it flat. The curvature of the slip should be slightly quicker than that of the gouge.

Scribing gouges are bevelled inside, and must be sharpened with the slip. To turn back the burr hold the outside of the gouge flat on the stone and half revolve it, keeping it flat.

Tools for Boring

The brace. You can obtain either the simple brace or the ratchet brace. The latter is well worth its extra cost, partly because it enables you to work in a corner where a full revolution of the brace is impossible, and partly because it is an advantage to have the hand in a certain position when boring a large hole as it gives more purchase. For average purposes a 200mm. (8in.) sweep is about right.

It is fairly easy to tell when the brace leans to right or left, but more difficult to detect whether it bears away from or towards you. You can often make use of this fact when the verticality of a hole is more important in one direction than another. For instance when boring dowel holes in a rail it would clearly be fatal if the holes were to lean sideways. Consequently it is advisable to stand at the end of the wood as shown in Fig. 22.

Using the brace. Various aids can be had as a guide, one being the square placed alongside the bit. In the case of a hole being bored in the end of a post two straight strips can be cramped temporarily to the post on adjacent faces as a guide as in Fig. 23. Another plan is to ask an assistant to stand alongside to indicate whether the brace is vertical.

Sometimes it is advisable to hold the head on the left hand when boring, as it helps both in steadying the brace and in increasing the pressure. Sometimes it is more convenient to hold the wood in the vice, and the pressure is increased by pressing with the body behind the left hand. For holes, the accuracy of which is important, the method is not recommended as it is difficult to tell whether the brace is square with the wood.

When a hole has to be bored accurately at an angle a guide should be made as in Fig. 24. This is cramped to the wood and the bit passed through the hole.

Bits. For dowelling the twist bit is invariably used. Owing to its straight spiral shank it is not liable to wander with the grain if properly started, and it cuts cleanly. Furthermore, its screw point draws it into the wood without undue labour. It is rather delicate, however, both its thread and cutters being easily damaged if contact is made with a hidden nail. For dowel work an extra short bit is

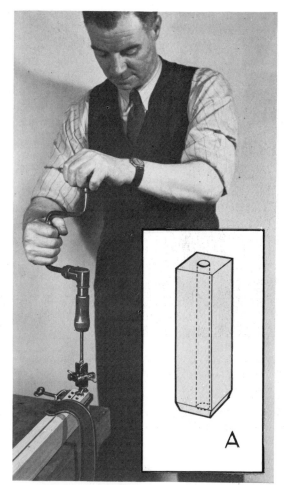

Fig. 22 Boring holes in stile preparatory to mortising

available. It is sometimes an advantage to use a morse drill. This, however, needs a jig as it is impossible to start the drill correctly in the right place otherwise.

For boring to a definite depth a stop is used. An adjustable metal type is available, but it is liable to mark the surface, and is especially awkward when the hole is being bored into an edge owing to the liability of the bearing surfaces to foul the edge of the wood. The simple devices in Fig. 25 are effective and make no mark that a single shaving will not remove. That at (A) is made specially fo-

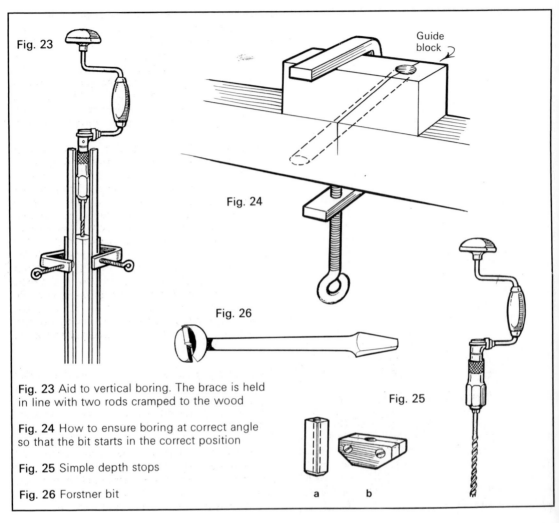

Fig. 23

Guide block

Fig. 24

Fig. 26

Fig. 23 Aid to vertical boring. The brace is held in line with two rods cramped to the wood

Fig. 24 How to ensure boring at correct angle so that the bit starts in the correct position

Fig. 25 Simple depth stops

Fig. 26 Forstner bit

Fig. 25

a   b

the particular job in hand, whereas (B) is adjustable to any position along the spiral of the bit.

For shallow holes, or holes right through thin wood, the centre bit is used. For the latter purpose the hole should be taken in from one side until the point emerges just beneath, when the hole is completed from the other side. The centre bit with thread point has an advantage in that it pulls itself into the wood and saves the necessity for pressure. The expansion bit (N), Fig. 2, p. 13 is useful for larger holes. It saves having to keep a wide range of centre bits.

Screw holes are generally bored with the morse or the drill bit, (J, Fig. 2, p. 12). Two or three sizes are kept to suit the general size of screws being used. These drills can be obtained with square shank to fit the brace, though generally the plain round drill is held sufficiently tightly. Many men keep a small hand drill in which to use the smaller sizes of drills.

Half-twist bits with gimlet points are quick borers, and are useful for tough hardwoods. They should never be used on softwoods or near the edge, however, as they are liable to split the grain.

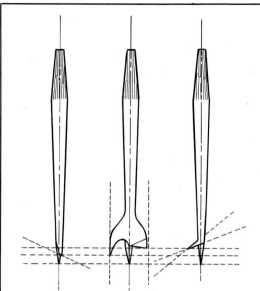

Fig. 27 (above) Details of the centre bit
Fig. 28 (below) Sharpening the cutters of the twist bit

For screw work, the snail countersink at (H, Fig. 2, p. 12) gives a clean finish. Sometimes it is necessary to enlarge the countersinking in a brass fitting, and the rose countersink (I) is used for this. For the rapid driving of screws and when considerable purchase is needed the turnscrew bit is useful. It is essential that a strong downward pressure is maintained.

As mentioned above, the morse drill is used for the shank hole for screws. For the thread hole a convenient tool for small screws is the bradawl. When the normal round type is used the cutting edge should be at right angles with the grain. A most useful type, however, is the bird-cage maker's or square awl. It cuts well and is not liable to split the grain even when used near an edge. Furthermore it has a point rather than a square end. For the screw holes of small fittings the reciprocating drill with spiral stem is useful. When the hole has to be extra small a needle can be ground to a cutting edge and used, the eye being broken off.

Forstner bit. This (Fig. 26) is a clean-cutting bit which can be used for some jobs which would be impossible with other bits. Although it has a slightly projecting centre, it is guided by its circular rim. It is especially useful when a hole has to be bored deeply without penetrating right through. This would be impossible with a centre or twist bit since the centre point would project at the other side. To bore a hole in an exact position calls for care in that the centre point has the minimum projection and is concealed by the rim. When starting it is often an advantage to give it a couple of backward turns first so that its rim cuts the circle before the cutters begin to scoop out the waste. Some makes of bit are more satisfactory in use than others.

Sharpening bits. The centre bit has three chief parts, and they should project in the following order: centre point, nicker, and cutter as shown in Fig. 27. Use a fine file to sharpen, sticking the point of the bit into a block of wood to steady it. Note that the nicker edge runs at an angle (Fig. 27) so that it cuts rather than scratches. This is sharpened on the inside. It is important that the outside is not burred over. The cutter is sharpened on top. The edges of the centre point may need a slight rub. The latter is generally triangular in section.

Twist bits are sharpened similarly, but the screw point must not be touched. If possible use a small file with a safe edge. Sharpen the nickers on the inside only, and the cutters on the side farthest from the screw point, as shown in Fig. 28. If a burr is set up on the outside of the nickers the bit can be rubbed flat on the oilstone.

Occasionally the countersink calls for a rub up with a small rat-tail and flat file. For the Forstner bit grind a small three-cornered file until the serrations are removed, and use this as a three-cornered scraper on the inside only.

Chapter three

How to Maintain and Use Tools (continued)

Planing

You plane wood for two reasons; to make it straight, flat, and square; and to make it smooth. For the former purpose the plane should be as long as possible in relation to the wood. A short plane would dip into the hollows too much, whereas a long plane is prevented from doing so by its own length. In the woodworking trades the craftsman uses either the fore plane or the jointer to make an edge straight or to make a joint. For the preliminary planing to remove saw marks or other roughness he uses the wood Jack plane. This is long enough not to dip into the surface, and, by setting it fairly coarse, it removes the roughness quickly. In this way the fore plane is reserved for accurate work, and thus keeps its edge longer and can always be set fine.

This is the ideal arrangement, but if you have not yet been able to get a trying or fore plane, you will have to use the Jack plane for jointing as well as for the rougher operations. Should this be the case you will find that your best plan when you have a number of similar pieces to prepare will be to set

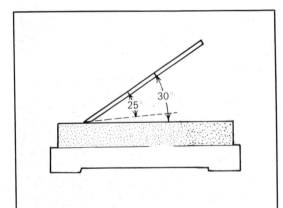

Fig. 1 (above) Grinding and sharpening angles

Fig. 2 (right) Plane cutter being sharpened on the oilstone

the plane slightly coarse and remove the roughness from them all. You can then re-set the plane (sharpening it if necessary) and make them all true.

The truing of wood enables all marking out to be done, and joints to be cut. It does not follow, however, that because wood is true that it is necessarily smooth. The grain of wood is liable to tear out if not planed in the right way, and a plane as set for truing is not adapted to deal with this. Consequently you have the smoothing plane which is of handy size for the work, and which is specially set to prevent the grain from tearing out. We shall see more about this under the heading of setting a plane.

Sharpening the plane. When you first buy a plane the cutter (or iron as it is generally termed) has been ground on a grindstone, but it is useless until it has been given a really fine edge on an oilstone. To save unnecessary work the grinding is done at a lower angle than that used on the oilstone. In this way only the extreme edge has to be rubbed. The idea is shown in Fig. 1.

To remove the cutter from a wood plane, hold the latter with the left hand so that the thumb passes into the escapement and bears on the back iron. Strike the front of the plane (on the striking button if it has one) and the wedge and cutter will slip out, but are prevented from dropping by the thumb. A wood smoothing plane is struck at the rear. In the case of a metal plane it is only necessary to raise the cam of the lever cap.

You will find that a back or cap iron is held to the cutter with a bolt. Holding the two on the bench and gripping the cutter at the unsharpened end release the bolt until it can slide along the groove in the cutter and out at the hole. There is no need to completely remove the bolt—in fact it is better not to do so as otherwise it may be lost in sawdust or shavings. Pour a few drops of oil on to the oilstone and place the cutter on it so that the ground bevel lies flat. Raise the hands a trifle so that only the extreme edge touches the stone, and you have the right angle. The latter is not critical, but if you aim at 30 deg. you will be about right. The grinding angle is 25 deg. (see Fig. 1).

Fig. 2 shows the sharpening operation. Hold the cutter so that it is skewed at a slight angle, and work it back and forth either straight or with an oval movement. Some prefer one, some the other. After a few rubs draw the thumb across the back. If it has been sharpened you will be able to detect a burr or roughness since the sharpening turns back the edge. When this appears reverse the cutter flat on the stone and rub it back and forth a few times to bend back the burr as shown in Fig. 3.

You need to get rid of this burr as otherwise it may be forced back on to the edge and blunt it. Draw the edge once or twice across a hardwood block as in Fig. 4. This will take it off but leave the edge rather rough. Put this right by giving a few rubs as in Fig. 2, and once again reverse flat as in Fig. 3. Finally strop it alternately on the bevel and on the back on a piece of leather dressed with oil and fine emery powder.

As you complete the sharpening look at the edge in the light. A keen edge cannot be seen, whereas

Fig. 3 Turning back burr on oilstone

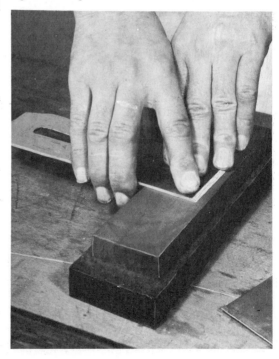

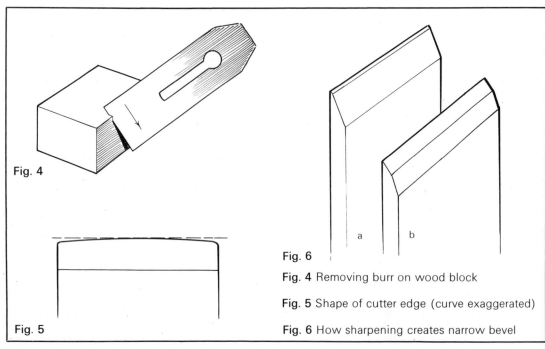

Fig. 4

Fig. 5

Fig. 6

a   b

Fig. 4 Removing burr on wood block

Fig. 5 Shape of cutter edge (curve exaggerated)

Fig. 6 How sharpening creates narrow bevel

a blunt one will reflect a thin line of light. In the same way any gashes will show as flecks of light. When you get used to it you will be able to tell by the appearance whether the edge is keen. The burr is an indication that the edge has been turned, but not reveal gashes.

For the fore plane and smoothing plane the edge should be slightly rounded as shown in exaggeration in Fig. 5, with the corners taken off. As the Jack plane has generally to take a heavier shaving the curvature can be slightly increased. After being sharpened several times the sharpened bevel will become wide as in Fig. 6, b, and it is time to have the cutter ground so that there is not so much metal to remove. Incidentally, some workers never have the cutter of a metal plane re-ground (unless it has been gashed) because it is quite thin and there is not much metal to rub away.

Setting. To set the plane place the back iron in position and turn the bolt until finger tight. The distance of the back iron from the edge depends on the work to be done. For the Jack plane which takes coarse shavings it might be about $1\frac{1}{2}$mm. ($\frac{1}{16}$in.) or more; for the fore plane which takes fine

shavings rather less. For the smoothing plane when set for cleaning up difficult wood with twisted grain it should be as close as it is possible to get it. When correct tighten the bolt right home.

All adjusting of the adjustable metal plane is by the screw and lateral lever. It is never struck with the hammer. Look along the sole as in Fig. 7, with a piece of white paper or light coloured wood beneath. The cutter should appear as a thin black line tapering to nothing at the sides. You can adjust the cutter until correct, using the rear screw to regulate the thickness of shaving, and the lever to give even projection at both sides.

In the case of the wood plane, place the cutter and back iron in the escapement, back iron uppermost, and hold in position with the thumb of the left hand. Place the wedge in position and lightly tap with the hammer. Take another look along the sole, and if there is insufficient projection tap the cutter out. If one corner sticks out strike the rear of the cutter at the side. When the cutter projects too much tap the striking button lightly. When all is in order knock the wedge home. There is no need to hammer it home really hard—you may distort the plane.

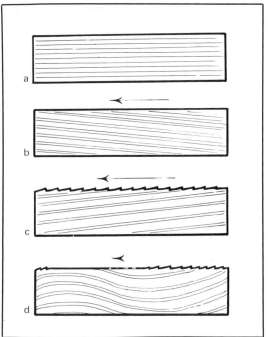

Fig. 7 (above) Sighting the cutter by looking along the sole

Fig. 8 (right) How grain affects direction of planing

Incidentally, the soles of all planes should be lubricated to assist working. With metal planes it is essential. A good plan is to keep a pad of cotton wool lightly soaked in linseed oil on a piece of wood and draw the plane across this occasionally, or rub a piece of candlegrease across the sole.

Use of the back iron. At this point perhaps we had better consider the purpose of the back iron. It is needed solely because of the tendency of some woods to tear out owing to the undulating grain, leaving little depressions in the surface known as tears (pronounced 'tares') which look unsightly. If the grain of the wood were always straight and parallel with the surface as in Fig. 8a there would be no tendency for the grain to tear out. As, however, a tree is never perfectly straight it is inevitable that the saw which cuts the boards will run across the grain in parts, and you get grain which either slopes or undulates. At (b), for example, the grain runs at

an angle. If planed in the direction shown by the arrow it would not tear out, but if turned the other way as at (c) it would inevitably tear as the plane was taken along it. First a split would start. It would run in the direction of the grain, that is downwards, but the raised shaving would be caught up by the cutter edge, wrenched up, and broken, and the same thing repeated over and over again until the end of the wood was reached. The trouble, you will observe, is that the cutter is not actually cutting most of the time because the split runs in front of it. It is only when the cutter edge catches up the split that it cuts and then the shaving is more or less wrenched up. If, therefore, you could break the shaving immediately it is raised it would lose its strength and the split would not develop. That is the purpose of the back iron, to break the shaving as soon as possible after it is raised.

The idea is shown in Fig. 9. The closer the back iron is to the cutting edge the sooner the shaving is broken, and the less liable it is to tear out the grain. Matters are helped, too, by having a small mouth to the plane. Fig. 10 shows how this restricts the lift of the shaving even when there is no back iron, causing it to break earlier than it would if the mouth were excessively wide. The fact that the smoothing plane is used only for thin shavings also helps in that the thin shaving is not so strong as a thick one and breaks earlier or just bends away.

It will be realized, however, that the close-set back iron has a disadvantage in that the resistance to the movement of the plane is increased. It is therefore a matter for compromise, the back iron being set farther back for medium or coarse shavings at cost of slightly increased liability to tear out.

In the case of the wood in Fig. 8c, the simplest plan would be to turn it the other way round as at (b), and it is always worth while looking at the edge of the wood before planing to see the direction of the grain. Sometimes it makes little difference as in the example at (d), which would tear out in parts whichever way the plane were taken. Another difficult case is when the grain runs in streaks side by side as in some varieties of mahogany. Alternate streaks will be smooth whilst the others tear out. If planing the other way the reverse happens.

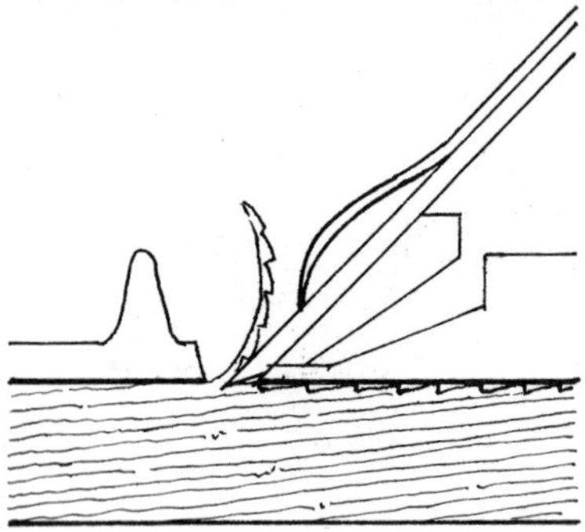

Using the plane. When the surface of the wood is planed the wood is generally laid on the bench and the bench stop knocked up to prevent it from moving. There is one precaution to take, however. Bench tops are frequently not flat, and the weight of the plane and the pressure used will cause the wood to bend. This may not matter a lot when it is merely being smoothed, but it may upset the accuracy when it is being trued. In Fig. 11 at (a), for instance, owing to the hollowness of the top, the wood is bent down under the pressure, and in all probability the plane would cease to cut when in the middle of the wood. At (b) the bench top is round, and consequently the far end of the wood is raised when the plane is started, and the whole thing is shot forward. These two illustrations are exaggerated, but they show the idea.

Generally the best plan is to use a planing board which is perfectly flat, and put the wood on this. This board is any plain, true piece of wood which is rather longer than the wood to be planed. A couple of screws driven part-way in at the far end serve as a stop. They can be given projection to suit the work in hand. When these are undesirable in that they might mark the wood, they are withdrawn and

Fig. 9

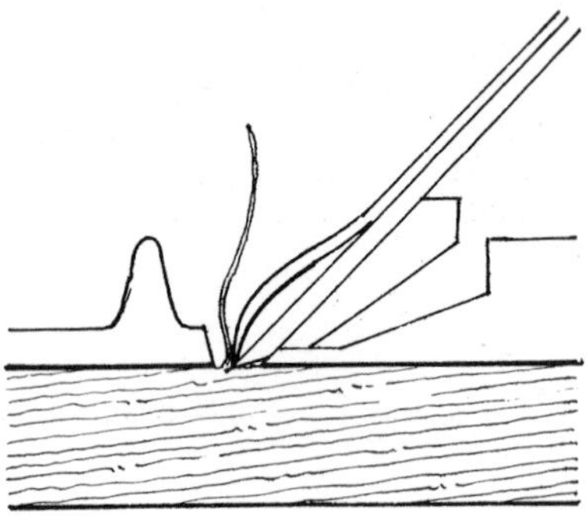

Fig. 10

Fig. 9 How cutter is liable to tear out grain

Fig. 10 Back iron helps to prevent grain from tearing

replaced by a crosspiece screwed on as shown by the dotted lines at (c), Fig. 11. Even when the planing board is used or when the bench top is true, it is usually a help to put a shaving beneath the middle of the wood, especially when narrow stuff is being dealt with. Incidentally if a large piece of wood is liable to shift about the bench top whilst being planed you can help to steady it by chalking the bench top, or sprinkling it with plaster of Paris.

The usual trouble the beginner finds is that he is inclined to make the surface round, especially at the

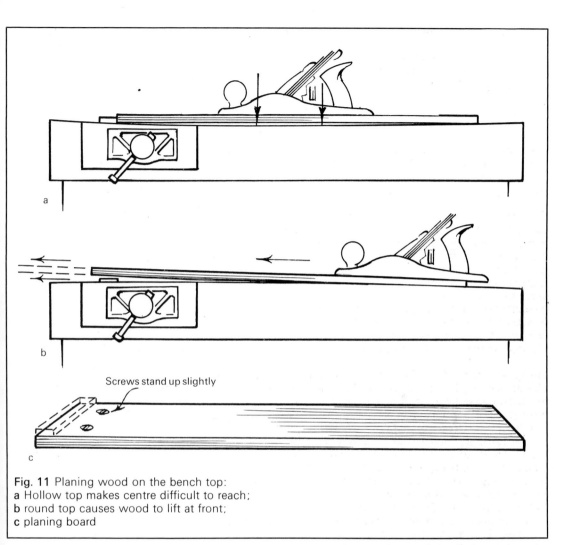

Fig. 11 Planing wood on the bench top:
a Hollow top makes centre difficult to reach;
b round top causes wood to lift at front;
c planing board

Screws stand up slightly

a

b

c

ends. To avoid this adopt the plan shown in Fig. 12. At the start of the stroke press well down at the front of the plane, and as the far end is reached transfer the pressure to the rear. After a while you will find that the process will be practically automatic.

Testing for wind. Nowadays most timber is bought ready planed, and requires little more than a skim to finish it after cutting to size, jointing, etc. When it is rough, however, it needs testing for truth, and this means that it must be straight in length, flat in width, and free of wind (pronounced as when you wind a clock). The straight-edge is used to test the straightness, but the winding strips are necessary to test for winding. However, a quick test is to look across the surface as in Fig. 13. Any serious winding will be at once obvious. For a closer test use the winding strips. If the wood is true the top edge of the near strip will appear parallel with the inlaid line on the back one. Fig. 14 shows the strips in use.

To correct a surface which winds work the plane

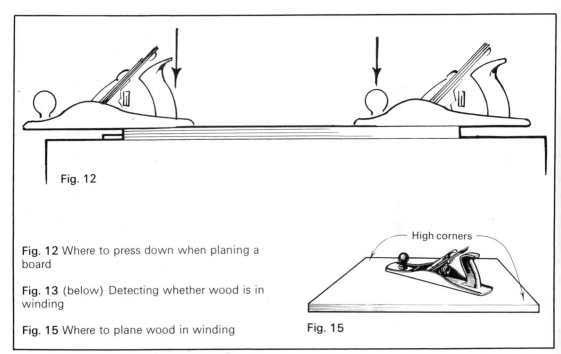

Fig. 12

Fig. 12 Where to press down when planing a board

Fig. 13 (below) Detecting whether wood is in winding

Fig. 15 Where to plane wood in winding

High corners

Fig. 15

diagonally from one high corner to the other as shown in Fig. 15. The plane itself is handy to use as a straight-edge. Laid at an angle across the wood it gives a quick indication of truth.

Edge planing. When an edge is being planed the plane is held as in Fig. 16. Note how the fingers of the left hand pass beneath the sole and bear against the side of the wood. They thus act as a sort of fence, so that the plane projects the same distance from the edge throughout the cut. This is important because correct manipulation enables an edge which is not square to be put right. The idea is shown in Fig. 17. The shaving is thicker at the middle of the plane than at the edges owning to the slight curvature of the cutting edge. When therefore an edge is out of square the plane is held so that it projects more on the high side. The sole is held flat on the edge, of course. Never attempt to rock the plane to correct an edge which is out of truth.

Sometimes an edge is square at one end and out of truth at the other; or out of truth at both ends but in opposite directions. Start the stroke with the plane towards the high side, and gradually shift the

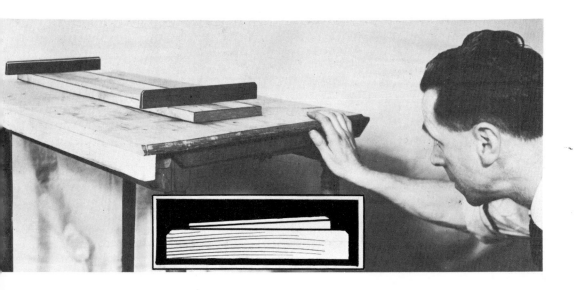

Fig. 14 (above) Testing a board for winding
using the winding strips
Fig. 16 (below) Planing an edge

Fig. 17 (below) How thickness of shaving varies
across the width

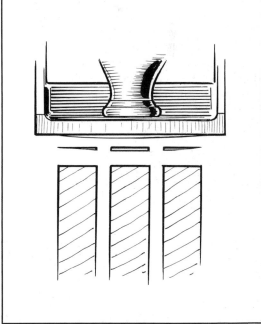

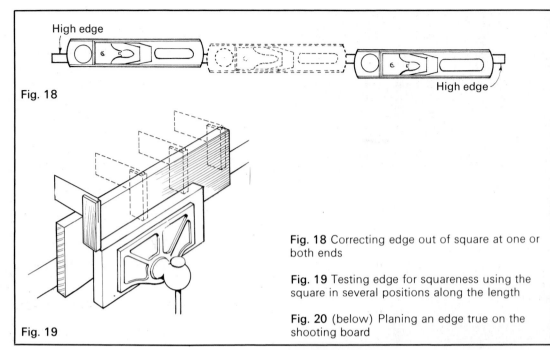

High edge

High edge

Fig. 18

Fig. 19

Fig. 18 Correcting edge out of square at one or both ends

Fig. 19 Testing edge for squareness using the square in several positions along the length

Fig. 20 (below) Planing an edge true on the shooting board

position of the fingers of the left hand on the sole so that the plane shifts to the other side as the end of the stroke is reached, as shown in Fig. 18. Fig. 19 shows how the edge is tested at various positions along the wood.

To test whether an edge is straight use a straight-edge. This, of course, is unnecessary when a joint is being planed because the two parts are tried together. A good working method of straightening an edge is to use the fore plane and remove shavings from the middle until the plane ceases to cut.

Follow with a shaving right through. A plane which has a true sole will plane an edge considerably longer than itself reasonably straight by this method.

The edges of wood about 12mm. ($\frac{1}{2}$in.) thick and over can be planed in the vice in this way. On thinner wood the plane would be liable to rock, and it is advisable to use the shooting board.

Shooting board. This is shown in Fig. 20 and is being used to plane an edge straight. The wood

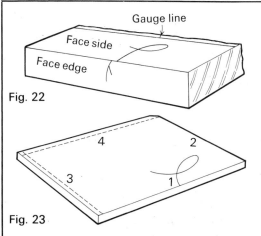

Fig. 22

Fig. 23

Fig. 21 (left) Trimming end grain on shooting board

Fig. 22 Identification marks of face side and edge

Fig. 23 Order in which edges of panel are planed

lies on the upper platform, and the plane rests on its side and is moved along the lower platform. The side of the plane must, of course, be square with sole if it is to plane the wood square. Since the plane makes the edge straight by virtue of the accuracy of its own sole, the wood is held so that it overhangs the upper platform by about 3mm. ($\frac{1}{8}$in.). Shavings are removed from the middle of the wood until the plane ceases to cut, after which a couple of shavings are taken right through. In the case of a butt joint, the one piece is planed with the face side uppermost, and the other reversed. Then if the plane is slightly out of square the two angles cancel each other out.

The method of using the shooting board is rather different when the end of a piece of wood is being trimmed. In this case the plane is kept up to the edge of the upper platform, and the wood held against the stop with sufficient inward pressure to keep it up to the sole of the plane as in Fig. 21.

Sequence in planing. In all planing operations there is a sequence to be followed. One side is made true first and one edge made square with it. These are known as the face side and face edge respec-tively. They are marked in pencil as in Fig. 22, and all subsequent marking made from one or other of them. For instance the try square has its butt resting against one of them, or the gauge is used with its fence bearing against either face side or face edge. There are exceptions to this rule, but it applies in most instances. When wood has been obtained machine planed it will already have been brought to an even thickness; otherwise the gauge will have to be set to the thickness required and both edges gauged from the face side. When the wood is wide the ends are gauged as well. The width will have to be gauged in any case as in Fig. 22.

When the edges of a wide board are to be planed they should be done in the order given in Fig. 23. This enables the rear corners to be taken off at an angle to prevent the grain from splitting out. The final trim at (4) takes out the chiselled corners. This method of taking off the corner to prevent splitting is shown in Fig. 24. (A) shows how the plain corner is liable to splinter out, whereas (B) shows the corner taken off. When the wood is not wide enough to permit this chiselling a block can be cramped on at the rear as at (C). Another plan is

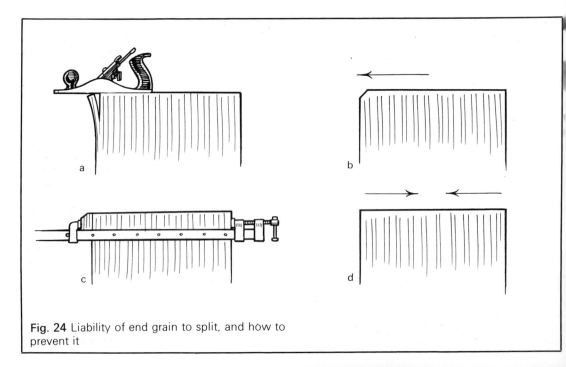

Fig. 24 Liability of end grain to split, and how to prevent it

to plane half-way in from each side as at (D). This applies equally when the wood is being trimmed on the shooting board.

Cleaning up. It will be seen that the wood Jack plane is used for the preliminary planing of rough timber, and the fore plane or its smaller counterpart, the panel plane, for truing it. At this stage all marking out, joint cutting and so on are carried out. Before the work can be assembled, however, certain parts require to be cleaned up finally, and the smoothing plane is used for this. The same plane is used for the cleaning up of table tops and similar parts, framed doors, and so on. Nowadays the adjustable metal plane is generally used. It is an extremely handy tool for bench work generally. Fig. 25 shows one of the older pattern metal smoothing planes in use in cleaning up a surface.

One other small plane which is extremely handy for trimming small parts is the block plane shown in section in Fig. 26. It is particularly handy for trimming the mitres of small mouldings and similar

Fig. 25 Cleaning up with the metal smoothing plane

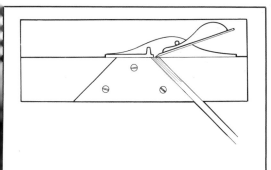

Fig. 26 Sectional view of block plane on mitre shooting board

parts because of the smallness of the mouth. The larger bench planes have the bevel of the cutter downwards so that, although the mouth itself may be small, there is an aperture behind it, and the end of a narrow piece may drop into this making accurate work impossible. The block plane has its bevel uppermost which necessarily reduces the aperture as shown in Fig. 26.

Planes for Special Purposes

Rebate plane. The most generally useful kind is the adjustable metal type which has a moving fence. It thus acts as a fillister plane. Once set, any number of rebates can be planed to the same size. A depth stop ensures that the plane ceases to cut when the required depth is reached. A spur is fitted to the right hand side, but this is used only when the plane is used across the grain. Its purpose is to cut across the grain so that it does not tear out. It is necessary to draw the plane backwards with a fair pressure a couple of times before using it in the normal manner. Otherwise the grain will not be cut through sufficiently. As the spur cuts quite deeply it is necessary to stop the rebate about a bare mm. short of the finished depth, and finish off with the spur taken out or reversed into a neutral position.

The wood rebate plane is preferred by some. It has no fence, and to start the plane the fingers of the left hand are curled beneath the sole to enable it

to be kept equidistant from the edge. Sometimes it is more convenient to fix a straight-edge to the wood to act as a guide. As no spurs are fitted it is essential that a saw cut is made first when cross grain is being worked. Otherwise the grain will inevitably tear out.

Fig. 27 shows a rebate being worked with a metal plane. Start at the far end of the wood and remove one or two short shavings. Then at each successive stroke bring the plane a little farther back until it takes a shaving along the whole length. In this way it is not so liable to drift from the edge. In any case, however, it is essential that a firm inward pressure is maintained. The cutter should stand a trifle proud at the side of the plane facing the wood — not more than the thickness of a piece of stout paper. Unless this is done the plane is liable to shift outwards a trifle at each stroke so resulting in a rebate which is not square.

Fig. 27 Working a rebate using the metal fillister plane

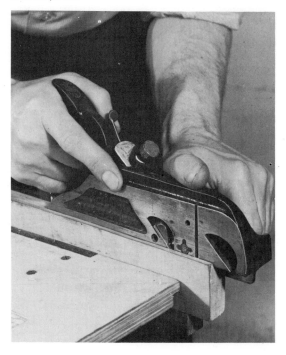

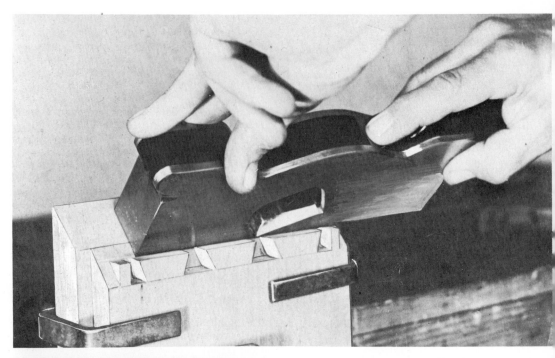

Fig. 28 (above) Typical use of the shoulder plane—it is especially useful for end grain
Fig. 29 (left) The bullnose plane in use

Shoulder plane. Although this is a special form of rebate plane, it is used for trimming rather than working a rebate. It is of special value for end grain. Thus wide shoulders can be trimmed with it, hence the name. The cutter has its bevel uppermost, and this means that it has close support practically up to the cutting edge. It is always set fine since its purpose is solely that of trimming. It is important that the edge of the cutter is sharpened square, because, although it is generally possible to knock the back of the cutter over slightly if not true, it causes the side of the cutter to protrude unevenly so that the plane does not bed down properly on its side. Fig. 28 shows a typical operation, that of trimming the mitred lap of a secret dovetail joint.

Bullnose plane. This again is another form of rebate plane, but the cutting edge is near the front of the plane so that it will work close up into a corner. Apart from this, however, it is an invaluable little tool for general work, and can often be used more conveniently than the shoulder plane. Fig. 29

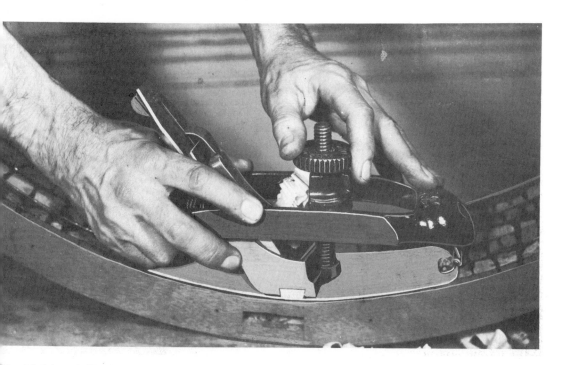

Fig. 31 (above) Planing a curved surface with the compass plane
Fig. 30 (right) The side rebate plane

shows it in use. A quite narrow type is also available.

Side rebate plane. This is not required often, but when it is wanted it is wanted badly. An example of its use is when it is necessary to widen grooves to hold polished or veneered shelves. Clearly the latter could not be planed in thickness. The side rebate plane is the only tool that can be used to widen the groove. It is shown in Fig. 30.

Compass plane. The metal type with flexible sole is shown in Fig. 31. It can be used for both concave and convex curves. Although provided with a back iron, the plane should be used *with* the grain as far as possible. Only curves which are struck from a circle can be planed. To set it hold the plane over the sawn wood and turn the adjusting screw till the sole takes up approximately to the shape. For concave shapes the sole should be of slightly quicker curvature, and rather flatter for convex shapes.

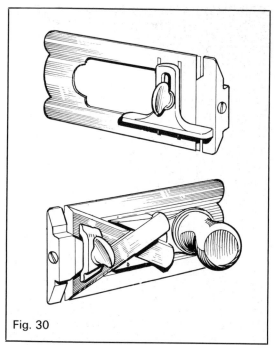

Fig. 30

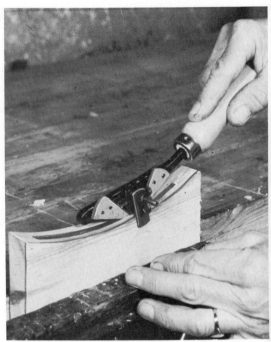

Fig. 32 (above) The Record plough plane (044C) in use

Fig. 33 (right) Working a groove around a curved edge using the Technikos plough. Two hands would normally be used on the tool but here the left hand is lowered to show details

Grooving plane or plough. There are a great many varieties of this, both in wood and metal. Metal grooving planes are of many forms from the simple small plane with three sizes of cutters to about 6mm. ($\frac{1}{4}$in.), to the multi-plane. These last named will work grooves up to any practical width, though for extra wide ones it is usual to use it twice, resetting the fence for the extra width. This is specially true when hardwood is being planed.

In addition to grooving this multi-plane can be used for rebating, though the fillister plane shown in Fig. 27 is more satisfactory for this work.

To set the tool fix the cutter with the required projection, secure the fence at the required distance from the edge, and set the depth stop so that the plane ceases to cut when the depth is

reached. Fig. 32 shows the Record plough plane No. 044C in use.

Whichever type of plane is used, it should be started at the far end of the wood and one or two short cuts taken. Then at each successive stroke it is brought a little further back until it can run right through. In this way the plough runs into a groove it has already worked, and any liability to drift from the edge is avoided. In any case a steady inward pressure must be maintained.

The above grooving tools are for straight work only. When a groove has to be worked around a curved edge the Technikos plough, Fig. 33, is invaluable. It has two opposed cutters and when a groove of odd width is needed the cutters can be staggered to give the required width. A narrow fence is incorporated to enable the tool to negotiate the curve, and a depth stop is provided. Grooves curved in either a horizontal or vertical direction can be cut.

Router plane. The metal type with adjustable cutter is used widely nowadays. It can be obtained with either open or closed mouth. The cutter is

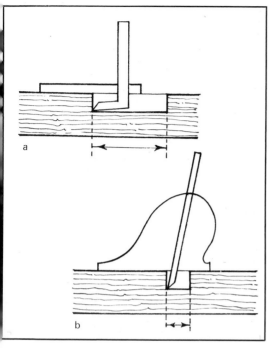

Fig. 34 (above) Section through (a) metal router and (b) wood router

Fig. 35 (right) The Stanley metal router plane in use

cranked and the cutting edge is almost horizontal so that it cuts easily. On the other hand it is liable to tear out woods with difficult grain. Furthermore it cannot work in a recess which is less than double the length of the cranked part of the cutter. This is made clear in Fig. 34. The tool in use is shown in Fig. 35. The old router or old woman's tooth still has its uses since it will work in a much more confined space (see Fig. 34.), and is not liable to tear out the grain since its action is more akin to scraping than cutting.

Moulding planes. These have only a limited use nowadays since most mouldings are machined. A small round plane is handy for working hollows, however. This has no fence and the angle at which it is held is a matter for judgment. The fingers of the left hand pass beneath the sole and act as a sort of fence. To work a hollow at an edge a plain chamfer should be worked with the bench plane first.

Other types of moulding planes to work special mouldings have a fence, and this is held hard up against the edge of the wood. Many planes require to be held at an angle. You can tell this by the fence member which must be upright when the plane is in use.

Toothing plane. This, shown at (Q), Fig. 1, p. 11, is used to roughen the surface before veneering and on certain wide joints. Its cutter, which is practically vertical, has a series of grooves at the face which produce a saw-like cutting edge. Apart from giving a suitable key for the glue, it takes out inequalities left by the ordinary plane. It is shown in use on page 132.

Chapter four

How to Maintain and Use Tools (continued)

General Tools

Hammer. The most useful type for general indoor woodwork, furniture making, etc., is the Warrington or London pattern (see A, p. 14). It has the cross pene at the back which is handy for starting nails, and also for rubbing down inlay strings, etc. A useful weight (including the handle) is about 11oz. For extra small nails the pattern-maker's type of about 6oz. weight is invaluable. The claw hammer is of little value for furniture making. It is used mostly by carpenters for whom the claw for withdrawing nails is useful. An inclusive weight of 1lb. 11oz. is a good size.

Hold the hammer by the end of the shaft and so take advantage of the leverage it gives. Always look at the point of the actual object you are striking. Thus, when using a punch, look at the head of the punch, not at the nail which it is driving.

Punches. Sometimes known as nail sets, these are required to drive nails beneath the surface of the wood. The most generally useful type is the hollow point which is not so liable to start from the nail head, though for flooring brads and other cut nails a square punch is mostly used. Pincers are a necessity, and a fairly large pair is desirable. When using them always place a spare block of wood or a scraper beneath to avoid damaging the surface.

Mallet. An all-round useful size is the 180mm. (7in.) head which weighs in the region of $2\frac{1}{2}$lb. Make sure that it has the tapered handle which fits the head with a wedge fit, so preventing it from flying off.

Screwdrivers. At least two are required, preferably three. The large one should be capable of driving 12 to 16 gauge screws, and be 250–300mm. (10–12in.) long. ((E), p. 14). For screws around the 8 gauge size a smaller driver is needed. The large one would not fit the slot, and would project at the sides.

The small screwdriver is needed for the screws you would use for small hinges, etc., say 4–6 gauge. An excellent type is the ratchet ((F), p. 15) which

Fig. 1 Use of the cork rubber when using glasspaper

can be used with one hand whilst the other supports the door, or whatever it might be. It is only necessary to turn the hand back and forth without altering its position. The finger grip is also a great convenience since the first turn or two can be made with the thumb and finger, the rest of the hand remaining still and just exerting pressure. For the smallest screws the long thin electricians' screwdriver ((G), p. 15) is invaluable.

Veneer hammer. This is usually made at home. It is used to force out glue from beneath the veneer. It consists of a main stock with a handle let into it at right angles (see (S), p. 15). A strip of brass fits in a slot in the stock, the edge of this being straight and rounded over in section. Exact sizes are not important. The brass strip might be about 150–180mm. (6–7in.) long.

Cork rubber. Always use this when cleaning up a flat surface, Fig. 1. Its use prevents corners and edges from being dubbed over. Use it always in the direction of the grain in a straight line. Working across the grain or in a circular path causes scratches to show badly, and results in stain taking

unevenly in patches. Sometimes it cannot be avoided. In a quartered panel, for instance, it is impossible to follow the grain, and the only way is to avoid coarse paper and work along the length of the panel as in Fig. 2.

Another occasion calling for compromise is when a door framework is being cleaned up. First the rubber is taken across the shoulder as at (a), Fig. 3, when it will inevitably work across the grain. If, however, the rubber is afterwards taken parallel with shoulder (b) it will take out the scratches previously made.

To clean up mouldings it is necessary to make small wood rubbers shaped to a reverse of the section as in Fig. 4. Unless this is done the edge will be dubbed over. In any case it is the only way of exerting any degree of pressure.

Spokeshaves. Both wood and metal shaves are available. The latter is similar to a plane in both the setting and sharpening. As the cutter is rather short to handle it is a good plan to make a holder having a slot in it. It can then be handled much like a plane

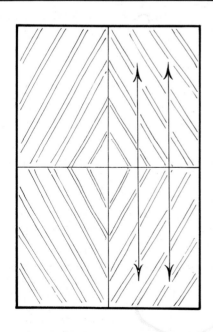

Fig. 2 (left) Direction in which glasspaper is used for a quartered panel—it is impossible to follow the direction of the grain

Fig. 3 (below) Glasspapering over a joint

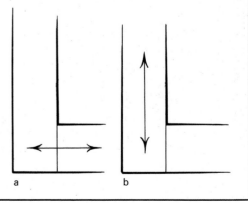

a   b

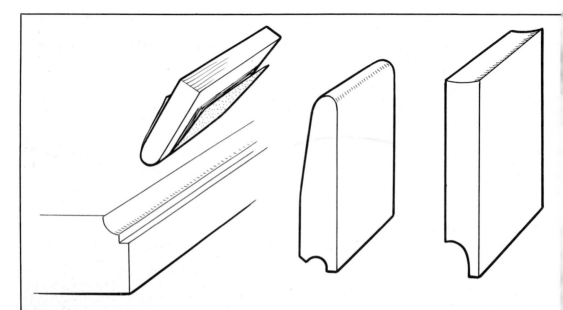

Fig. 4 Glasspaper rubbers used for cleaning mouldings

Fig. 5 (below) The round-faced metal spokeshave in use

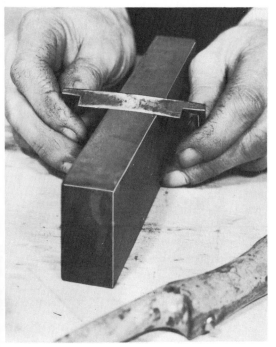

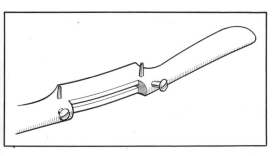

Fig. 6 (above left) Sharpening the cutter of the wood spokeshave

Fig. 7 (left) Loose cutter held with screws

Fig. 8 (above) Cleaning up a concave edge with the wood spokeshave

cutter. Fig. 5 shows the tool in use. To sharpen the wood type one way is to hold the cutter in the jaws of a handscrew or in the bench vice, and work an oilstone slip on the bevel. Another method is to use the edge of the oilstone as in Fig. 6. As a rule the tool works better if no attempt is made to remove the burr.

The cutter is held purely by the friction of the tangs. and these are tapped one way or the other to give the required setting. After prolonged use the tangs tend to become loose and liable to drop out. Round-head screws with the points nipped off can

be driven in as in Fig. 7. Fig. 8 shows the wood spokeshave in use.

Two chief points need to be watched when using the spokeshave; to work in the direction of the grain, and to keep the edge square. The former point is obvious from Fig. 9. Squareness of edge, however, comes only with practice, and the only plan is to test the work frequently and at various points.

Clearly the spokeshave cannot reach into the extreme corners, noted at (X), Fig. 9, and such

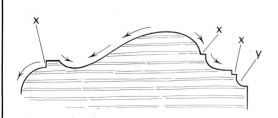

Fig. 9

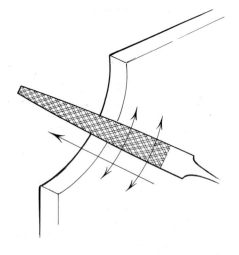

Fig. 9 Direction in which spokeshave is used

Fig. 10 Compound action of the rasp or file over a shape `

Fig. 11 (below) Cleaning the edge of abrasive material with the shaper

Fig. 10

parts need rubbing with the file followed by the scraper, and finally glasspaper. In the same way a concave curve of small radius could not be reached by the spokeshave (Y). For this either a small half-round file or a rat-tail file would be needed.

File and rasp. The file is used with a sort of compound movement as shown in Fig. 10. As it is pushed forward it is partly revolved. In this way it takes out lumps and removes saw marks. In its turn it leaves file marks, of course, and these are removed by the scraper. When a lot of wood has to be removed it is quicker to begin with the rasp, the coarse face of which takes out inequalities quickly. It is followed by the file, which should be of rather quicker curvature than the curve being cleaned.

Shaper. This has similar uses to the rasp and file, and has the advantage that it is not liable to clog since there are open spaces between the cutting edges. The shaper is made in various patterns; flat, curved, and circular. Its chief value is in the rapid removal of unwanted wood, and for use on abrasive materials such as chipboard, etc. It is shown in use in Fig. 11.

Scraper. No matter how carefully a surface is planed, the plane is bound to leave some marks. Furthermore some woods tear up in parts no matter in which direction the plane is taken. The only way of taking out such blemishes is to use the scraper. A handy size is about 130mm. (5in.), the thickness being about 1·2mm ($\frac{3}{64}$in.). A thin scraper heats up quickly and becomes painful to use. A thick one is difficult to bend and is therefore tiring to use.

Fig. 12 shows it in use. It is pushed forward by the thumbs, the fingers at the ends bending it back slightly. In this way the edge is slightly curved, the centre part touching the wood. Note that it leans forward at an angle, the exact slope depending upon the way it is sharpened. Trial shows the most effective slope. Fine shavings should be removed, not mere dust.

The most awkward part of scraping is the start at the near edge, and the best way is to hold the scraper at a slight angle as in the plan view, Fig. 13. In this way part of the scraper is already lying on the wood, and there is no difficulty about starting the cut.

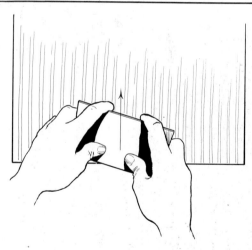

Fig. 12 (left) Cleaning up a surface with the cabinet scraper

Fig. 13 (above) How scraper is started at the end of wood

Fig. 14 (top left) Rubbing down the scraper edge with the file

Fig. 15 (above) Finishing the edge on the oilstone

Fig. 16 (middle left) Rubbing the sides on the oilstone

Fig. 17 (bottom left) Flattening the sides with the gouge or burnisher

Sharpening the scraper. To sharpen the scraper hold it in the vice and with a fine flat file make the edge straight and square, taking out any rounding-over that may have ocurred at the edges, see Fig. 14. To remove the file marks hold the scraper in a pad and work it on the oilstone, changing the direction of the movement so that wear on the stone is equalised. Some prefer to use the edge of the stone, working it between the case and its lid, as in Fig. 15. A slight burr will be set up at the edges, and this is removed by laying each side of the scraper on the stone and rubbing flat as in Fig. 16.

The edge is now ready to be turned. Hold the scraper flat on the bench about 5mm. ($\frac{1}{4}$in.) from

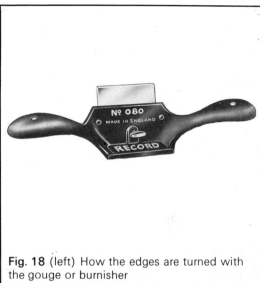

Fig. 18 (left) How the edges are turned with the gouge or burnisher

Fig. 19 (above) The scraper plane

he edge and draw a hard steel tool such as a gouge along it once or twice as in Fig. 17. Take care not o catch the fingers with the gouge. A special ounded sharpener known as a burnisher or icketer is available. Bring the scraper forwards so hat it overhangs the edge of the bench by about 5mm. ($\frac{1}{4}$in.). Wet the side of the gouge in the mouth and, holding it at a slight angle, draw it along the scraper, first in one direction, then the other, using strong pressure, as in Fig. 18. This hould turn up a strong edge. Some prefer to hold he scraper upright, and draw the gouge upwards.

After being in use for a while the edges will become dull. They can be restored a few times by turning ack as in Fig. 17 and re-turning as in Fig. 18. Eventually, however, this will fail to turn up a atisfactory edge, and it is necessary to use file and ilstone again.

'or some purposes the scraper plane, Fig. 19, is useful, especially for woods with hard and soft grain. Whereas the ordinary steel scraper is liable o dig into the soft parts of the grain, the plane avoids this. The cutter of the tool is filed and honed t about 45 deg. and the edge turned up to hook

form with a burnisher. The cutter is held vertically in the vice and the burnisher held flat on the bevel and gradually brought up to within about 15 deg. of the horizontal in successive strokes. To set the cutter the plane is held on a flat board with the fixing screws entirely free. The cutter is dropped into its slot when it will fall to the wood by its own weight. The two fixing screws are then tightened and the rear adjusting screw fed forwards, thus bending the cutter slightly and giving it projection beyond the sole.

Oilstone and oilstone slips. Nowadays the manufactured stones such as the India, Carborundum, and Unirundum are widely used in preference to the natural stones, because of their consistent quality combined with rapid cutting. They can be obtained in three grades, coarse, medium and fine; also in combination form. For cabinet work the fine grade is recommended. Use a thin lubricating oil, and wipe clean after use. Make a container for it immediately as it is easily broken.

One or two oilstone slips are needed, and it is advisable to choose those of tapered section, as these give rounded edges of varying curvature.

Chapter five

Rules, Gauges, Dividers, Square, Bevel, Parallel Strips

How to Maintain and Use Tools (continued)

These are most important because accurate work is impossible unless the wood is set out correctly.

Rule. For general bench work the 1 metre (2ft. or 3ft.) rule is convenient, though there is a tendency to replace it with the flexible metal type, which has the advantage of opening up to a much greater length, yet taking up little space when closed. The type with combined metric and Imperial markings has advantages.

Always hold the rule so that the calibrations actually touch the wood. Thus in Fig. 1 the rule is on its edge and there is no doubt of the measurement as there might be if the rule were held flat. In the latter case the measurement would appear to vary according to whether the wood were seen from the right or left. This illustration is also of value

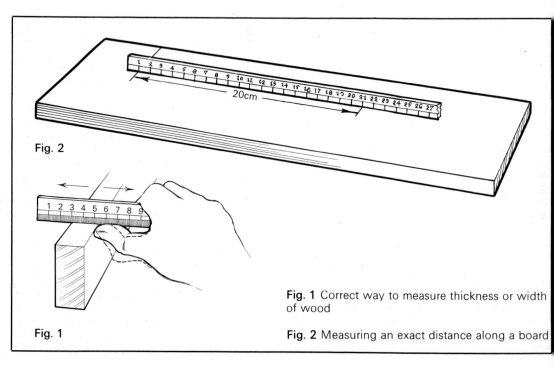

20cm

Fig. 2

Fig. 1

Fig. 1 Correct way to measure thickness or width of wood

Fig. 2 Measuring an exact distance along a board

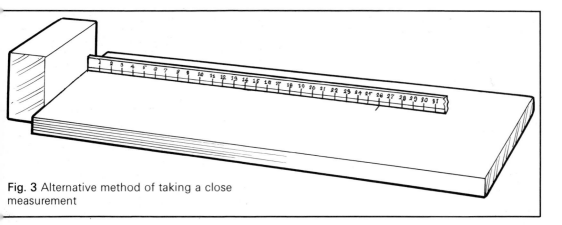

Fig. 3 Alternative method of taking a close measurement

n that it shows how the thickness (or width) of a piece of wood is measured. Note that measurement s not taken from the end of the rule, but from one of the calibrations. It is far easier to judge when a mark is level with the edge of the wood rather than the end of the rule. By rocking the thumb over one way or the other the rule can be made to slide the most minute distance, and the exact measurement can be noted with ease. In any case the thumb acts as a bearing in keeping the rule steady.

The same idea is followed in Fig. 2 when an exact distance is being marked. Instead of the end of the rule being placed on the mark, the first 1cm. (10mm.) calibration is used. Then in measuring the distance 10mm. is added. Thus, suppose the distance to be noted is 200mm., the mark is made opposite the 210mm. calibration on the rule. Another way is to place a block of wood exactly on the mark and put the end of the rule against this. The same idea can be followed when the distance has to be taken from the end of the wood as in Fig. 3. All these methods are used for close work. They are unnecessary for approximate measurements.

The rule can often be used for drawing a pencil line parallel with an edge as in Fig. 4. Although it does not give the close accuracy of a gauge line, it is quite suitable for, say, the marking of a board for ripping out. Sometimes the finger gauge method in Fig. 5 can be used for rough marking. Rather more accurate is the use of notched wood as in Fig. 6. This is specially useful when chamfering when a gauge mark would be unsightly.

One other occasional use for a rule is in marking a board of odd width into approximately equal parts. Thus, suppose a board say 142mm. wide has to be divided into five equal parts. Take the first figure above the width into which five will go easily. Clearly it is 150. Set one end of the rule at one edge of the board, and 150 at the other, the rule sloping at an angle. Mark the wood at 30, 60, 90, and 120mm. as shown in Fig. 7.

Gauges. The three chief kinds are, marking, cutting, and mortise. In addition there is the panel gauge which is similar to the marking gauge but is much bigger and has a pencil in place of a steel marker. It is used for marking wide boards.

Fig. 8 shows how the marking or cutting gauge is held. The first finger bears down on the top of the gauge, whilst the root of the same finger and the thumb push forward. The remaining three fingers press inwards towards the edge. This last is of great importance in that it is vital that the gauge does not drift outwards. This may easily happen, especially if the grain tends to run in that direction. Only marks *with* the grain or at *end* grain should be made with the marking gauge.

For cross grain the cutting gauge is necessary; the other would merely scratch. This tool has a knife rather than a marker. It is used in the same way but it is advisable to set the cutter at a *slight* angle as in Fig. 9 so that it tends to run *into* the wood. The fence, of course, prevents it from actually doing so; the great thing is to stop any tendency for it to run outwards.

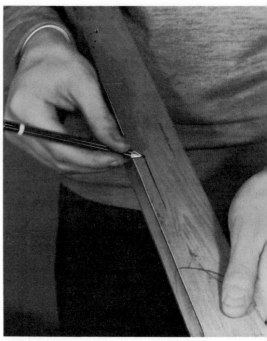

Fig. 4 (above left) Drawing a pencil line parallel with an edge

Fig. 5 (above right) The finger-gauge method showing a line parallel with an edge

Fig. 6 (left) Use of a rebated slip for drawing a pencil line parallel with an edge

Fig. 7 (below) Dividing an odd measurement into equal parts

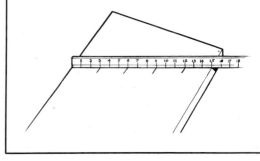

Fig. 8 (above) How either the cutting gauge or the marking gauge is held

Fig. 9 (below) Setting of cutting gauge. The cutter inclines at a slight angle so that it tends to draw the gauge inwards

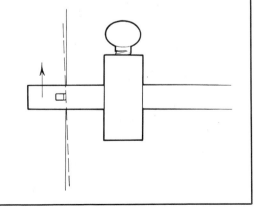

In addition to marking, the cutting gauge is used to cut right through thin wood. The cutter is given a fair projection, and a deep cut made from each side. Softer varieties of wood can be cut up to about 6mm. ($\frac{1}{4}$in.) thick in this way.

The gauge can either be set with the rule, or to the item for which it is needed. In the former case the end of the rule is held against the fence of the gauge and the latter adjusted until the cutter or marker is level with the required measurement. Final fine adjustment is made by tapping one end or the other of the stem on the bench. When a fitting such as a lock or hinge is being fitted the gauge is set to the fitting itself, the latter being placed on the fence and the marker set to the pin or whatever it may be. When dovetailing the gauge is held to the wood itself so that it can be set to its thickness.

The mortise gauge has two markers, one fixed and the other adjustable. The distance between them is regulated to the width of the chisel to be used in mortising, the latter being held to the gauge. The fence is set afterwards to whatever position is required. In the case of a mortise and tenon joint to

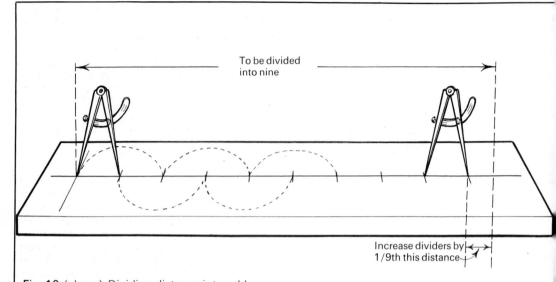

To be divided
into nine

Increase dividers by
1/9th this distance

Fig. 10 (above) Dividing distance into odd
number of parts using dividers

Fig. 11 (below) Testing squareness of rebate

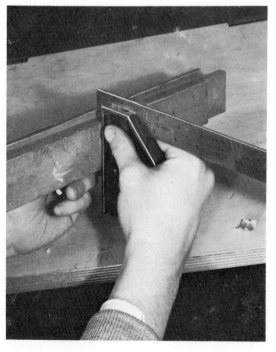

fit flush, the gauge is used from the face side of
both pieces.

Dividers. These have various uses, from scribing
a circle to dividing a distance into an odd number
of parts. Fig. 10 shows how the latter is done. It is
assumed that the distance has to be divided into
nine equal parts. Set the dividers to what you think
is one ninth, and step along as to the left. If badly
out re-set until approximately right—some trial and
error is inevitable. If nine steps are short increase
the setting by what you estimate one ninth of the
remaining distance, and step out again. This will
bring the setting much nearer, and a second
adjustment will put it right. If on stepping out the
nine moves takes the point beyond the mark, the
setting is decreased by one ninth of the distance
over-run.

Square. The adjustable type of engineer's square
shown at (W), p. 13, has many advantages. Apart
from normal use in marking and testing, it can be
used for rebate work as in Fig. 11, and as a set
square in Fig. 12. The ordinary wood-metal square
could not be used for either purpose. In any case
this latter type of square is often inaccurate.

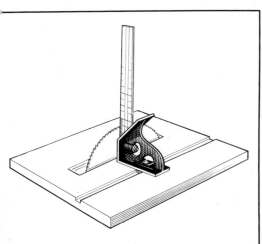

Fig. 12 Testing squareness of circular saw or any other item

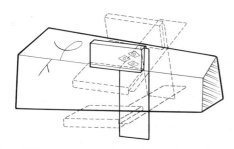

Fig. 13 Use of square from face side and edge

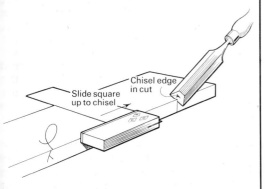

Chisel edge in cut

Slide square up to chisel

Fig. 14 Marking shoulder with chisel and try square

A rule to keep in mind is that the square should be used from either face side or face edge whenever possible. There are exceptions, but since these two have been made true and square with each other the desirability of working to them is obvious. Fig. 13 is an exaggerated example of the application of the rule. Lines such as might be required for the shoulders of a joint are to be marked round all four sides of a piece of wood. This particular piece is shown intentionally inaccurate, but if the butt of the square rests always against either face side or face edge the marks should meet.

When two or more pieces have to be marked alike it is an advantage to cramp them together and square the marks across all. They can then be separated and the mark squared round each independently. A typical example is in the rails or stiles of a door. For close accuracy always make a knife or chisel cut rather than a pencil line. The latter is for approximate or rough working only, or when the knife marks might appear as a blemish. As a typical example of marking with the square, take the rails of a door, the shoulders of which have to be marked. Cramp the rails together flush and, using the rule, make marks with a sharp pencil at the shoulder positions. Placing the knife or chisel on each mark in turn, square lines right across both rails. Separate the rails, and square the marks round each independently. To do this place the knife at the corner of the wood, its edge resting in the slight cut already made as in Fig. 14, and slide the square up to it. In this way the position is bound to be correct. Note that the chisel or knife should bear over to the right so that the bevel is about square with the edge. Otherwise the bevel may prevent the blade of the square from sliding to the correct position. This sliding up of the square to the knife is invariably more accurate than trying to position the square by eye only. For large work the wood square shown at (Q), p. 13, is necessary. It is usual for the craftsman to make his own.

Mitre square. This is needed for marking and testing 45 deg. mitres. There is no special point in its use, except that when mitre lines have to be squared on to all four surfaces, care has to be taken to position the square exactly, otherwise the lines may not meet owing to the angle.

Sliding bevel. This is used mainly for odd angles —for instance the rail shoulders of a stand with

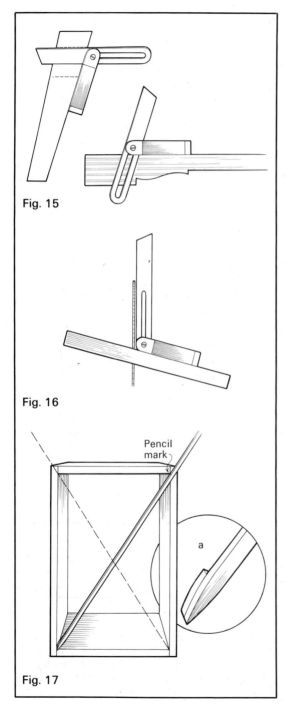

Fig. 15

Fig. 16

Pencil mark

a

Fig. 17

legs set at an angle. The angle can be set by a protractor or by a drawing. For some work it is an advantage to have the blade set centrally in the stock as this gives the acute angle and its complementary obtuse one. Fig. 15 shows it in use when marking the joint of a stand with leg set at an angle. In the leg the bevel must be worked from inside the leg owing to the taper, whereas the rail owing to its shaped edge, needs to be marked from above. On the other hand, in Fig. 16, which shows the table of a circular saw being set at an angle, the blade projects at one side only.

Straight-edge and parallel winding strips
Both of these are usually made by the worker himself. The former should be in well-seasoned straight-grained hardwood. A test for the working accuracy of the edge is to place it on a flat board and draw a line along the edge with a keen pencil. When reversed on to the other side it will align with the pencil line if true. It has many uses for marking out and testing generally, and can be of any convenient size. Many workers keep two; about 500mm. (20in.) and 1m. (3ft.) respectively. Incidentally the accepted scientific method of testing is to plane three straight edges, each of which should match up to the other two when tried in both directions, but this is scarcely necessary for the woodworker.

Parallel strips (winding strips) are used mostly to test whether a surface is free from winding, see Fig. 14, p. 39. Another use is in testing whether the four legs of a cabinet will stand square on the floor. If the strips are not long enough to reach across the legs they are placed on longer strips of wood, the edges of which are parallel.

Diagonal strip. When a large carcase has been assembled it may be misleading to test with the square since any curvature in the wood would give a false reading. It is therefore advisable to use the diagonal strip or squaring rod shown in Fig. 17. Placed across the job the diagonal length is noted with the pencil. When reversed into the opposite corners it will show the same length if true.

Fig. 15 Marking stand with splay legs, using sliding bevel
Fig. 16 Testing angle using sliding bevel
Fig. 17 Diagonal strip used to test squareness

Appliances

All of these can be made by the craftsman himself.

Shooting board. There are various ways of making this. The simplest is shown in Fig. 18. Exact sizes are not important, but those given can be taken as a general guide. Two are handy; a short one, say 600mm., (2ft. or 2ft. 6in.) for general trimming and short joints; and one from 1m. to ·5m. (3ft. to 5ft.) for long joints in thin wood. Note the chamfered lower corner of the upper platform which forms a dust trap and avoids false working. The effective edge of the stop is at 90 deg. Its wedge formation ensures a tight fit. It can always be tapped in in the event of its becoming loose, and the projecting end levelled. If possible use quarter-cut wood throughout as this is not liable to warp.

The shooting board is used in two distinct ways. The first is in planing joints in thin wood, or in planing an edge straight and square. Its advantage for thin wood is that there is no liability for the plane to wobble. The operation is shown in Fig. 19. Note that the wood overhangs the upper platform by about 6mm. ($\frac{1}{4}$in.), and that the plane makes the edge true by virtue of the truth of its own sole. It does not run along the edge of the upper platform. The usual plan is to remove shavings from the middle until the plane ceases to cut, then take a couple of shavings right through. Generally this will automatically make the edge straight, though in the case of a joint the parts are tried together, or the edge tested with a straight-edge in the case of a single edge.

Theoretically the edge should be square, assuming the sole of the plane to be square with its side. In the case of a joint, however, it is always advisable to plane one piece with the face side uppermost, and the other with it downward. In this way any angularity in the one is cancelled by that in the other, and the parts go together in alignment.

The second use of the shooting board is in trimming the ends of wood square. In this case the wood is held tight up against the stop, and the plane is worked along the edge of the upper platform. The wood is pressed towards the plane and in this way is fed steadily out as planing proceeds. As the far

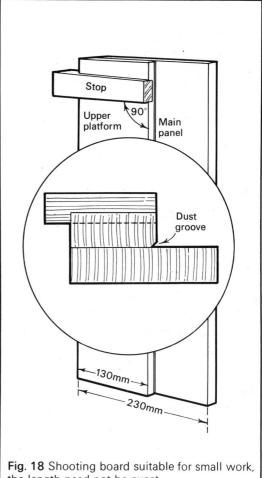

Fig. 18 Shooting board suitable for small work, the length need not be exact

corner is liable to splinter out, it is advisable to chisel it off. If this is impracticable owing to there being insufficient width the plane will either have to be taken halfway in from each edge, or a spare piece of wood with parallel edges placed behind it as in Fig. 20.

Mitre shooting board. This has similar uses to the normal shooting board but is for trimming mitres. It is shown on p. 16 at (B). The direction of the plane is reversed when the wood has to be placed on the far side of the stop.

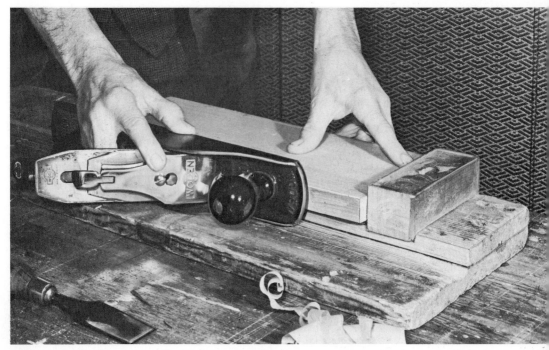

Bench hook. Used chiefly to hold the wood steady when being sawn, this is a useful item (see (E), p. 16). An important point about it is that the strip which bears against the edge of the bench should be dowelled on, not screwed or nailed—at any rate at the end over which the saw is used. The reason for this is that with continual use the wood is worn away by the saw and fixing screws or nails may ultimately become bared and foul the saw. Fig. 12, p. 23, shows how it is used, the wood being held firmly against the back of the bench hook.

Mitre block and box. These are needed for sawing mitres, the former for small mouldings. The only special point about the mitre block is that the wood must be kept firmly up against the stop, and whenever possible the saw should cut *into* the section not out of it. In other words the back of the moulding should be against the stop of the mitre block, so that any rag created by the saw occurs at the back where it does not matter. Fig. 21 shows the mitre block in use.

The same thing applies to the mitre box. Thus when cutting, say, a large cornice moulding it is advisable to place it upside down and saw towards the

Fig. 19 (above) Truing the edge of a board on the shooting board
Fig. 20 (below) Avoiding splintered corner when trimming end grain

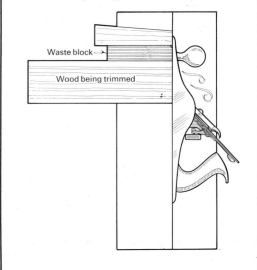

Waste block

Wood being trimmed

waste piece

Fig. 21 (above) Use of the mitre block. The waste piece (inset) avoids cutting into the base of the block

Fig. 22 (below) Pitched cornice moulding being mitred

Fig. 23 (right) Trimming moulding using mitre template. The thumb is normally on the chisel to steady it but to avoid hiding the blade is shown here at the side

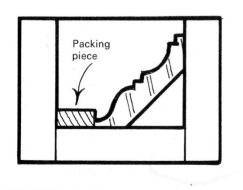

Packing piece

BOW—5**

moulding as in Fig. 22. In this way the teeth cut into the section in both a horizontal and vertical direction. This illustration is also interesting in that it shows the way to deal with a pitched cornice moulding which has no backing. To form a true mitre the top and back faces of the moulding which are at right angles with each other must bear against the back and bottom of the mitre box, and, to ensure this, a packing piece is planed so that it fits exactly between the edge of the moulding and the side of the box. This makes the position definite. It does not matter if the saw cuts right through it.

Mitre template. Fig. 23 shows the use of this in cutting the mitre needed in a door frame having a moulding worked in the solid. It is placed over the moulding and its sloping end (at 45 deg.) used as a guide for the chisel. For small mouldings it can be held in position with the hand. On larger ones a thumbscrew can be tightened over it.

Cramps

These are used to pull the parts of joints together and to hold them whilst the glue sets, and also to hold the wood to the bench whilst being worked.

Sash cramps. For assembling a door frame or a butt joint these are a necessity. Length ranges from 600mm. (2ft.) upwards, and size should be selected to suit the average work done. Blocks should be placed beneath the cramp shoes to prevent damage to the surface.

Tests for both squareness and freedom from winding should be made as soon as possible after tightening the cramps. If the square reveals an inaccuracy as in Fig. 24 the position of the shoes should be shifted in the direction shown by the arrows. A winding test is made by looking across the work. Both near and far rails should appear parallel. If out as shown in exaggeration in Fig. 25 the cramps should again be adjusted in the direction of the arrows.

A point to remember is that cramps are necessarily heavy and may pull a framework out of truth by their weight and so give a false reading. They may also cause a framework to appear true when the weight of the cramps is pulling it down. The frame

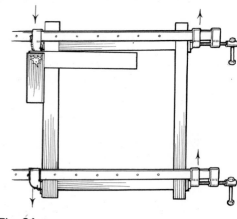

Fig. 24

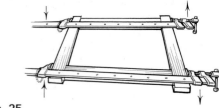

Fig. 25

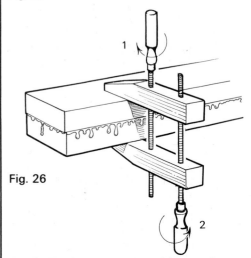

Fig. 26

Fig. 24 Testing squareness of frame when cramping
Fig. 25 Cramped framework in winding
Fig. 26 Order of tightening screws of handscrew

may spring into winding again after the cramps are removed.

When an extra large framework has to be assembled and the available cramps are not long enough, two can be held together by nuts and bolts passed through them. In this way the length can be adjusted to suit the job in hand. The two shoes are removed, enabling the screws to be tightened from either end.

G Cramps, handscrews, and thumbscrews.

These are used chiefly when wood is joined in its thickness. Their application is fairly obvious. The handscrew is particularly useful. To use it open the jaws to the approximate size by grasping a handle in each hand and revolving the one about the other. Rapid adjustment can be made in this way. The inner screw is then tightened (1) Fig. 26 (see arrow), and lastly the outer screw, again in the direction of the arrow. This has the effect of levering the jaw on to the wood. When finally tightened the jaws should be approximately parallel.

The thumbscrew is just a small edition of the G cramp and is used for small work.

Bench holdfast. This (I, p. 17) is used to hold wood still on the bench whilst being worked. Its stem passes through a hole in the bench and it exerts its power by being levered over sideways. It is therefore effective only on a thick bench top. If the latter is thin it is necessary to thickness it locally. Some holdfasts have a metal socket for recessing into the bench top. When a hole is bored through the bench to receive it it is clearly necessary to avoid doing so over a drawer or cupboard.

Improvised cramps. These can always be made from lengths of wood with stops screwed on at the ends to act as shoes. Pairs of folding wedges are knocked in at one end to give the necessary pressure. For the light cramping of odd shapes springs can be used. These are simply old uphol-stery springs cut down and partly straightened out in the form of a C. They are specially useful in repair work in which moderate pressure only is required over surfaces of awkward shape.

Fig. 27 Testing squareness of a cramped-up framework

Chapter six

Light Machines for Woodwork

Although most home woodworkers follow hand methods, there is an increasing tendency to install a machine of one kind or another to cut out some of the more tedious and back-aching operations. The most obvious choice in this connection is a small saw since sawing is probably the most laborious task connected with woodwork. It is as well to point out at the outset, however, that there is a great advantage in having a basic machine to which various machine attachments can be added. This basic machine usually takes the form of a wood-turning lathe, for which circular saw, bandsaw, planer, sander, and mortising attachments are available. There is also the small universal machine which may include circular saw, planer, and borer, but is not a lathe.

As a general rule a machine which is designed for a single purpose is more satisfactory than one which has to be adapted to various uses, but taking into account the limitations of workshop space and the fact that it costs less, the single adaptable machine is generally the better proposition for home craftsmen than several separate machines. A typical machine is shown in Fig. 2, and the various attachments are detailed below the illustration. The use of the individual machines is much the same whatever the type or make, though slight variation in method of use or of sharpening may be needed in accordance with the particular type. The following general principles apply.

Circular Saw

For general woodwork this is the most useful type of saw to have because not only can ripping, cross cutting, and mitreing be done on it, but rebating and grooving are also possible. An essential feature is a table which can be raised or lowered so that the depth of rebates and grooves can be adjusted. Preferably too it should be adjustable at an angle up to 45 deg. to enable wood to be cut at angles other than a right angle. In some machines the saw is adjustable rather than the table, and this has the advantage that, since the table remains flat, there is no tendency for the wood to slide sideways when bevel cuts are being made.

Fig. 1 Use of a light machine in the workshop

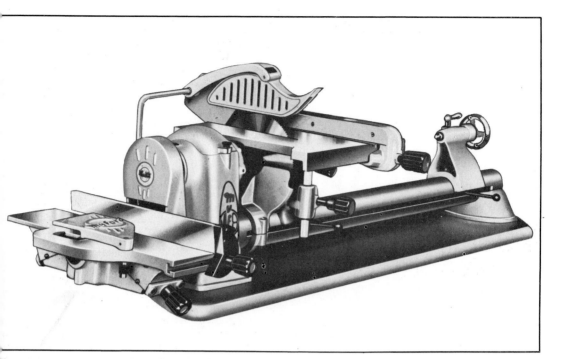

A fence is an obvious requirement so that wood can be ripped to width; also a grooved bench top so that the mitre gauge can be used for cross-cutting at right angles or any other angle. A riving knife is a necessity so that the wood does not tend to bind on the saw in the event of the kerf closing. Lastly an efficient guard should be fitted both above and below (though in many machines the lower casing acts as a guard beneath the top).

For general use either the combination saw (B), Fig. 3, or that with radial cross-teeth (A) should be fitted, as either can be used for both ripping and cross-cutting. Here a word of warning is necessary: keep the saw sharp. A dull saw will burn the wood, and an endeavour to force the wood may result in inaccurate work and possibly cause an accident. Saws with tungsten carbide tipped teeth (C) have the advantage that they remain sharp for a long period and can be used on hard or abrasive materials such as chipboard and other resin-assembled boards without losing their edge.

Ripping. When the timber already has a straight edge it is only necessary to set the fence to the required distance from the saw (the latter cutting

Fig. 2 (above) The Myford ML8 lathe showing circular saw and planer attachments. Other attachments are bandsaw, disc sander and mortiser

Fig. 3 (below) Types of saw teeth

Fig. 4 (above) Use of pusher stick to avoid
bringing fingers close to saw
Fig. 5 (right) Cross-cutting using the mitre gauge

on the waste side), and push the wood through,
keeping the edge close up against it. For long
boards it is a help to have someone at the back to
take it off, pulling and supporting the boards as the
cut nears completion. If this is not possible the
wood can be cut half-way from one end, reversed,
and the cut completed from the other end. In all
cases avoid putting the fingers near the revolving
saw and never have them between the saw and the
fence where they might be trapped. The pusher
stick shown in Fig. 4 should always be used to push
the wood at the end of the cut.

If there is no straight edge to start off with, you can
either plane it straight first (by machine or hand)
and work from this, or you can draw in a pencil line
with the straight-edge, and, standing behind the
wood, pass the wood through without using the
fence. All subsequent cuts can be made from this,
using the fence as a guide.

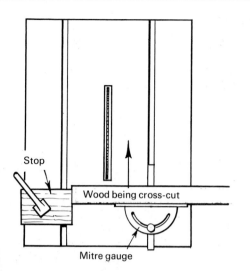

Stop

Wood being cross-cut

Mitre gauge

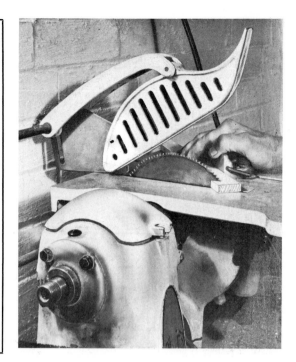

Fig. 6 (above) Cross-cutting to length
Fig. 7 (right) Cutting a mitre on the circular saw
using the mitre gauge. The guard is shown
raised to reveal the saw

Cross cutting. Fig. 5 shows a typical operation.
Note that both hands are kept to the side of the
saw. When several pieces have to be cut all to the
same length the method shown in Fig. 6 can be
followed. A block of wood to act as a stop is fixed
near the front of the saw table with a G cramp.
Its position is adjusted so that its distance from the
saw equals the length of the pieces to be sawn.
The wood is held against the mitre gauge and
pressed up to the stop. The gauge is pushed up to
the saw, and the process repeated until the
required number of pieces has been sawn.
Mitreing is done similarly to square cross-cutting,
Fig. 7, and in the case of compound cuts the table
is also tilted.

Grooving. Frequently on light machines it is
necessary to pass the wood over the saw for as
many times as may be needed to give the required
width of groove. If a drunken saw is available this
can be set to the width, though the bottom of the
groove is not flat, but slightly curved. For most
work, however, the curve is so slight as not to
matter. Some saws can be fitted with a dado head
which will cut grooves. Light machines, however,
are frequently not made to take these, partly

because there is insufficient spindle room, and also
because the cut would be too heavy.

The table (or saw) is first adjusted so that the saw
projects by an amount equal to the required groove
depth. The fence is positioned so that the cut is
level with one side of the groove to be cut. If the
fence reaches only to the saw, a lengthening piece
must be screwed on so that the wood can bear
against it until it is past the saw. After a trial cut all
the parts are run through. The fence is shifted to cut
to the other side of the groove, and again all the
parts cut. For narrow grooves this second cut will
probably give the required width, but third or even
fourth runs may be needed. Remember in every
case to keep the face side of the wood to the fence.

The pusher stick, Fig. 4, is needed for completing
the cut, though the push block is sometimes an
advantage, as shown in Fig. 8. It enables downward as well as inward pressure to be maintained.

Rebating. Narrow rebates can be worked by
taking parallel cuts side by side as at (a), Fig. 9, the
wood being passed through as many times as may
be needed to give the rebate width. For a larger

71

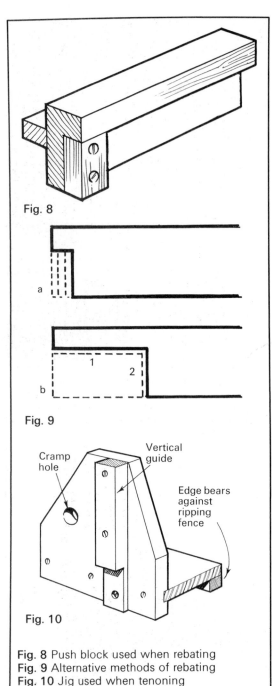

Fig. 8

a

b

Fig. 9

Cramp
hole

Vertical
guide

Edge bears
against
ripping
fence

Fig. 10

Fig. 8 Push block used when rebating
Fig. 9 Alternative methods of rebating
Fig. 10 Jig used when tenoning

rebate, however, two cuts at right angles are the simpler method as at (b). Other things being equal cut No. 1 should be made first because, at the completion of the second cut the waste piece drops away, and it is desirable to have the broad surface of the wood bedding on the saw table where it is not liable to tilt over. Once again the pusher stick is used towards the completion of the cut. This is specially desirable since the riving knife cannot be used, and quite possibly the guard (this depends on the size of the wood being rebated).

Tenoning. It would not be economical in time to set up the saw to cut a single tenon or pair of tenons, but considerable saving in time occurs when a whole series is required. The simplest plan is to make the special device shown in Fig. 10. The parts are glued and screwed together. Exact sizes are not important, but the length might be about 150mm. (6in.), height 175mm. (7in.), and width 100mm. (4in.). In use the wood to be tenoned is held against the vertical guide with a thumbscrew, the latter being either passed through the cramp hole or fixed at the side according to the width of the wood being tenoned. The far edge bears against the ripping fence, the latter being positioned so that the saw cuts to the side of the gauge line. A lengthening piece must be screwed to the fence so that the device is supported throughout its cut. The height of table or saw is arranged so that the shoulder line is just reached. One cut is made at each tenon, the saw readjusted, and the other side of all the tenons cut. Fig. 11 shows the operation. It is usual to cut the shoulders by hand.

It will be realized that the over-all length of all tenons must be alike, otherwise the saw will over-cut some tenons, and under-cut others. This means that a different system must be followed as compared with that usually used for hand work. Exact over-all length including tenons must be fixed beforehand. Apart from actual cutting there is a further saving in time in that only one piece need be marked with the gauge.

Speed. The theoretical optimum speed of an 20cm, (8in.) circular saw is in the region of 4,500 r.p.m., but few small saws are designed for so high a rate. The more usual speed ranges from 1,500 to 2,500 r.p.m., and the saw should cut perfectly well if kept sharp. As a guide to the power required, the following are average.

Saw diam.	H.P. motor
(7in.)	$\frac{1}{3}-\frac{1}{2}$
(8in.)	$\frac{1}{2}-\frac{3}{4}$
(9in.)	$\frac{1}{2}-1$

Band Saw

Next to the circular saw this is the most useful machine saw to have, Fig. 12. It can be used for straight cuts much as the circular saw is used, and also for curves for which the latter is useless. On the other hand, it will neither rebate nor groove, though tenons can be made on it.

Adjustment. There are several adjustments to be attended to on the bandsaw. First the table is usually made to tilt, and the correct angle should be tested with try square or protractor. The top wheel has a tensioning screw which is slackened off when the saw is not in use. When a new saw has to be fitted the locking device has usually to be un-screwed at the front of the table to enable the saw to be passed through the slot. The purpose of the device is to hold the table rigid.

Tracking is the first adjustment of the saw itself, and is accomplished by tilting the top wheel one way or the other. It should be carried out without guides or thrust wheel. Turn the wheel by hand and note whether the saw tends to keep central on the wheels or run to front or rear. If it is inclined to run towards the rear tilt the top of the wheel slightly forward at the top. Continue to adjust until it runs in the required position. It is advisable to vary this from time to time so that wear on the tyres can be equalized.

When satisfactory bring forward the thrust wheel so that it barely touches the back of the saw—it should turn only when the saw is being pressed against it in use. The guides may be blocks of metal or hardwood, and they are adjustable horizontally. They should be just short of touching the sides of the saw—not the teeth, of course. As a rule the upper guides form a complete unit with the thrust wheel, the whole being movable vertically. In use it should be set to clear the wood being sawn with just sufficient space above to enable the line to be followed.

Practical sawing. When possible avoid backing

Fig. 11 Cutting a tenon on the circular saw—the lower guard is shown removed to reveal saw
Fig. 12 (below) Bench bandsaw of the three-wheel type. Coronet Tool Company

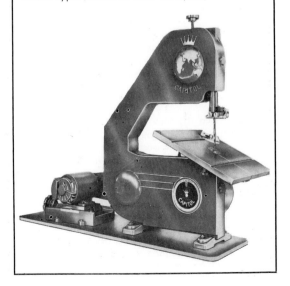

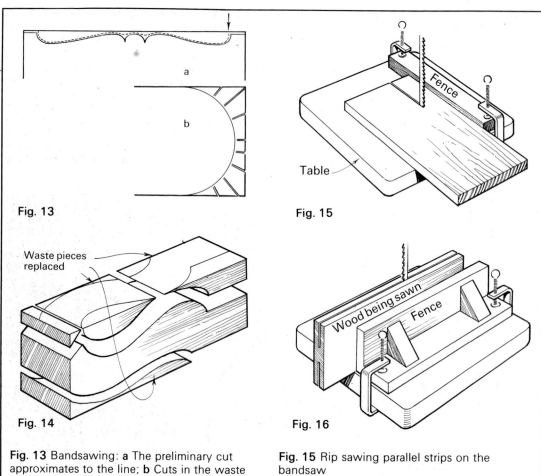

Fig. 13

Fig. 15

Waste pieces replaced

Fig. 14

Table

Fence

Wood being sawn

Fence

Fig. 16

Fig. 13 Bandsawing: **a** The preliminary cut approximates to the line; **b** Cuts in the waste enabling it to fall away easily
Fig. 14 Stages in bandsawing a cabriole leg

Fig. 15 Rip sawing parallel strips on the bandsaw
Fig. 16 Re-sawing on bandsaw. Wide wood is already part sawn from each side on the circular saw

the wood from the saw. Sometimes it cannot be helped, when it should be done carefully and the path of the kerf followed. When a line is fairly intricate follow the main sweep first, ignoring the smaller detail. For instance, in Fig. 13 (a), the first cut would be shown by the dotted line. This would clear away the bulk of the waste without backing, and enable the acute corners to be cut afterwards. Note that the cut is made to the waste side of the line, allowing for later cleaning up. In the case of Fig. 13 (b), the preliminary cuts enable the waste to fall away when the acute curve is being sawn.

Some items call for sawing on two surfaces. For example, the shape of a cabriole leg is marked out on two adjacent faces, and saw cuts made at right angles, producing a square section ready for rounding. The shapes on one side having been cut, the waste parts are replaced as in Fig. 14 enabling the remaining cuts to be made. In some cases the lower waste is also replaced to act as a sort of supporting cradle. It is scarcely necessary in the present case because the back curve reaches practically to the bottom and there is no tendency for it to be unsteady.

When the saw is used for ripping straight cuts a fence is used. This may be a special adjustable item made for the table, or simply a straight piece of wood cramped to the table as in Fig. 15. Make sure that it is fixed parallel with the edge so that the saw is in alignment with the cut.

Sometimes it is useful to use the bandsaw for resawing—that is cutting a board in its thickness. It is a great help if preliminary saw cuts can be made on the circular saw as it lessens the work the bandsaw has to do. The operation is shown in Fig. 16 which shows the tall fence used to ensure that the wood is upright. Fig. 17 shows the bandsaw in use for tenoning.

Planer

Two kinds of machines come under this heading; the surface planer and the thicknesser. The latter, as the name suggests, is used to bring timber to an even thickness, but is not much used in the small home workshop because it is expensive. It is, however, possible to obtain a thicknessing attachment for most planers.

Parts of the surface planer. The diagram in Fig. 18 shows the chief parts. There is the main body in the centre of which the cutter block revolves. This block may have either two or three cutters. In front and to the rear of the cutter block are two tables which are adjustable along two inclined beds. Their height in relation to the cutters is thus adjustable. A fence is fitted to the front table, this being adjustable to any position and also free to cant to any angle. On many machines a rebating table (which is really a side extension of the front table) is fitted. Invariably, too, there is a guard which should be capable of extending right across the cutter block, and also be variable in height.

Sharpening and setting. Although ground, the cutters of a new machine require to be honed on an oilstone to give a fine edge. A simple jig is shown in Fig. 19, and variations can be worked out to suit the individual cutters. The device enables the correct angle to be maintained. When regrinding is needed it is necessary to mount the cutters upon a special carrier which runs back and forth across the

Fig. 17 (above) Sawing a tenon on the bandsaw
Fig. 18 (below) Diagram showing chief parts of the planer

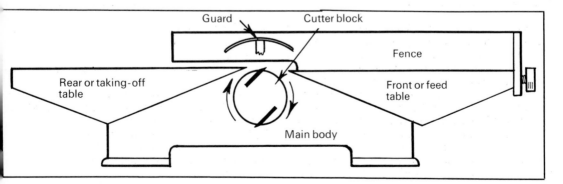

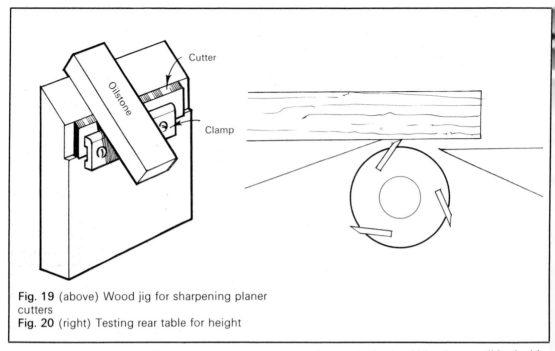

Fig. 19 (above) Wood jig for sharpening planer cutters

Fig. 20 (right) Testing rear table for height

face of the grinding wheel, thus ensuring even grinding.

The cutters are held in the block in various ways, some with wedge pieces held by bolts, or by a separate cap again bolted. As a rule there is some means of adjustment for height—either an adjustment screw at each end or a hole at the rear which enables the cutter to be tapped. Turn the bolts finger tight only when placing the cutters in the block and carry out all adjustment before finally tightening. When there is no adjustment the cutters must all be ground and honed to exactly the same extent.

In use the rear table must be exactly level with the tips of the cutters when in the highest position, and once set is never moved for normal planing until sharpening is required again. Deal with one cutter at a time. Place a piece of wood having a straight edge on the rear table, as in Fig. 20, towards one side and turn the block by hand, adjusting the height of the rear table until the cutter just barely touches the wood. When one side is correct bring the wood to the other edge and test this side of the cutter. The latter will probably need raising or

lowering, and this should be done until both sides just touch the wood, no more. From this point on the rear table must not be moved (the front table is set well down below the level).

Now deal with the second cutter, adjusting this until both sides of this also just touch the wood. When all is in order tighten the fixing bolts and make a second test. The thickness of the cut is fixed by the height of the front table. To ascertain this hold the straight wood on the back table as before. The thickness of the cut will be equal to the gap between the wood and the front table. Some machines have a scale showing thickness of cut, but this requires adjustment after each sharpening. To do this set a gauge to exactly 3mm. ($\frac{1}{8}$in.) and mark along the edge of a straight piece of wood. Set the front table to what is obviously less than 3mm. ($\frac{1}{8}$in.), and, setting the machine in action, pass the wood part way over the block. Lower the front table until the gauge line is just reached and set the pointer to the 3mm. ($\frac{1}{8}$in.) mark. All thicknesses will then be correct to this.

Surfacing. Set the fence to slightly more than the width of the wood, and the guard so that the wood

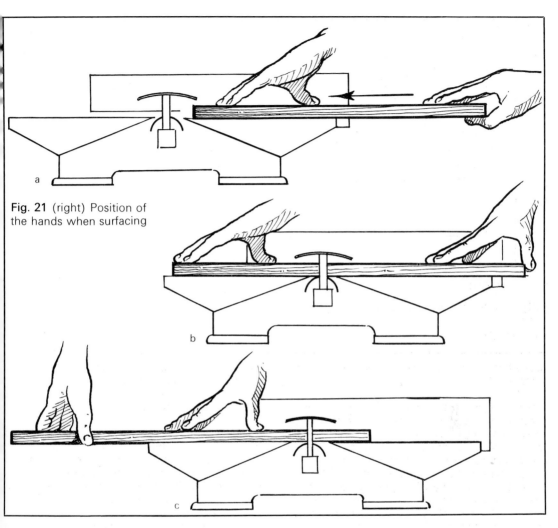

Fig. 21 (right) Position of the hands when surfacing

will pass beneath with comfortable clearance. The front table is also adjusted to the required thickness of cut. Push the wood forward with the right hand and press steadily down with the left on the front table. As the wood passes over the block withdraw the left hand so that it does not approach near to the block. When a reasonable length has passed beyond the block take the left hand over to the wood on the rear table and again press down. As the end of the wood approaches the block take also the right hand over to the rear table where it assists in both pressing down and moving the wood. Done in this way neither hand is ever immediately over the revolving block. Fig. 21, 22.

When a short piece has to be planed it is advisable to use a pusher block as given in Fig. 23. At the start of the cut the wood is fed with the hands in the usual way, but once the rear end is fairly on the table the pusher block is used. When practicable put the hollow side of the wood down on to the table as it is easier to get it straight. If this cannot be done it is necessary to take shavings from the middle first before passing the wood right across.

Edging. This is a similar operation, but the wood

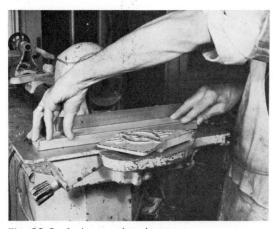

Fig. 22 Surfacing on the planer

Fig. 23 Use of the pusher block when surfacing

Fig. 24 Use of thicknessing attachment to bring wood to constant thickness

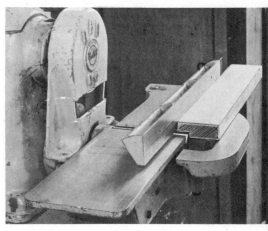

Fig. 25 The planer set up for rebating

must be held firmly up against the fence so that the edge is planed square. If the guard is of telescopic form it is usual to set it low over the block and leave just sufficient gap between its end and the fence for the wood to pass through. In the case of extra wide wood it is as well to increase the height of the fence by screwing a wood fence to it. This gives an increased bearing surface against which the wood can bear. As a fair amount of pressure is required in all planing operations it is as well to wipe over the surface of the tables and the fence with a lightly oiled rag. One last word. Examine the wood and

pass it through in the direction in which it is less likely to tear out the grain.

Thicknessing attachment. This is attached to an ordinary surface planer as in Fig. 24, and is used after one surface of the wood has been planed true. The main pillar of the attachment is secured to the front table, the thicknessing plate thus rising or falling with it. The rear table is set as for normal planing and the distance between it and the thicknessing plate equals the finished thickness of the wood after planing. If much wood has to be

removed pass the wood through twice, the machine being reset for the second pass.

Rebating. Many machines are provided with a rebating table which is a lateral extension of the front table. This supports the wood as it passes through. The rear table is unaltered, that is it remains level with the tops of the cutters. The front table is lowered to the rebate depth, and the fence brought over so that it leaves exposed a length of cutter equal to that of the rebate width. Normally the wood can be passed through in a single operation, but if the rebate is large or the wood extra hard it is as well to set it to half the depth first and pass the wood through twice. At the start of the cut feed the work slowly; otherwise the cutters may snatch the wood and jolt it backwards. Fig. 25 shows the rebating process.

Fig. 26 (left) Stopped chamfer being worked on planer

Fig. 27 (below) Working tapered legs

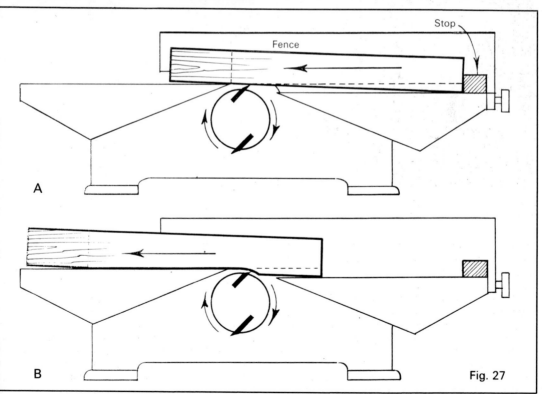

Fig. 27

Bevelling and Chamfering. When these run right through the procedure is much as in normal edging except that the fence is set over at the required angle.

Stopped chamfers are different, and it is necessary for both tables to be exactly level with each other, the cutter block standing up by an amount equal to the chamfer depth. A wood facing is fixed to the metal fence, and stop blocks are screwed to this so that the chamfer begins and ends in the required positions. The wood is held firmly against the near stop and the far end slowly lowered on to the revolving block. The cutters tend to grab as this happens, but the rear block prevents it from being knocked back, and once it lies on the table all grab ceases. The wood is fed forward until the front stop is reached. Fig. 26 shows wood being stop-chamfered.

Fig. 28 Trimming wood on the disc sander

Tapering. The rear table is level with the top of the cutters as in normal planing, and the front one lowered by an amount equal to the wood to be removed at the thin end. A stop is fixed either to the table or to the fence so that the cutters begin to operate just short of the required point as at (A), Fig. 27. The near end of the wood rests against the stop. The wood is pushed forward as at (B).

If the entire length of the wood is to be tapered, the cut will have to be started short of the end because it is essential that the end of the wood drops on to the lip of the rear table. The stop fixed so that there is at least 6mm. (¼in.) of wood resting on the lip. Without this there would be a heavy throw back.

Sanders

There are two chief kinds of sanders used in the home workshop; disc and belt. The former of these is shown in Fig. 28, its chief use being to trim wood rather than to smooth it. For instance it is invaluable for trimming mitres after sawing, or for cleaning up squared ends of wood. Another use is in cleaning the shaped edges of wood when the curvature is convex. Clearly the table must be at right angles to the disc, and the groove along its surface must be parallel with it. The mitre gauge is used as a guide for the wood, and this is slid back and forth so that wear on the abrasive is equalized. Only the down-coming side of the disc is used, as otherwise the wood is liable to be lifted.

Perhaps the chief way in which the disc sander saves time is when a number of pieces have to be trimmed all to the same length. One end of all the pieces is first made square by holding it against the mitre gauge. A jig is then made as shown in Fig. 29. A notch is cut in it, and its length is such that when pressed against the end of the work it touches the end of the table when the far end of the work is hard up against the sanding disc. In use the jig is held against the end of the work and the two pressed forward until the jig touches the table and the sander thus ceases to cut. For large pieces it is advisable to hold the jig to the work with a cramp.

Mitreing is done in much the same way as square trimming, but with the mitre gauge set to the required angle. If necessary a jig similar to that in Fig. 29 can be made, but with its notch cut to accommodate the mitre cut. In all cases the face of the moulding should be uppermost so that the inevitable rag is formed on the underside where it will not show. Compound mitres which slope in both thickness and width can be trimmed readily on the sander.

Renew the abrasive paper as soon as it ceases to cut, otherwise it will merely burn the wood. One of the cold tube glues such as Seccotine gives good adhesion. Place over a flat board, if necessary with a weight above, so that the paper is in close contact with the disc. One of the special sanding discs sold for the purpose can be used, or garnet paper can be stuck down. Avoid allowing it to become damp

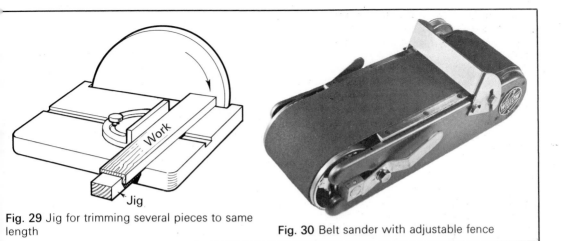

Fig. 29 Jig for trimming several pieces to same length

Fig. 30 Belt sander with adjustable fence

Belt sander. This type can be used for trimming much as the disc sander is used, but it has two advantages; the movement is in a straight line so that it can be used for cleaning up polished work for which the disc sander would be quite un-suitable; and the drums around which it passes enable concave shapes to be smoothed. Fig. 30 shows a belt sander.

Nearly all belt sanders are provided with a stop of some sort, and in the better models an adjustable table is fitted. When this is not provided it is usual to build up one, the details being adapted to suit the individual machine. It should include a table which can be set to various angles so that mitres, etc., can be trimmed. A tracking device is invariably included which ensures that the glasspaper remains on the drums.

Powered Hand Tools

Just as the lathe is the basis of a series of attach-ments for sawing, planing, sanding, etc., so the electric drill is the basic powered tool for which saw, sanding disc and grindstone can be obtained, although of course individual portable machines are available.

The drill gun itself will generally take drills up to 6mm. ($\frac{1}{4}$in.) (larger and heavier drills go up to 12mm. ($\frac{1}{2}$in.) but their use in woodwork is limited). The usual metal-worker's morse drills can,

of course, be used, but it is necessary to pop all holes with a centre punch, as morse drills have no centre point, but an edge. Special twist bits with round shanks can be obtained, but if there is any difficulty the square end can always be sawn from the ordinary twist bit intended for use in the brace. Many of these twist bits have a screw centre and, owing to the speed of the drill, are inclined to grab into the wood and when the hole is large the machine may stall. It will generally be more satisfactory if the screw is filed into the form of a square pyramid, as the drill can then be fed into the wood at whatever speed is required. For holes which must be dead upright it is advisable to use a drill stand which enables the drill to be lowered into the wood. There are two advantages; the hole is perfectly square or at whatever angle is desired, and the hole can be stopped at any depth without the necessity of individual testing.

Slik bits, Fig. 31, used with the electric drill bore clean holes. They are interchangeable on a common shaft and work with a scraping rather than a cutting action. The edges are ground at a low angle which has the advantage of avoiding digging in. They are ground on a small wheel.

A small circular saw attachment is shown in Fig. 32. It is provided with a depth gauge and adjustable fence, and both square cuts and cuts at an angle can be made. The advantage of the tool is in work in which it is more convenient to take the machine to the wood rather than vice versa.

CBOW—6**

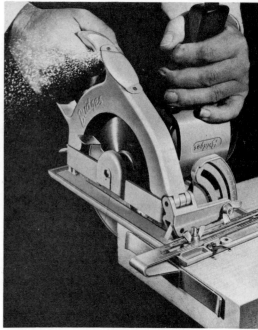

Fig. 31 (above left) The slikbit used in the electric drill
Fig. 32 (above right) Portable saw attachment
Fig. 33 (below) The portable jig saw. Photo: courtesy Black and Decker Ltd.

Jigsaw. This is used for cutting curves and ha the advantage that it can be used for interior cut It is shown in Fig. 33. It is at its best for woo 12mm. ($\frac{1}{2}$in.) thick and under, but can be used fo the occasional cutting of thicker stuff. It can b used in one of two ways, the choice dependin upon the job. For a large panel the saw can b taken to the wood, but small items are best done i reverse. The saw is fixed reverse way up on th bench or in the vice, and the wood passed across i

Sanders. Of the various types of portable sander the orbital (Fig. 34) is the most generally useful fo flat surfaces. It can be obtained as an individua machine or as an attachment for the electric dri It does not rotate in the ordinary sense, and perhap the simplest way of describing the action is t imagine a series of pencil dots on the surface o the pad each of which moves round in a tiny circl somewhere in the region of 2—3mm.

High speed electric router. For such work a recessing, grooving, rebating and moulding, etc this machine has great advantages. It is somewha expensive, however, and for this reason, plus th fact that it may be difficult to fit a suppressor to i

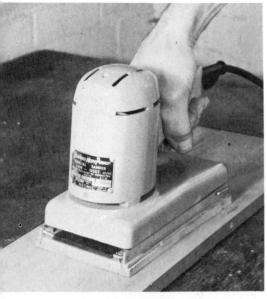

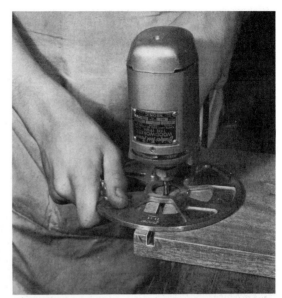

Fig. 34 (above) The orbital sander in use
Fig. 35 (top right) Cutting a groove with the
portable high-speed electric router
Fig. 36 (middle right) Working a rebate with the
Arcoy rebater—the rebate is formed by two cuts
at right angles with each other
Fig. 37 (bottom right) Cutting dovetails with the
Arcoy dovetailer—the variable pitch comb is
shown

is not often found in the home craftsman's work-shop. It will however perform many operations which would be difficult or impossible by other means. It is shown working a groove in Fig. 35.

Rebater. This is virtually a small circular saw used as an attachment to the electric drill. It forms a rebate by making two cuts at right angles with each other as shown in Fig. 36.

Dovetailer. This is an effective machine for cutting lap-dovetails. It cuts both tails and pins in one operation. Apart from the standard equipment there is a variable pitch device, Fig. 37, which enables dovetails to be spaced on wood of varying widths without part of a dovetail being exposed at one end. There is also an attachment for cutting slot dovetails.

Chapter seven

Construction

There is a growing tendency today to use man-made materials rather than solid wood. This is largely because it is almost impossible to obtain many of the more attractive hardwoods in the solid. Consequently veneer has to be used over a groundwork of plywood, laminboard, or chip-board, the edges being lipped with strips of solid wood or veneered. Only such parts as legs, narrow rails, and items to be turned, shaped or carved are made in the solid. Since such manufactured materials are free from liability to shrink there is considerably more freedom in methods of construction than was possible when only solid wood was used. On the other hand each of these materials has its own peculiarities that have to be allowed for in construction, especially in the types of joints to be used.

Items such as doors and drawer parts are frequently made in these modern materials, either ready-veneered boards being used or veneer being laid over the basic panel later. Thus flush doors are popular, these needing only to be lipped or provided with wide edgings suitable to receive hinge and lock screws, etc. On the other hand panelled doors are still preferred for some jobs and have their advantages in some circumstances, though even here panels are frequently in plywood. Traditional methods of construction in solid wood still require to be known, especially by those to whom reproduction furniture appeals.

A point to be kept in mind is that some modern materials require the use of machines if they are to be used effectively. An example of this is chipboard which needs to be cut dead to size on the circular saw because it is difficult and sometimes even impossible to trim the edges really cleanly. The plane removes only dust and in any case loses its edge quickly owing to the abrasive nature of the bonding adhesive. A cut with the handsaw leaves only the roughest of edges and trimming is essential. It is therefore far more satisfactory to use the circular saw which, on a reliable machine, makes a straight cut perfectly square and with a clean finish. The use of a saw with tungsten-tipped teeth avoids the rapid dulling of the teeth.

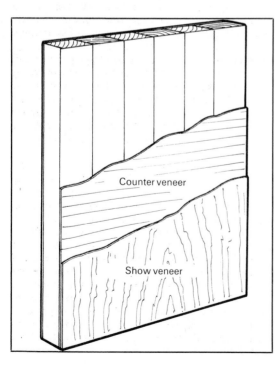

Counter veneer

Show veneer

Fig. 1 Strips glued together side by side and veneered

Another point in this connection is in the use of boards which are ready-veneered on both sides. The use of the handsaw would almost certainly cause the veneer to splinter away at the back, and when only hand methods are possible it is necessary to make the cut well on the waste side so that any splitting out can be planed out later. Better still the cuts are made on the circular saw, the saw itself being given the minimum projection above the board so that the oncoming teeth cut more nearly in alignment with the board rather than striking downwards when they would be more liable to split out the veneer on the underside. Sharp teeth are essential. In really important cases it is advisable to cut through the veneer on the underside first with the cutting gauge (or chisel and straight-edge) so that the grain of the veneer is severed. There is no difficulty about trimming plywood or laminboard with the plane.

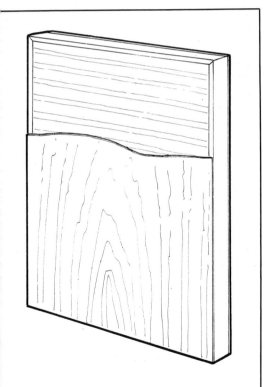

Fig. 2 Laminated or plywood door, edged and veneered

Flush Doors

These are generally in accordance with modern ideas of design, and have become practicable largely owing to the introduction of materials such as plywood and laminated board which are available in wide panels and are free from shrinkage.

Jointed and veneered door. In smaller sizes the method in Fig. 1 can be followed, this being the original way of making such doors, and still used to an extent. Straight-grained, dry, reliable wood is used, strips about 50mm. (2in.) wide being glued together with the heart side alternately front and back. Both sides are levelled and laid with a plain veneer, the grain of which runs crosswise. Over these counter veneers the face show veneers are laid. It is important that veneers of equal thickness are laid on both sides. Sometimes the counter veneer is omitted, but the result is not so reliable.

Lamin board or multi-ply. This is shown in Fig. 2. Whichever substance is used, the veneers should have their grain at right angles with that of the outer surface. In the best way counter veneers are used as in Fig. 1, but frequently this is omitted. Both sides should have the same treatment. To conceal the layers at the edges a lipping is needed, and in many cases this is added before veneering as this gives an unbroken effect at both front and back. If, however, the panel is liable to be subjected to much wear at the edges it is better to veneer first. The edging then affords protection, and it is so narrow that it does not show up unduly.

Methods of arranging the edging are shown at (a), (b), and (c), Fig. 3. The simplest, that at (a), is about 5 or 6mm. ($\frac{3}{16}$ or $\frac{1}{4}$in.) thick and is glued round, the corners being mitred. The veneer is taken right over it. A stronger method is that at (b) and is widely used in the trade. As, however, the edging section is rather awkward to make by hand methods owing to the two rebates having to be of exactly the same depth, the edging at (c) may be preferred. Here only a groove is needed, and the rebates on the ply which form the tongue are more easily worked because there is a much larger area to grip. The rebates could be marked out with cutting gauge and worked independently from each side.

85

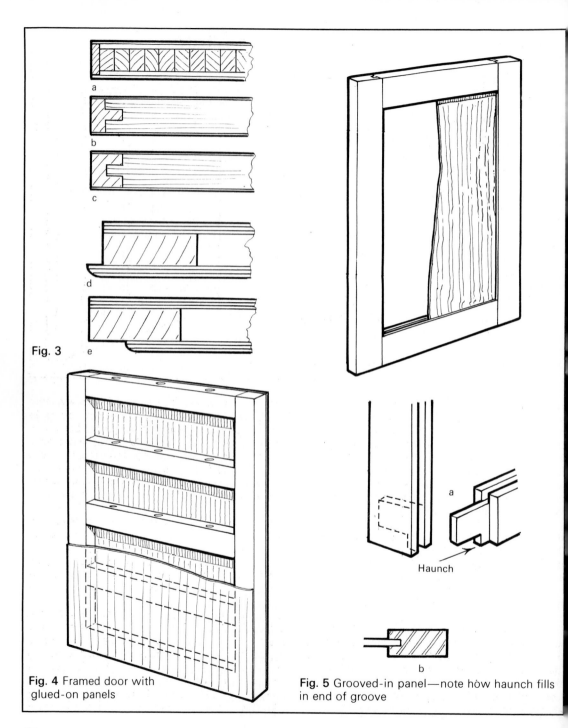

Fig. 3

Fig. 4 Framed door with glued-on panels

Fig. 5 Grooved-in panel—note how haunch fills in end of groove

Haunch

a

b

a

b

c

d

e

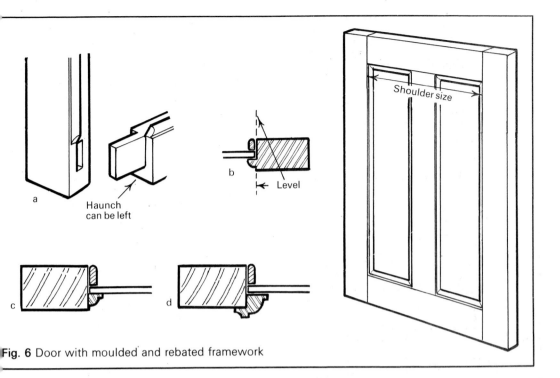

Fig. 6 Door with moulded and rebated framework

ramed and covered door. The method in Fig. 4 frequently used, especially for painted work. In he best way both sides are covered with ply, hough the back one is often omitted. Intermediate ross-rails are desirable to stop any tendency for he panels to sink in locally. When both sides are overed complications are sometimes caused wing to the air necessarily trapped between the anels not being equalized with that of the urrounding atmosphere. To get over this a series f holes can be drilled through all rails as shown. he front ply can either finish flush with the aming at the edges, or it can be made to project s at (d), Fig. 3. The latter is useful in that it forms rebate and helps to keep out dust. Alternatively he set-in panel at (e), Fig. 3, can be used.

ramed doors. These consist of a main framework ut together with mortise and tenon joints, and one r more panels fitted either into grooves or rebates. he idea is that the framework provides the trength, the panel being simply a filling-in piece. of solid wood it is free to move in its grooves or ebates as shrinkage or swelling occurs.

Grooved-in panel. The grooved-in type is shown in Fig. 5. It is used chiefly for painted doors in which there is no difficulty about the application of the finish since the brush is used. It is undesirable for a polished finish in that it is difficult to work the rubber into the internal edges and corners. The panel should preferably be of plywood, laminboard, or hardboard depending upon the particular job.

Note that grooving automatically cuts away the tenon at the inside; consequently the mortise must be set in at the inside correspondingly. Another point is that a haunch is left at the outside of the tenon as at (a) to fill in the groove which necessarily runs right through in the upright.

Moulded and rebated door. For cabinet work with polished finish this is widely used since the panel can be polished separately and fitted afterwards. The front edges are moulded in the solid in the best work, as at (b), Fig. 6, (as distinct from an applied moulding), and an essential feature is that the bottom of the moulding is level with the rebate as shown. This is because

87

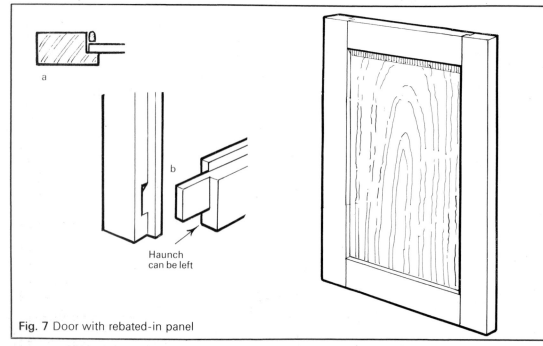

a

b

Haunch
can be left

Fig. 7 Door with rebated-in panel

the moulding is cut away locally opposite the joint, and this produces a flat surface for the shoulders of the tenon.

When setting out notice that the shoulder length is taken up to the rebate, not to the edge of the stiles. This seems obvious enough after moulding and rebate have been worked, but it is not so clear beforehand when the wood is still square-edged. It makes a stronger job if a haunch is cut at the bottom as suggested in (a).

For cheaper work the moulding is applied separately (c), Fig. 6, being mitred round. It is quicker to make because only a plain square-edged frame is needed, and the moulding can be obtained ready-made. A more legitimate use is when a bolection moulding is required as at (d). This could not easily be worked in the solid.

Rebated panel. When the panel is to be rebated in and there is no moulding, the joint at (b), Fig. 7 is used. This calls for long- and short-shoulders to the tenon, the back shoulder being longer than the front one by the rebate depth. Here again a haunch can be allowed with advantage. In all these

examples the joints are marked out and cut firs This is followed by the rebating or grooving, th moulding being worked last. Any mitreing (as i (b), Fig. 6) is the final process and is carried ou during the fitting.

Making a framed door. Fig. 8 shows the genera procedure. Details would be adapted in accordanc with the particular kind of door being made. In th example given at (a) the framework is moulde and rebated, and the joint used would be tha shown on p. 104, at d. Having planed stiles an rails true, mark out the rebate and moulding dept with the gauge (the two are equal). Holding a stil against the cupboard carcase (b) mark with penci the door height, adding about $1\frac{1}{2}$mm. ($\frac{1}{16}$in.) t allow for trimming and fitting. To mark th shoulder size of the rails place the two stiles at th bottom of the carcase and lay the rail on them as a (c). Transfer the line of the rebate, again addin about $1\frac{1}{2}$mm.

To ensure both stiles being alike they should b cramped together temporarily as at (d) and th marks squared across both. Note that in addition t the over-all width it is necessary to square in th

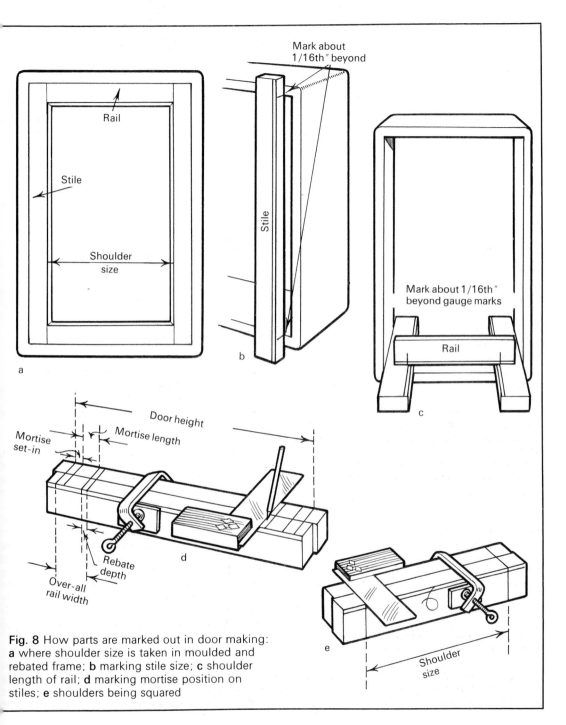

Mark about
1/16th″ beyond

Rail

Stile

Stile

Shoulder
size

Mark about 1/16th″
beyond gauge marks

Rail

a

b

c

Door height

Mortise length

Mortise
set-in

Rebate
depth

d

Over-all
rail width

e

Shoulder
size

Fig. 8 How parts are marked out in door making:
a where shoulder size is taken in moulded and
rebated frame; **b** marking stile size; **c** shoulder
length of rail; **d** marking mortise position on
stiles; **e** shoulders being squared

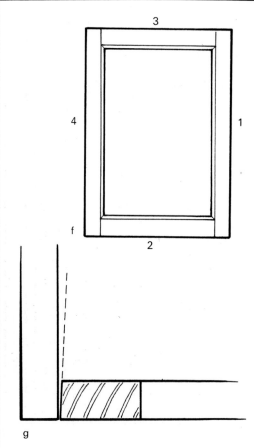

Fig. 8 f order in which door edges are trimmed; g how closing edge slopes

rebate depth and the mortise set-in at the end. The two latter lines give the mortise length. All marks should be put in with pencil.

A similar procedure is followed for the rails, but the marking knife or chisel is used (e). Afterwards the parts are separated and the marks squared all round each rail independently. The butt of the square should be against face side or face edge in every case.

Cutting the joints follows, after which the rebates are worked, and lastly the mouldings. The shoulders should not be sawn until the last two processes have been completed. The mitreing of the moulding is described at (f), page 16, done with the mitre template.

After assembling level the joints and fit the door in the order shown at (f). If, after planing the No. 1 edge to fit the cupboard, the door is appreciably too wide, plane the surplus equally from both edges. Otherwise they will not balance. The same thing applies to the top and bottom edges.

Large Doors

Ledged and braced door. The simplest form of door is the kind one might make for a shed. It consists of tongued and grooved boards, usually 22mm. ($\frac{7}{8}$in.) or less for a light door, with ledges or cross pieces of heavier stuff—say 32mm. ($1\frac{1}{4}$in.) — nailed across. To prevent sagging diagonal braces are added as in Fig. 9, these fitting into notches cut into the ledges. It is unlikely that the width can be made up by an exact number of boards, and the procedure is to go beyond the width and reduce the two outer boards so that the effect is balanced Remember that the outer tongue and groove have to be removed from these outer boards in any case. It may occasionally happen that very narrow strips are left at the outside, and it is then advisable to reduce the width of all the boards, re-grooving them where necessary; or, better still, choose a width of board which is more convenient.

Prepare the ledges, remembering to set them in where necessary to clear the door jamb. Bevel or chamfer the edges as shown. Ledges are usually inside, but for outside work the lower edges should be left square and a drip groove worked. It is convenient to cut the notches to receive the braces before fixing as it is merely a matter of sawing across the grain and chiselling the sloping notches. Nail all three ledges to one stile as in Fig. 10, test for squareness, and turn the whole over. With straight-edge and pencil mark the positions, and nail the boards, punching in the heads. In this way the nails pass through the thinner wood to the thicker.

Once again reverse the door and cut the braces to make a close fit in their grooves. Nail on finally from the other side, pencil lines being drawn in as

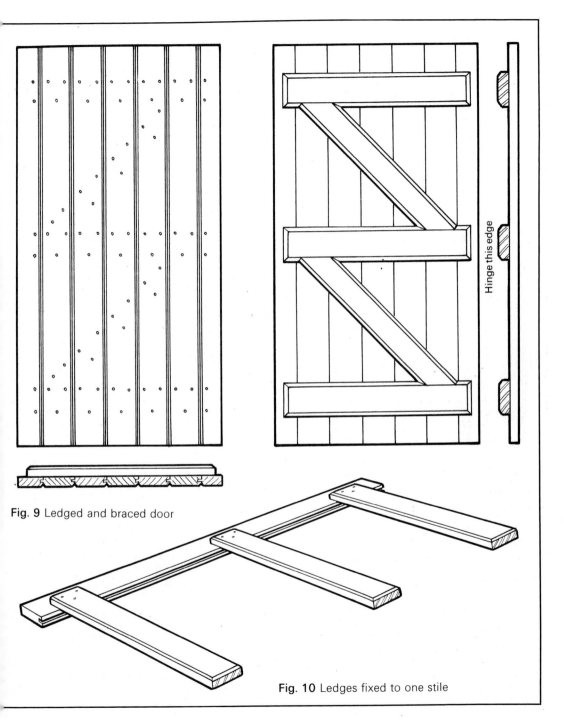

Fig. 9 Ledged and braced door

Hinge this edge

Fig. 10 Ledges fixed to one stile

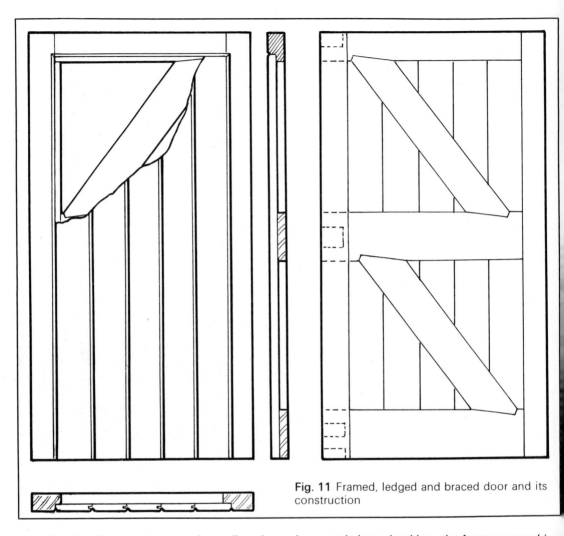

Fig. 11 Framed, ledged and braced door and its construction

a guide. In all cases stagger the nails when possible to avoid splitting.

Framed, ledged and braced door. This is used in better class work. A framework is put together with mortise and tenon joints, and braces fitted to prevent sagging. Tongued and grooved boards are nailed on to one side as in Fig. 11.

Top rail and stiles are rebated to receive the T and G boards, but the mid and bottom rails are thinner by the thickness of the boards and have bare-faced tenons. (a) shows the top rail joints. Note the long- and short-shoulders, the front one reaching down to the rebate. The bare-faced tenons of mid and bottom rails are given at (b). All are taken through and wedged from outside.

Assuming that the boarding has a V joint at the tongue, the main frame should be chamfered to agree before assembling. That of the top rail runs right through, but that of the stiles should run out short of the joint and be finished with a mason's mitre cut in the solid after gluing up. Cut in the braces, and fix with a nail at each end driven through the edge.

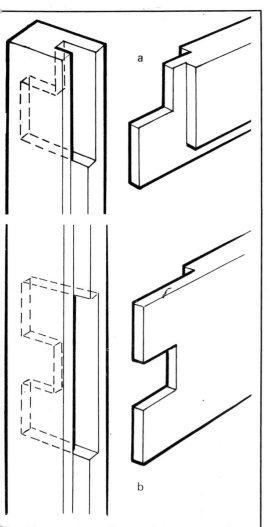

Fig. 11 a mortise and tenon joint at top; **b** bare-faced tenon of mid-rail

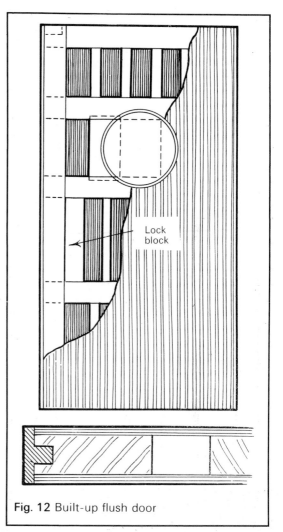

Fig. 12 Built-up flush door

he T and G boarding should be even as far as
ossible. Any reduction that may be needed should
e taken equally from the outside boards. Nail in
osition, and punch in all heads.

lush door. These are of many kinds. An
ttractive pattern with or without glass panel is
hown in Fig. 12. A main framework is put
together with mortise and tenon joints and a
veneered plywood panel glued on at each side. To
prevent sinking between the rails a number of
slats are inserted. Also a lock block is set in to
enable a mortise lock to be cut in, and uprights to
enable the circular window to be cut. Tongued
edges are added finally, partly to give a neat finish,
and also to protect the veneer edges.

It is essential that the door frame is entirèly free
from winding; also that the whole is kept completely flat when the panels are being pressed.
Otherwise any winding will be perpetuated.

93

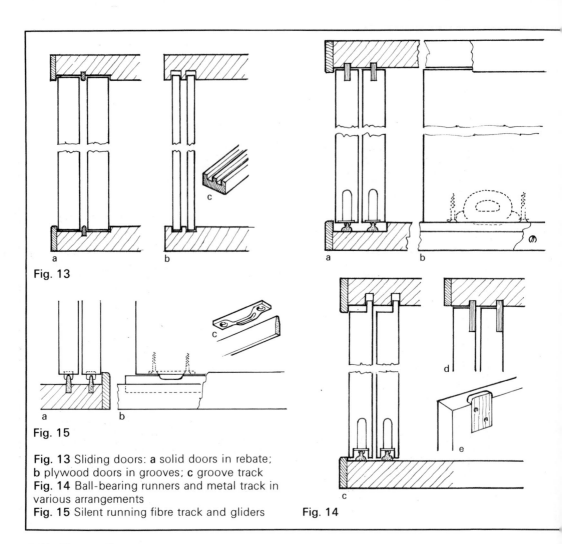

Fig. 13 Sliding doors: **a** solid doors in rebate; **b** plywood doors in grooves; **c** groove track
Fig. 14 Ball-bearing runners and metal track in various arrangements
Fig. 15 Silent running fibre track and gliders

Sliding Doors

There are many ways of arranging these.

Solid wood doors. A simple method for wood doors is given in Fig. 13 at (a). There is a rebate wide enough to take both doors with a separating bead between. It is successful up to a point, but the bearing surfaces are wide, and there is consequently considerable friction. Furthermore the wear takes place on the surface and edge of the door itself, and an unsightly wear mark is eventually

formed. The use of candlegrease as a lubricant is help in reducing friction.

The separating bead is inserted when the doors ar being put in position. Make it a tight fit and us only one or two dabs of glue so that removal is no unduly difficult. If preferred the top bead can b glued in permanently beforehand. The lower on can be in two lengths with a short spliced join One piece only is glued in permanently. Th allows the door to be passed in and slid along after which the remaining piece is tapped in wit two dabs of glue to hold it.

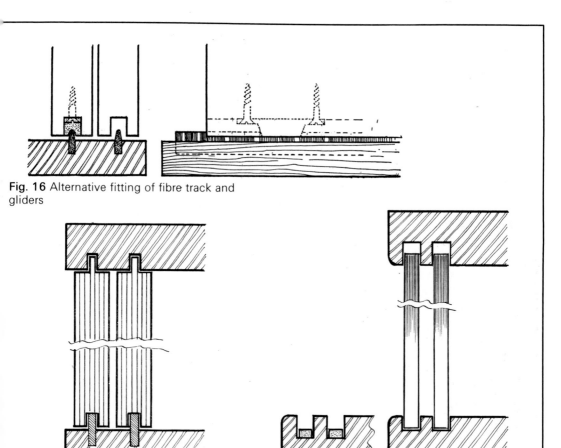

Fig. 16 Alternative fitting of fibre track and gliders

Fig. 17 Sliding doors tongued and grooved top and bottom

Fig. 18 Sliding glass doors running in grooves

Lighter doors in plywood can be arranged as at (b). The top grooves are double the depth of those at the bottom so that the doors can be raised and pulled forwards to remove them. Alternatively the special grooved section at (c) can be inserted in a rebate.

Special tracks and runners. For heavy doors the ball-bearing runner and track in Fig. 14 is often used. The runners are let into the underside of the door as at (a) and (b), and the track is screwed to a rebate in the cupboard bottom. When a facing-fillet can be fixed the arrangement as shown is satisfactory. Otherwise it is necessary to groove the underside of the door so that it fits right over the track as at (c). At the top are simple wood tongues. A simple alternative is that shown at (d) and (e). Pieces of hardwood are let into the backs of the doors and fixed with screws. They slide in grooves as shown and can be screwed in after the doors are in position. In this way the doors can be released easily.

A specially successful fitting is the fibre track and gliders in Fig. 15. The fibre track is let into grooves worked in the cupboard bottom, and when a

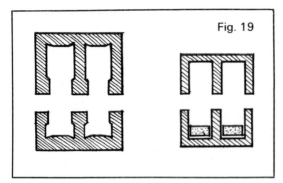

covering bead can be used the gliders are merely recessed into the underside of the door. A better method, however, is to work grooves in the door so that the latter fits closely down to the cupboard bottom as in Fig. 16. An alternative is the scheme in Fig. 17, often used for multi-ply doors. The top tongues are slipped in first and the bottom beads again arranged in separate lengths.

Glass doors. A simple method is given in Fig. 18 in which grooves to give a free fit are worked in top and bottom. It will be noted that the top grooves are extra deep to allow the doors to be lifted up and dropped into the bottom ones. This allows for the removal of the doors at any time. Rather sweeter running is obtained by placing strips of fibre in the bottom grooves as shown to the left. Tempered Masonite does very well for the purpose. An alternative is to glue strips of felt along the grooves, though this does not wear so well.

Special metal and fibre channelling is also available as in Fig. 19. In both of these a large groove is worked in top and bottom to receive the channelling as a whole.

One last word with regard to any scheme which has projecting beads at the bottom is that it is a good plan to stop both beads about 50mm. (2in.) short at one end so that the bottom can be dusted out easily.

Tambours

A tambour consists of a series of narrow strips of wood glued down on to a canvas backing. The

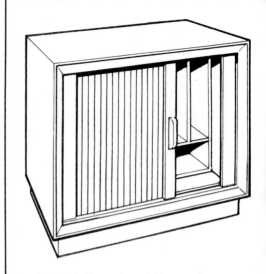

Fig. 19 (left) Examples of fibre tracks

Fig. 20 (above) Small cabinet with tambour front

ends fit in grooves worked in the cabinet, Fig. 20 and it can travel around any curve of reasonable radius. Generally only convex curves can be negotiated (the canvas fitting on the inner side because the joints can open as the tambour passes around the bend. Some tambours, particularly those fitted to the older type of writing desk, have wires passing through them to hold them together in place of canvas. This makes it simple to use a tambour which can bend either way since the pivoting point is in the middle of the wood in line with the wire.

Various sections. Some sections of tambours are given in Fig. 21. The simplest is that at (a). In this particular case the surface is veneered but solid strips could be used. For the latter a common practice is to use alternate strips of light and dark wood. When veneer is used as at (a), the grain is often taken cross-wise, and a single sheet of veneer is used so that the grain is continuous. In making such a tambour the work is prepared in a width sufficient for all the strips to be cut, two or more pieces being jointed together. It is then veneered, and the whole cut into strips afterwards each being numbered so that it can be replaced in

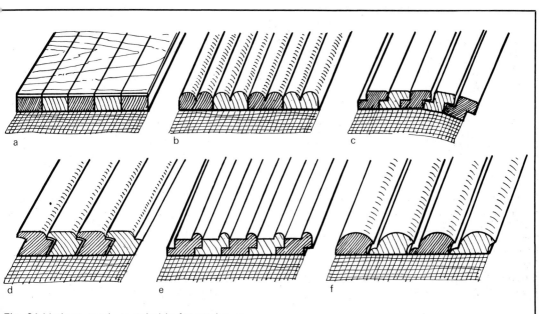

Fig. 21 Various sections suitable for tambours

he same order and so preserve the continuity of grain. To avoid casting both sides can be veneered.

When a bead section is required the strips can be prepared to form single beads each, unless they are extra narrow, in which case they can be formed two to each strip as at (b). It will be realised that in both this section and that at (a) the joints necessarily open as the tambour passes around a curve. As a rule this does not matter because it is generally concealed around the curve. Where this cannot be arranged an overlapping section is advisable as shown at (c).

A rather neater section is that at (d), in which the small curved portion is struck from a centre in line with the canvas backing. The two parts thus fit neatly within each other. It is, however, an awkward section to work by hand. (e) is simply a variation of (c), whilst (f) has the advantage that it can bend in either direction.

Assembling a tambour. It is necessary to make an assembly board on which the parts can be put together as shown in Fig. 22. This has edging pieces nailed down on three sides, the thickness of the strips being rather less than of the tambour pieces. The last named must be all of exactly the same thickness, and the edges should be planed perfectly square, and straight. Before placing in position rub a piece of candlegrease along the edges to prevent any glue which may penetrate from adhering. They are assembled side by side and the fourth edging piece passed on at the end. This should be lightly tightened with a cramp then nailed, thus bringing all the pieces close together. To prevent any tendency for the pieces to be lifted up by the pressure hold a batten across the face of the tambour pieces until the nails have been driven into the edging piece. In any case only light pressure is needed.

For the backing use a good quality piece of fine canvas. Stretch it as far as possible by drawing it back and forth over the rounded edge of a straight bar of wood. Fix it to one end of the board with a few tacks, and fold it back clear. Glue the tambour pieces, draw the canvas right across to the far end, and fix down with one or two tacks. Smooth out any creases in the canvas, and fix down a top board with cramps, (Fig. 23). A sheet of paper prevents any glue which may have squeezed

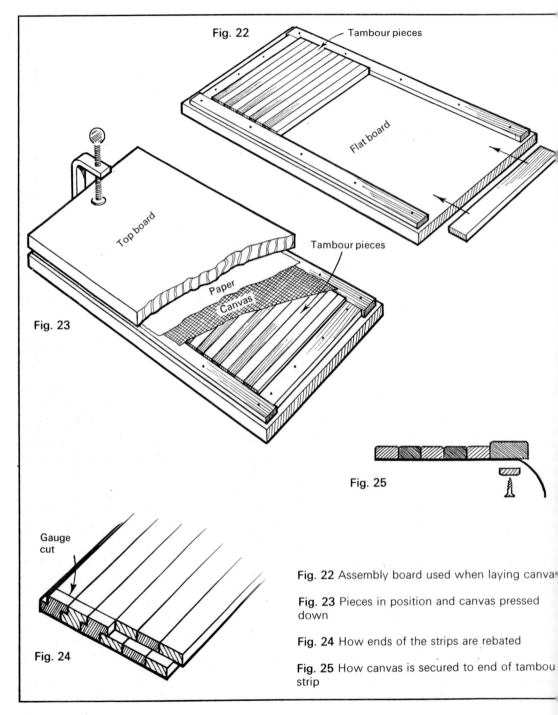

Fig. 22

Tambour pieces

Flat board

Top board

Tambour pieces

Paper

Canvas

Fig. 23

Fig. 25

Gauge cut

Fig. 24

Fig. 22 Assembly board used when laying canvas

Fig. 23 Pieces in position and canvas pressed down

Fig. 24 How ends of the strips are rebated

Fig. 25 How canvas is secured to end of tambour strip

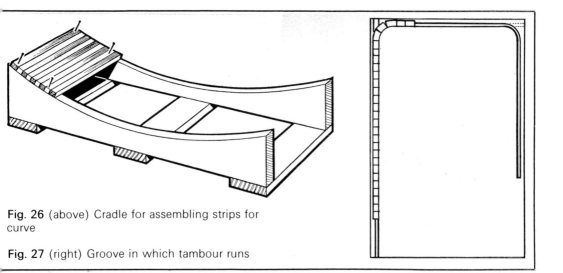

Fig. 26 (above) Cradle for assembling strips for curve

Fig. 27 (right) Groove in which tambour runs

rough from sticking to the board. Often it is not ecessary to use the top board, the canvas being st smoothed down by hand. Make sure that all eases are got rid of.

tting. Allow ample time for the glue to set and y the movement, making sure that every joint ens. The ends are then trimmed so that they ter the groove. Sometimes the groove is rrower than the thickness of the tambour eces, a rebate being worked at the front of the mbour as in Fig. 24 to form a shoulder. The lvantage is that the groove is entirely hidden by e shoulder even after considerable wear. It is ecially useful for moulded tambour pieces as herwise the groove would be visible in the cesses. To work the rebate cut the face of the mbour with the cutting gauge and use the oulder or bullnose plane.

/hen the tambour is fitted to a bow shape which is sible it is usual to have the members in the form f beads and to glue up flat. The slight opening at e curve scarcely shows. If, however, the flat ction ((a), Fig. 21) is required it is desirable to t on a cradle which has the same curvature as the b as shown in Fig. 26. The pieces are cut about 8mm. (1½in.) over length and are placed face ownwards on the cradle. When the joints are shot e shooting board should be arranged so that the dge is a trifle out of square thus ensuring a close

joint when the parts are in the curve. The first strip has a couple of nails driven half way in, about half a dozen strips laid in and pushed tightly home, and another piece nailed. You can turn the cradle upside down to see that there are close joints on the face side.

As a rule the end member is made extra large as this enables a handle to be fixed to it. The canvas is glued about half way across it and 50 or 75mm. (2 or 3in.) free end left as in Fig. 25. This is taken around a fillet or bead and the latter screwed at the back so locking the canvas. Alternatively the bead is screwed straight down over the canvas.

Tambour grooves. The groove in which the tambour works has usually to be cut in with the chisel. The router can be used to finish off to even depth, and for the straight portions a fence can be fixed to enable it to be used as a plough. Do not have the curves too sharp. As a rule it is necessary to cut the groove rather fuller at the curves to enable the tambour to pass easily. There must of course be a place (generally at the rear) where the tambour can be started (see Fig. 27). This can be blocked up after the tambour is in position or a stop can be fitted. Sometimes it is practicable to make a separate lining for the cabinet in which the grooves can be worked. The Technikos plough is useful for working the groove, especially round flat curves. The tool is shown in use in Fig. 28.

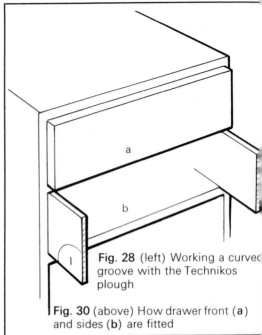

Fig. 28 (left) Working a curved groove with the Technikos plough

Fig. 30 (above) How drawer front (a) and sides (b) are fitted

The tambour should not be finally fitted until both it and the cabinet have been polished because it would be impossible to polish cleanly. In fact, in the case of a moulded tambour the individual members should be polished—or at least bodied up before the canvas backing is glued on. Otherwise it would be impossible to reach the quirks with the rubber. When the whole thing has been fitted and the working tried, the ends of the tambour should be lubricated with candlegrease. This will both ease the running and make it silent.

Drawer Making

In the best way drawers are dovetailed, and the joints are still cut by hand in good cabinet work. Fig. 29 shows the setting out for the usual form of drawer at (A). The lapped dovetails at the front have the pins running almost to a point, this giving a very neat appearance. Note that, since the bottom fits in a groove worked in the front it is necessary for this groove to be contained within the bottom dovetail (see dotted lines). Otherwise a gap would appear at the sides. The sides are not grooved since an applied grooved moulding is

used (see sections (B) and (C)). At the back th bottom fits beneath the square lower edge of th back.

In the case of a small shallow drawer in which th utmost interior depth is required, the bottom fi flush with the lower edges of the sides and rests i rebates. This necessitates a small square membe being cut at the bottom as at (D), Fig. 2! Sometimes the drawer sides have to be set in fror the ends, in which case the slotted dovetail at (F is used. This is stopped at the top. At (A) th bottom is shown projecting at the rear. This needed only when solid wood is used, its purpos being to enable the bottom to be pushed forward i the event of shrinkage. If it is of plywood hardboard it can finish level.

Making a drawer. Plane the drawer front to mak a close fit in the opening ((A), Fig. 30). It helps t make it slightly tapered—no more than th thickness of a thin shaving. Plane the bottom edg first, and trim one end to align with the openin Mark the length, trim to fit, and plane the top edg lastly. The back is treated similarly but the width less owing to its resting on the drawer bottom, an

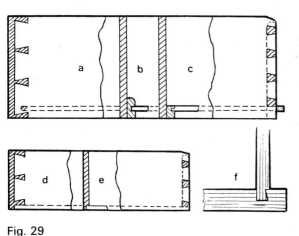

Fig. 29

Fig. **29** Setting out of dovetailed drawers

Fig. **31** Board screwed to bench enabling drawer to be cleaned up

Fig. **32** Simple drawer construction

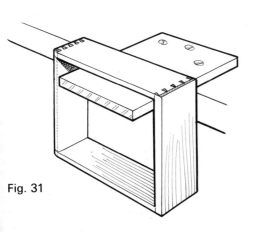

Fig. 31

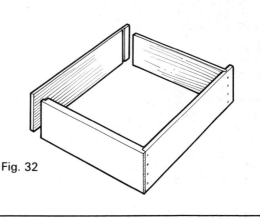

Fig. 32

e set-down from the top. Trim the bottom edges the sides, plane the ends square, making both ke, and plane the top edge until a fairly tight fit is cured ((b), Fig. 30). Dovetailing follows (see 114), and, after assembling, the drawer is fitted fore the bottom is added. A convenient way of aning without danger of racking is shown in g. 31. Candlegrease rubbed cold over the earing surfaces is a good lubricant, but should t be used until after polishing.

r a quick and cheap alternative the construction Fig. 32 can be followed. A lapped joint is cut at

the front, and a simple groove at the rear. The whole is assembled with glue and nails, the last named being driven in askew so that they slope towards each other dovetail fashion.

Window Frames

It is seldom that the home craftsman needs to make a house window, but he often requires one for a garden shed or garage. A light double frame casement window is given in Fig. 33.

101

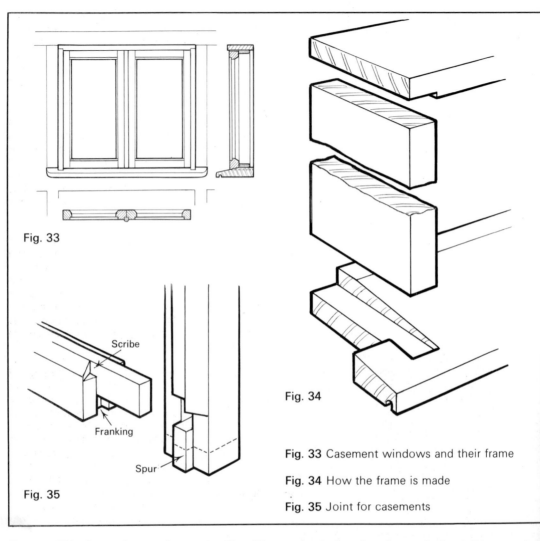

Fig. 33

Fig. 34

Fig. 35

Fig. 33 Casement windows and their frame

Fig. 34 How the frame is made

Fig. 35 Joint for casements

Frame. This is made as shown in Fig. 34. Uprights and top have a simple rebated joint. At the bottom the uprights fit into a sill which is planed at its top outer surface to give a slope. Under the front edge is a drip groove. A simple checking is to cut to receive the upright, and it is advisable to do this before working the chamfer because this enables the router to be used.

Casements. A standard section is used for this. The joint shown at Fig. 35 is used, and it will be noticed that in place of the cabinet maker' haunch is a franking. The mortise width is mad equal to the width of the centre square. Wedge through-tenons are used, and the chamfer i scribed rather than mitred. Note how the chamfe is cut away locally opposite the mortises, enablin equal shoulders to be used on the tenon. Th centre closing bead should fit in a rebate as i Fig. 33, and this necessitates each frame bein rebated. It is necessary to bevel the bottom edge to align with the sloping sill.

Chapter eight

Joints

The number of joints used in woodwork is little short of staggering when their variations in detail and size are taken into account. One need only bother with the relatively few basic joints, however, and we give these on the following pages. Their application will be found in the designs for things to make.

Mortise and tenon joints. The chief kinds are shown in Figs. 1 and 2. Generally the tenon is as near as possible one third the thickness of the wood, and it is a case of selecting a chisel for mortising which is the nearest to this size. Thus for 19mm. ($\frac{3}{4}$in.) stuff a 6mm. ($\frac{1}{4}$in.) chisel is used; for 22mm. ($\frac{7}{8}$in.) and 25mm. (1in.) wood an 8mm. ($\frac{5}{16}$in.) size is suitable.

A simple stub-tenon joint and the method of cutting is given in Figs. 1, 3 and 4. At the outset it should be realized that when several corresponding joints are to be cut, as in, say, a door, all tenons would be marked out at the same time, the shoulder marks being squared across all. This is explained more fully on p. 88, where door construction is dealt with. Here, however, we give the procedure in a single joint for clearness.

Square the rail width in pencil across the edge of the stile as at (b), Fig. 3, noting that the whole thing is invariably set in from the end of the wood leaving a waste piece as it lessens any liability for wood to split (a). A third line is put in to give the mortise length. Now set the pins of the mortise gauge to the width of the chisel being used, (c), and fix the fence so that the pins are as near as possible central on the edge of the wood (in the case of rebated frames the mortise is generally level with the corner of the rebate). Mark the wood (c) with the fence bearing against the face side of the wood.

Much of the waste can be removed by boring, using a bit slightly smaller than the mortise width. This is shown more clearly on page 27. The mortising is shown at (d), Fig. 3. The wood is cramped over a solid part of the bench, and a thumbscrew put on at the end with a waste piece of wood beneath the screw. This reduces any liability for the wood to split. Make the first cut at about the middle, and cut in a little way only. Shift the chisel a little way along and chop down again, this time a little deeper, and so work

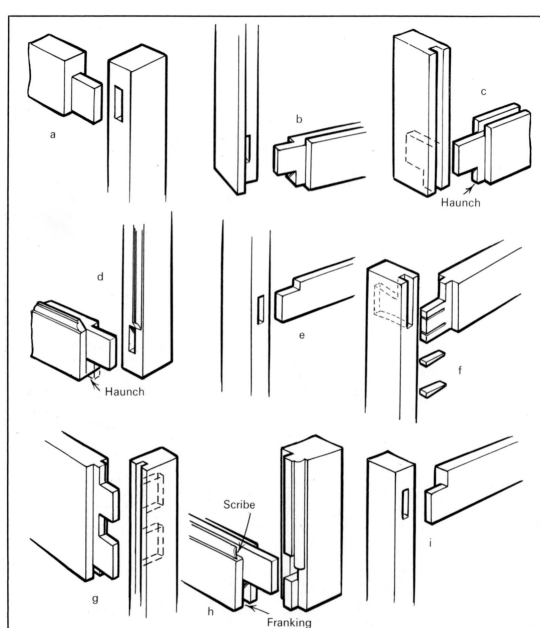

Fig. 1 Varieties of the mortise and tenon joint: **a** stub mortise and tenon (a haunch could be added as at **c**); **b** mortise and tenon for rebated frame, note long and short shoulders; **c** mortise and tenon for grooved frame; **d** mortise and tenon for rebated and moulded frame; **e** bare-faced mortise and tenon; **f** wedged-through-mortise and tenon; **g** double mortise and tenon; **h** mortise and tenon for window frame; **i** bare-faced mortise and tenon

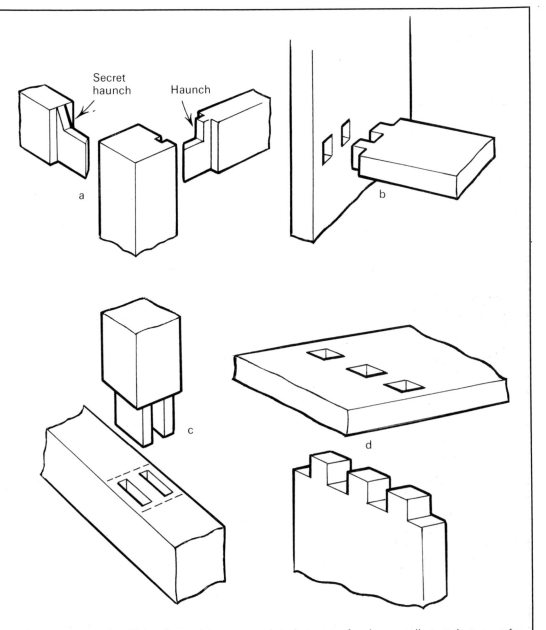

Fig. 2 Further examples of mortise and tenon joints: **a** mortise and tenon for leg and rails, alternative haunches are given—tenons are cut at an angle at ends to meet in thickness of wood; **b** twin tenons for drawer rails; **c** twin tenons for heavy framing; **d** pinned joint for carcase partitions, etc.

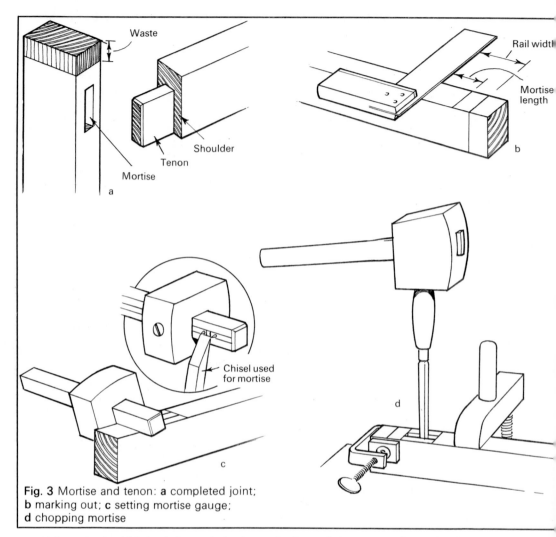

Fig. 3 Mortise and tenon: **a** completed joint; **b** marking out; **c** setting mortise gauge; **d** chopping mortise

up to about 1mm. ($\frac{1}{16}$in.) of the end. A piece of paper stuck to the chisel shows the depth to which the chisel is taken.

Reverse the chisel and repeat the process in the other direction. Levering over the chisel will remove the centre waste. Finally cut down on the pencil lines, keeping the chisel upright. These final cuts take out the dubbed-over ends caused by the levering-over with the chisel.

The tenon shoulders should be squared round with the chisel or a knife as at (a), Fig. 4. Hold the butt of the square always against either the face side or face edge of the wood. Mark the tenon with the mortise gauge, again used from the face side. End and both edges should be marked. Hold the wood at an angle in the vice as shown at (b) when sawing, and place the saw to the waste side of the gauge line. To complete the cut reverse the wood as at (c), this time upright. A properly cut tenon should fit as it is with no further attention.

To enable the shoulders to be sawn make a sloping cut with the chisel on the waste side as shown

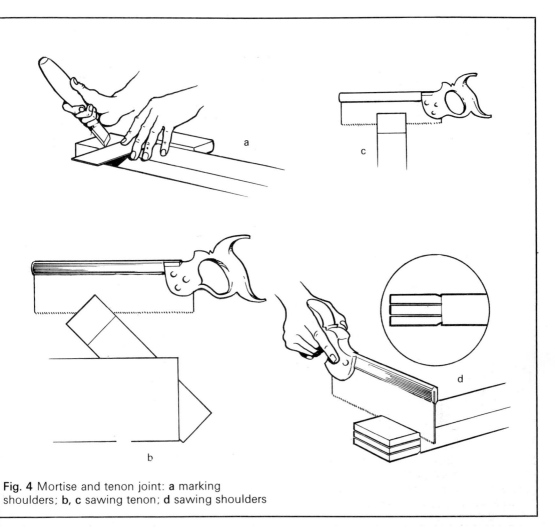

Fig. 4 Mortise and tenon joint: **a** marking shoulders; **b, c** sawing tenon; **d** sawing shoulders

inset at (d). This provides a channel in which the saw can run. Lastly mark the amount to be cut away at the side of the tenon and cut. It is advisable to put a thumbscrew on the wood at the mortise end to prevent splitting when the joint is being fitted. In some cases a haunch is left on the tenon as in Fig. 1C.

Dowelled joints. Although these have a perfectly legitimate place in some work, they are often used as a quick substitute for the mortise and tenon joint for some types of framework as in Fig. 5B. Chairmakers frequently use dowels for

joining seat rails to the legs. Although there are various ways of marking out the joint the method chiefly used today employs a special proprietary dowel guide. The only marking out required with this tool is a centre line, the dowels being spaced equally at each side. Apart from a saving in time in marking out, the bit is guided by the sleeves fitted to the guide, and the holes are therefore perfectly true. Several sizes of sleeves are available to suit different sizes of bits. The tool is shown at D and E.

A groove should be formed along the length of all

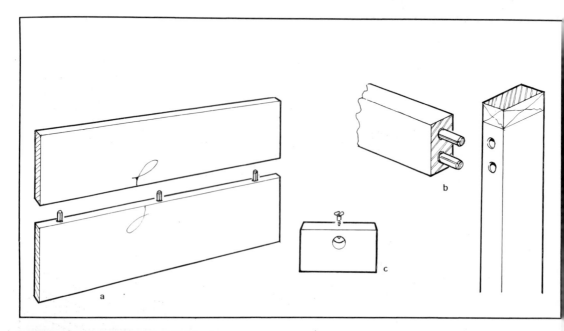

Fig. 5 a edge joint strengthened with dowels;
b framing joint; c appliance for grooving dowels;
(left) The Record dowelling jig
(below left) The Woden dowelling jig

dowels to enable surplus glue to escape when the dowels are knocked in. Without it the wood would be liable to split out. A simple means of forming this groove is the appliance at Fig. 5C. A hole slightly larger than the dowel size is bored in a piece of hardwood and a screw driven in at the edge so that the point protrudes at the hole. The dowel rod is pushed through the hole whilst in a long length, the screw point forming the groove.

Another detail is that it is advisable to lightly countersink the bored holes as glue is awkward to remove cleanly after the dowels have been inserted in the one piece. It helps, too, if the ends of the dowels are lightly chamfered as it enables them to be started easily in the holes. A special dowel sharpener for the brace is available.

Halved joints. These are used in the construction

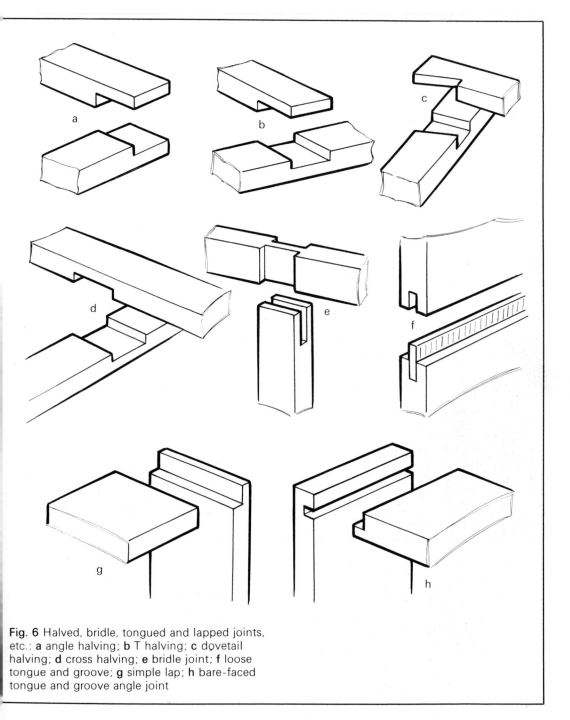

Fig. 6 Halved, bridle, tongued and lapped joints, etc.: **a** angle halving; **b** T halving; **c** dovetail halving; **d** cross halving; **e** bridle joint; **f** loose tongue and groove; **g** simple lap; **h** bare-faced tongue and groove angle joint

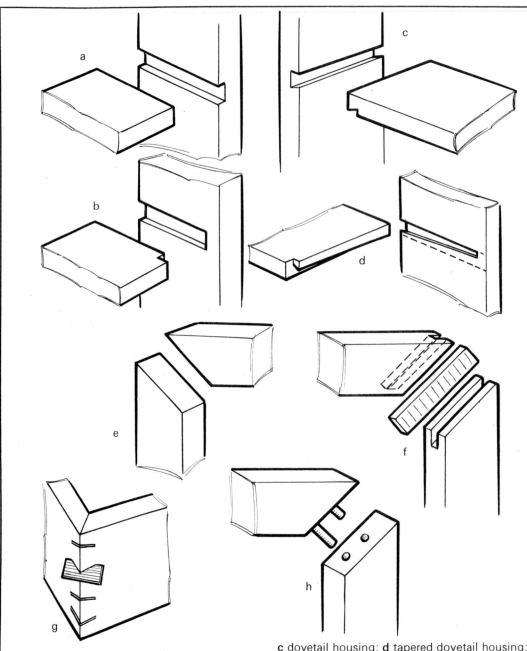

Fig. 7 Examples of housed joints, mitres, etc.: **a** common housing; **b** stopped housing; **c** dovetail housing; **d** tapered dovetail housing; **e** simple mitre; **f** tongued mitre; **g** veneer keyed mitre; **h** dowelled mitre

f frames, etc., often as a simple substitute for the mortise and tenon. Their chief value is when he material is too thin for the mortise and tenon to be cut. The positions in which the joints are used are obvious from Fig. 6 (a, b, c and d). A centre line is marked with the gauge from the face side in a, b and c, and a saw cut made immediately to the waste side of the line. The shoulder line is squared across with chisel or knife, and a sloping groove cut similarly to that of the tenon, (d) Fig. 4. When the joint has to withstand any strain (as in the loose seat of a chair, for instance), it should be screwed as well as glued. In the case of the cross-halving (d) the parts should be just hand tight. Too tight a fit may cause distortion.

he bridle joint (e) is handy when a sideboard, table, or similar piece has three legs at the front. The top rail can be in a single length and the centre leg bridled into it.

The grooved joint (f) with loose tongue is used for strong joints required when boards are glued side by side—table tops, carcase ends, etc. The lapped joint (g) is often used as a simple alternative to the lapped dovetail. It requires to be both glued and nailed. (h) is used similarly, but is not very satisfactory owing to the short grain at the end which is liable to split away.

Housed joints. The simple housing (a), Fig. 7, is used chiefly for shelves, partitions, etc. When its front appearance is an objection the joint is stopped as at (b). In the case of (a) the groove is simple to cut. Two lines are squared across the wood with knife or chisel, sloping grooves chiselled on the waste side, and the tenon saw worked in these. The bulk of the waste is chiselled away, and the depth made even with the router.

It is not quite so simple with the stopped groove. The method is to chop a recess immediately against the stop as in Fig. 8. This enables the saw to be worked back and forth in short strokes until the depth is reached. The removal of the waste is with chisel and router as before.

For a stronger joint the dovetail housing at (c) can be used. This can be cut right through as shown, or it can be stopped similarly to (b). As a guide to holding the saw at the correct angle a

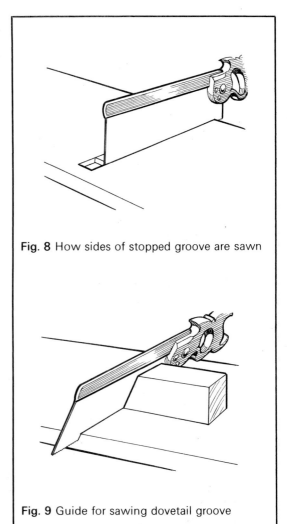

Fig. 8 How sides of stopped groove are sawn

Fig. 9 Guide for sawing dovetail groove

block of wood can be fixed to the side of the line as in Fig. 9, being either cramped or nailed down.

Just as easy to cut and certainly simpler to fit is the tapered and shouldered dovetail housing at (d). Its advantage is that the joint is quite slack until pushed right home. This makes it much easier to tell just where the joint may need easing.

Mitred joints. The simple mitre is given at (e), Fig. 7. It is cut on the mitre block or box according

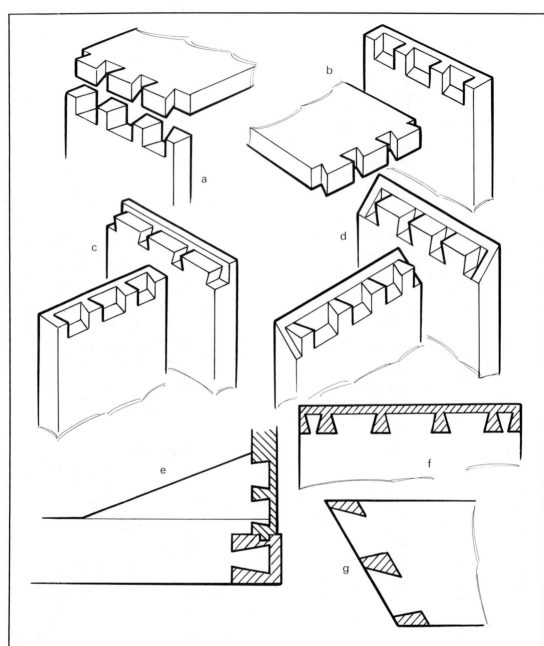

Fig. 10 Various types of dovetail joints: **a** through dovetail; **b** lapped dovetail; **c** double-lapped dovetail; **d** mitre secret dovetail; **f** lapped dovetail for carcase—note narrow end dovetails to prevent corners from curling away; **g** angle dovetails

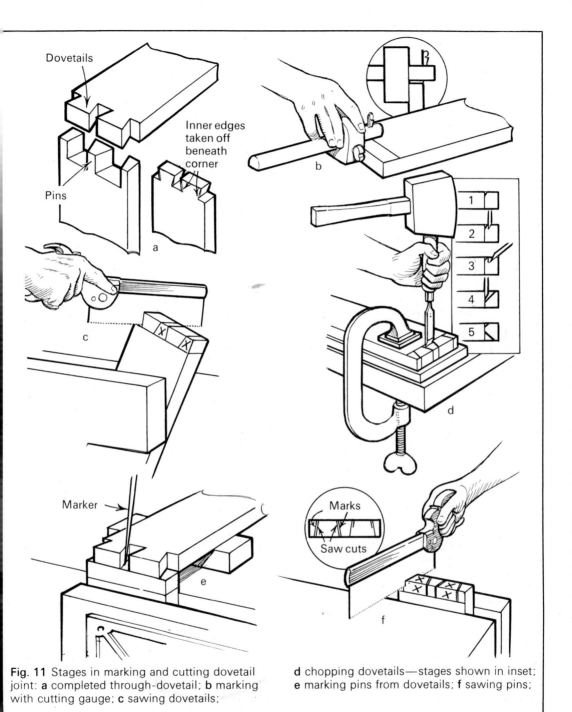

Dovetails

Inner edges
taken off
beneath
corner

Pins

a

b

1
2
3
4
5

c

d

Marker

e

Marks

Saw cuts

f

Fig. 11 Stages in marking and cutting dovetail joint: **a** completed through-dovetail; **b** marking with cutting gauge; **c** sawing dovetails;

d chopping dovetails—stages shown in inset; **e** marking pins from dovetails; **f** sawing pins;

113

to its size. Small mitres can often be glued up straightway from the saw but larger ones need trimming on the mitre shooting board, (b), p. 16.

Various ways of strengthening mitres are given at (f), (g), and (h). The first and last are used chiefly for frames, whereas (g) is handy for strengthening a small mitred box to be veneered. Saw cuts are made across the mitre, and slips of veneer glued in, these being levelled after the glue has set.

Dovetails. These make the strongest joint for such structures as boxes, etc. When the appearance of the dovetail does not matter the through dovetail (a) Fig. 10, is the simplest and strongest. The lapped dovetail (b) is used when one side must be plain, as in carcase sides, drawer fronts, etc. At (c) the joint is concealed on both sides except for a thin line of end grain formed by the lap. At (d) it is entirely hidden.

The application of the lapped dovetail to the joining of a top rail to a cabinet side with corner post is shown at (e). (f) is for a wide carcase where the narrow end dovetails prevent any tendency for the wood to curl away at the corners. When one piece slopes at an angle the arrangement at (g) is followed.

The method of cutting the through dovetail is given in Fig. 11. The thickness of the wood is gauged across as at (b). When the thickness of the two varies, the thickness of the one is gauged on to the other. Do not cut in deeply as the mark has later to be planed away. Pencil in the dovetail positions. In an important position they are measured and marked with a template. The slope is 10mm. ($\frac{1}{2}$in.) in 60mm. (3in.) as shown in Fig. 12. Place the wood in the vice at an angle so that the saw can be held upright and cut down as at (c). Put crosses on the waste pieces. Much of the latter can be cut away with the coping saw at about 1mm. from the line.

Chop away the waste as at (d). Make a sloping cut up to the gauge line (1), and chop down about 1mm. ($\frac{1}{16}$in.) from the line (2). Make a sloping cut at (3) so that the actual corner is not removed. Repeat the process right on the gauge line, (4), and finally turn over the work from the other side (5).

Place the part with the pins in the vice, and lay the dovetailed piece on it in position as at (e). A waste piece at the back will support it in the correct position. Run a marker around the dovetails as shown, and cut as at (f). The saw should be held just to the waste side of the mark, this giving a comfortable hand-tight fit. Note the crosses which denote the waste pieces. It makes it obvious which parts are to be removed. The chopping is much the same as for the dovetails. Before assembling the inner edges of the dovetails are lightly chiselled away as at (a) so that they start together easily.

The lapped dovetail is cut similarly, but the pins can only be chopped from the one side. In the mitre dovetail the pins must be cut first as otherwise it is impossible to mark the one from the other.

Carcase joints. When solid wood is used for a carcase such as a cupboard the lapped dovetail shown at (a), Fig. 13, is used for work for which it is desired to conceal the joints. It is assumed that a separate top is used which covers the dovetails at the top. At the sides the lap of the dovetails conceals the joint. An alternative sometimes used at the top is the use of rails at front and back with angle braces glued on at the inner edges, as at (b). If there is no objection to the joints showing, ordinary through dovetails can be cut as at (c), in which case they need to be nicely spaced and neatly cut. In the case of a carcase in which there is no separate top and in which the joints have to be concealed the double-lapped dovetail at (d) is used. In this the only indication of the joint is the thin line of end grain showing at the side. The joint at (e) is sometimes used for a cheap job and is a simple lap, the parts being glued and nailed together, though sometimes a dovetailed bracket such as that shown in Fig. 17 can be added, at the inner angle.

Man-made materials. These include plywood, blockboard, and chipboard, and special forms of construction are invariably necessary when they are used. In one sense they have an advantage in that they are free from the shrinkage and swelling that is a feature of solid wood. On the other hand their construction often means that normal joints cannot be used. For multi-ply and blockboard the method in Fig. 14 is useful. Rails

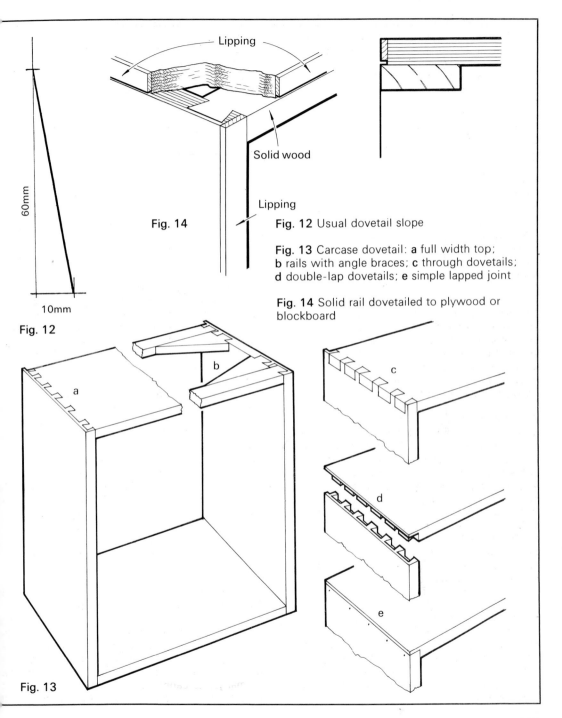

Lipping

Solid wood

Lipping

Fig. 14

Fig. 12

60mm

10mm

Fig. 12 Usual dovetail slope

Fig. 13 Carcase dovetail: **a** full width top;
b rails with angle braces; **c** through dovetails;
d double-lap dovetails; **e** simple lapped joint

Fig. 14 Solid rail dovetailed to plywood or
blockboard

Fig. 13

a
b
c
d
e

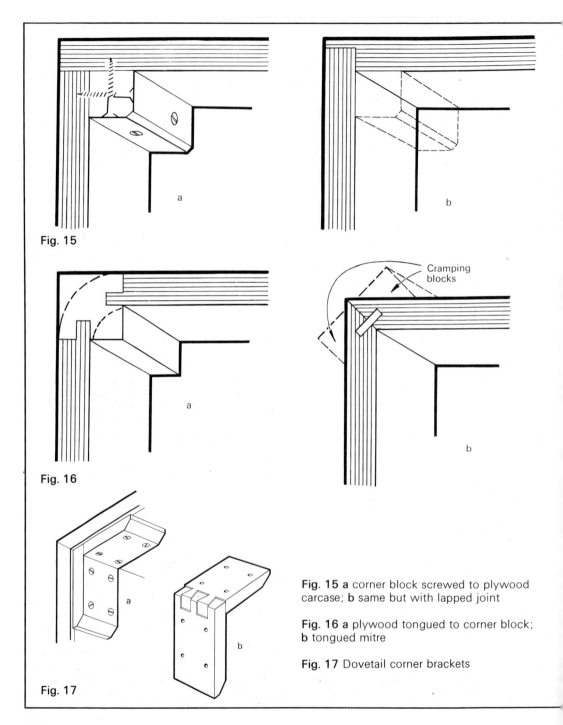

Fig. 15 **a** corner block screwed to plywood carcase; **b** same but with lapped joint

Fig. 16 **a** plywood tongued to corner block; **b** tongued mitre

Fig. 17 Dovetail corner brackets

Fig. 15

Fig. 16

Cramping blocks

Fig. 17

the top are used at front and back and possibly the middle, these being dovetailed in. This can be done successfully if somewhat coarse dovetails are used. The front edges of the ends are lapped; also the edges of the top which is fixed with screws driven upwards through the rails. It gives an attractive appearance if a narrow rebate is worked round the underside of the top.

Another method also suitable for either multi-ply or blockboard is either of those in Fig. 15. At (a) the parts are merely butted together and strengthened with blocks glued and screwed in the angle. A rather neater method is (b) in which the top is rebated so that only a thin line of plywood shows at the end. The glue block is fitted as in the previous case as shown by the dotted lines.

Sometimes the design allows a double-grooved block to be used, the top and side being tongued into it as at (a) Fig. 16. If preferred the rounded corner effect can be given (dotted lines). A neater effect is the mitred and grooved joint at (b), Fig. 16. The grooves, however, are awkward to work by hand as the short grain of the plywood is liable to crumble under the plough. If a circular saw or high-speed router is available, however, it makes a strong joint. Triangular blocks can be glued on temporarily as shown by the dotted lines to enable cramps to be applied when assembling.

The use of screwed brackets is sometimes an advantage for a mitred, butted or rebated joint as shown in Fig. 17. These can be glued and screwed at front and back as at (a). They are dovetailed together, and when making the dovetails, it is an advantage to set the gauge bare of the thickness so that when the parts are assembled the end grain of both pieces stands in slightly as at (b), Fig. 17. Unless this is done the wood, being liable to shrink slightly in its thickness, may eventually leave the ends of the pins and dovetails slightly projecting, causing a loose joint. In some pieces of furniture this bracket method can be used for solid wood such as the rebated joint at (e), Fig. 13.

Coarse dovetails can sometimes be used for blockboard as at (a), Fig. 18. It does, however, depend to an extent on the grain direction of the material. Pelleted screws can also be used for

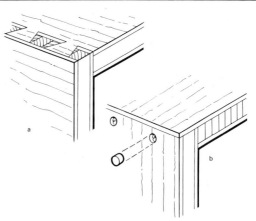

Fig. 18 Joints for blockboard a coarse dovetails; b lapped and screwed

Fig. 19 Bolted knock-down fittings

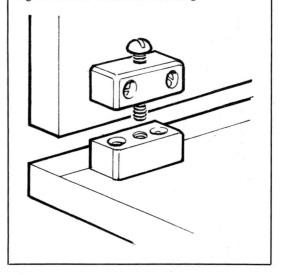

blockboard as at (b). Note however that it is only practicable when the core of the rebated piece runs crosswise as shown. Otherwise the screws enter end grain where they have poor hold.

In the case of some veneered chipboards the only really practicable method is the use of special bolted fittings shown in Fig. 19. The fittings, in two pieces, are screwed in the angle of the joining parts. Bolts draw the parts tightly together.

Chapter nine

Metal Fittings, etc.

Locks

There are many kinds of locks made for special purposes. Fig. 1 shows those most commonly used. (a), (b), (c), (d), (e), (f) and (g) are furniture locks; (h), (i) and (j) are for house doors.

Kinds of locks. (a) is the straight cupboard lock which is screwed to the inside of the door and is not let in. Mostly these locks shoot both right and left, and can so be used for doors opening right or left. The cut lock at (b) is much neater, but requires recessing into the wood. As the bolt shoots in one direction only the lock must be ordered R or L. To tell which you need, face the door from the outside. If the lock is on the left you need a L.H. lock. Thus the lock shown is L.H.

Similar in form is the drawer lock at (f). This has to be let into the drawer front. The box lock (g) is also let into the wood, but in addition is a plate which needs recessing into and screwing to the lid.

The lock at (d) is known as the link-plate lock and is used for a door which closes over the face of the cabinet. It is recessed into the back of the door, and the link-plate into the front edge of the cabinet. The link passes through a slot in the lock, the bolt passing through it. Since the bolt shoots right or left it can be used at either side. For sliding wood door the lock at (e) is used. The lock at (n) is used for glass sliding doors. It is held with a thumb screw to the leading edge of the rear glass. The detachable lock is slid on to this bar and prevents either door from being moved. (1) and (m) are two forms of ball catches, and (k) is a mortise bolt for a room door.

Of locks for house doors the simplest and cheapest is the rim lock at (h). It is simply screwed on, though there is sometimes a projecting plate which need to be recessed into the edge (i) shows the Yale pattern latch in which the cutting-in is reduced to a minimum. The mortise lock at (j) requires to set right into the edge of the door.

Fixing a cut door lock. This is widely used on furniture. The stages of fixing are given in Figs 2–7. Square across the surface and edge of the

Fig. 1 Examples of locks and bolts used in furniture and house doors

door a centre line. Set the gauge to the distance of the pin from the outer plate as in Fig. 2, and mark across the pencil line. This gives the keyhole position, and a bit is selected which will give a close fit to the rounded portion of the escutcheon. A hole is bored right through the door and the escutcheon laid in position as in Fig. 3. A slight tap with the hammer will give an indentation of the shape, the sides of which can be sawn with the keyhole saw. A narrow chisel will remove the waste.

Place the lock with the pin level with the pencil line, and mark the door in line with the body of the lock as in Fig. 4. Set a gauge to the thickness of the body including the plate, and mark the edge of the door. This gives the position and extent of the wood to be cut away. Make a series of saw cuts across the grain down to as far as they can be taken as in Fig. 5. The door should be held down on the bench with handscrews. Remove the waste with the chisel as shown, and chop down at the ends and back. The latter needs to be done carefully to avoid splitting along the grain. Once again ease away the waste.

Place the lock in position, making sure that the pin is level with its hole, and mark round the ends of the plate with a marking knife. It is of little use marking the sides of the plate as at this stage the lock cannot be pushed right home. The simplest way of marking these sides is to use the gauge in conjunction with a waste piece of wood with parallel sides. Set the gauge as shown in Fig. 6. Then, holding the waste piece right over the lock recess (this waste piece must be longer than the lock) mark the door edge. The back plate is marked similarly. Fig. 7 shows the completed recess.

Screw on the lock and try the action with the key. To find the position of the recess to be cut to take the bolt, shoot out the latter and smear its surface with thin paint, or, say, the dirty oil from the oilstone. Shoot the bolt back and close the door. Now turn the key as far as it will go. This will leave a mark on the cupboard side which can be chopped out with a small chisel.

Drawer locks are fitted similarly, but the keyhole is the other way round. It may also be necessary to use the special drawer-lock chisel (p. 12) when the space is restricted. In the case of a box lock (g), Fig. 1, the link plate also has to be attached. To find its position place it on the lock and turn the key. Bring down the lid and thump it. There is generally a small spike at the back of the plate which will be driven into the lid. Turn the lock, and raise the lid, the plate being lifted with it. Mark round its edge and chop the recess to receive it, finally screwing it in position.

Mortise lock. Assuming that you are fixing the lock to a framed door, the vertical position will be decided by the main centre horizontal rail. The tenons of this rail run right through and there is a fair distance between them. The lock should be let in here, as shown in Fig. 8.

Marking the position. Wedge open the door and, holding the lock in the position shown in Fig. 9, mark lines across the edge level with the top and bottom of the body of the lock. The lock should extend equally into both tenons. Now turn the lock into the position it will occupy, and, keeping the body level with the marks made just at the edge, mark the position of the spindle hold and keyhole as in Fig. 10, using a pointed scriber. Mark all round the holes. Work from the inside of the door because the edge is frequently planed at a slight angle to allow it to clear easily. The holes cannot be bored directly over these marks because they do not allow for the face plate. The bit must therefore be started farther in by a distance equal to the thickness of this plate. The usual sizes are 9mm. ($\frac{3}{8}$in.) for the keyhole and 16mm. ($\frac{5}{8}$in.) for the spindle. When the point of the bit just emerges finish the hole by boring from the reverse side.

The mortise. Turning now to the edge again, draw in a pencil line exactly down the centre (see Fig. 10), using the rule and finger as a gauge. With a twist bit of the same size as the thickness of the body of the lock bore a hole on the centre line so that it is just inside the top horizontal line. A lath of wood cramped to the door as in Fig. 11 will enable you to judge whether the bit is being held square. A series of holes is bored right along the mortise, and it is desirable to bore them as close together as possible so that the subsequent chopping out is minimized. To enable this to be done, knock a plug of wood into the first hole before you bore

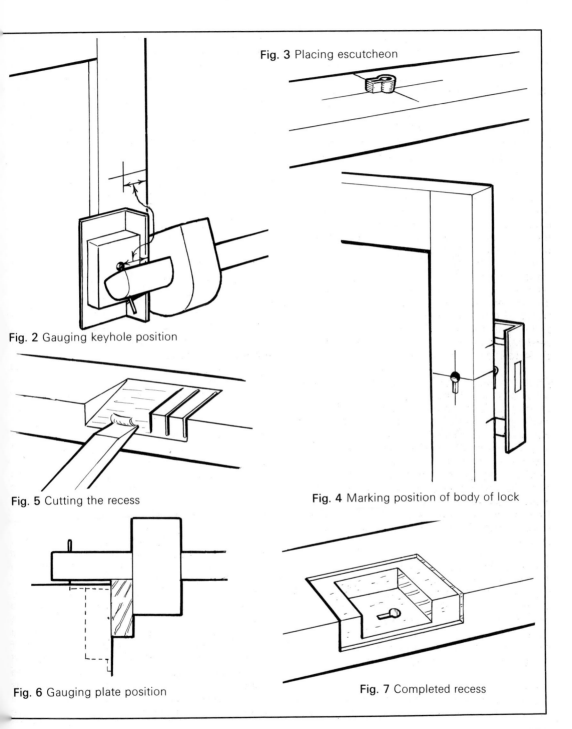

Fig. 2 Gauging keyhole position

Fig. 3 Placing escutcheon

Fig. 4 Marking position of body of lock

Fig. 5 Cutting the recess

Fig. 6 Gauging plate position

Fig. 7 Completed recess

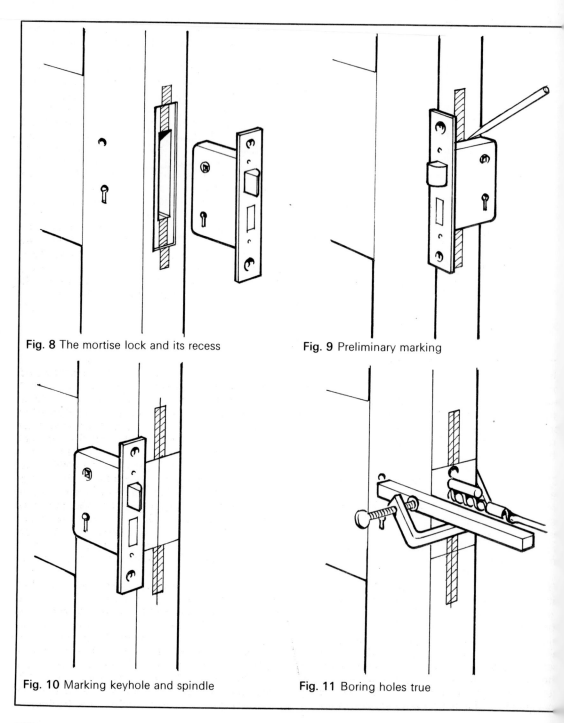

Fig. 8 The mortise lock and its recess

Fig. 9 Preliminary marking

Fig. 10 Marking keyhole and spindle

Fig. 11 Boring holes true

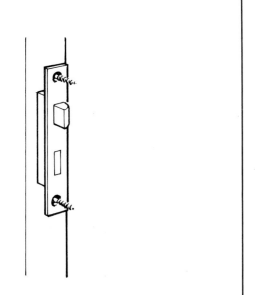

Fig. 12 Hint when fitting face plate

outer one being held with metal screws. This should always be removed during re-painting.

Fitting the striking plate. To fix the striking plate, nearly close the door and scribe a line where both bolts occur. Square this across the door rebate. Now open the door, shoot out the bolts and put a film of the dirty black oil from the oilstone on the faces. Shoot the bolts, close the door tightly, and open the bolts as far as they will go so that they leave a mark on the jamb. This gives the position for the striking plate which can now be placed level with the top of the marks and a line scribed round. Always work to the top, because this allows for subsequent dropping of the door. Screw on the plate and mortise the holes. You will probably find that part of the plate projects at the front. This should be bent over, partly to enable the latch to close more easily, and also because a projecting corner is liable to catch the clothing of anyone passing.

Hinges

Kinds of hinges. Some of the more generally used hinges are shown in Fig. 13. Of these the butt (a) is the kind mostly used in furniture making, windows, and internal doors, etc. It is intended to be recessed into the wood, and its comparatively narrow shape makes it suitable for the edges of doors. The back flap (b) is let in similarly but is wider, and is used for bureau falls, flap table tops, etc., where there is plenty of width. For the special kind of flap table having what is known as the rule joint, the fixed edge rounded and the flap edge hollowed, the table top hinge (c) is used. Note that the screw holes are countersunk on the side opposite to the knuckle, and that one flap is longer than the other to bridge across the hollow.

The ornamental hinge (d), sometimes known as the butterfly hinge, is screwed straight to the surface without being let in. For narrow edges the strap hinge at (e) is used. The acorn hinge, (f), is used when for some reason the hinge has to project well beyond the face of the door. The acorn ends have an ornamental effect. When the pivoting point has to be at the outer corner of a door which closes over the face of a cabinet the lift-off hinge, (g), is used. This enables the door to

e second. Remove it and put it into the second efore boring the third, and so on. This will nable you to start each hole right up against ne previous one without danger of the wood rumbling away and making the bit run out of 'ue. A piece of paper stuck to the bit will mark ne depth to which each hole should be taken.

:hop out the mortise with the chisel. The pro-essional carpenter has a swan-necked chisel for nishing, this enabling the cross grain of the nons to be cut in the corners, but it is not ssential. You can now finish the keyhole with ad saw or with the chisel. A waste block in the nortise will prevent the wood from splitting.

'he face plate. The face plate has now to be tted. The lock is put in position and a line cribed round. As it may be awkward to withdraw ne lock when it is pushed right home a useful int is to put a couple of screws in the plate the everse way round as in Fig. 12. These give you omething to grip when you want to withdraw ne lock. Test to see that the spindle hole and eyhole coincide with those bored, and screw up. ncidentally, some locks have two face plates, the

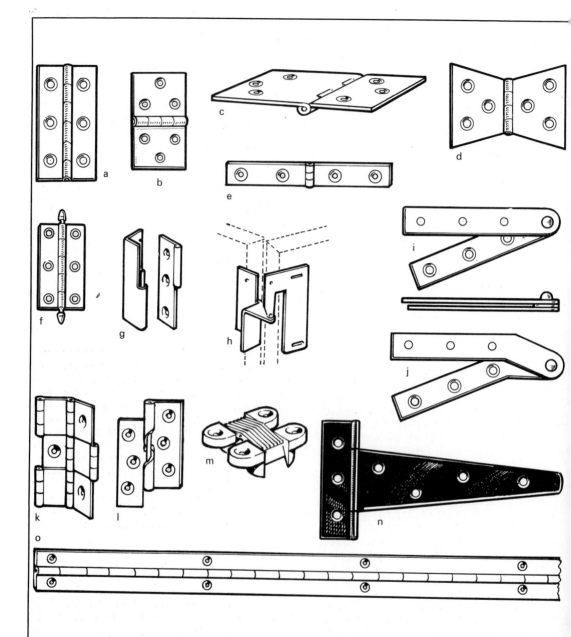

Fig. 13 Common types of hinges for various purposes: **a** plain butt hinge; **b** back flap hinge; **c** table top hinge; **d** butterfly hinge; **e** strap hinge; **f** acorn hinge; **g** lift-off cabinet hinge; **h** pivot hinge; **i** centre hinge; **j** cranked centre hinge; **k** reversible screen hinge; **l** rising butt; **m** soss hinge; **n** cross-garnet hinge; **o** strip hinge

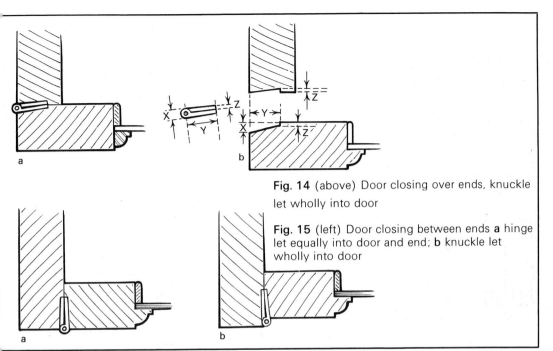

Fig. 14 (above) Door closing over ends, knuckle let wholly into door

Fig. 15 (left) Door closing between ends **a** hinge let equally into door and end; **b** knuckle let wholly into door

pen without projecting sideways. That at (h) has similar effect.

he centre hinge, (i), fitted at top and bottom dges, is generally used when the pivoting points f butts would not be practicable. The cranked ype (j) brings the centre to yet another position. or such items as screens the reversible hinge at k) is used. The centres of the knuckles equal the hickness of the wood. If the latter is more than his the hinge will bind. Rising butts, (l), are used or a room door which has to clear a centre carpet. hey are made R and L hand. To tell which is equired stand outside the door. If the hinges are the right then the RH hinges are required, and ice versa. The soss hinge at (m) is let into the oining edges of, say, a table top and is com-letely hidden on the surface. The leaf can move hrough 180 deg. The cross garnet hinge (n) is for arge external doors of the ledged and braced type. he strip hinge (o), sometimes known as the piano inge, is used for wide falls.

Position of butt hinges. These can be fitted in arious ways, according to the position and detail f the door. At (a), Fig. 14, the door closes over the face of the cupboard. If preferred the hinge could be let equally into the door and cupboard. Usually, however, the method shown at (a) is followed because a bead is generally worked along the edge of the door to give a neat finish, and the knuckle of the hinge lines up with this. The knuckle is let into the door in its entirety, but to make the appearance as neat as possible and relieve the screws of the entire strain it is usual to cut sloping recesses in the cupboard edge. Note that only the opening edge is let in; at the knuckle side the wood is uncut. (b) shows how the sizes taken from the hinge are marked on door and cupboard.

When a door is contained between the sides of the cupboard either of the methods in Fig. 15 can be used. At (a) the door is flush at the front with the cupboard ends, and the butt is let equally into door and cupboard. At (b) the door is recessed and the butt knuckle is let entirely into the door, though sloping recesses for the flange only are cut in the cupboard. To enable this door to swing through 180 deg., the centre of the knuckle is brought forward so that it is midway between the surface of the door face and the outer edge of the cupboard.

125

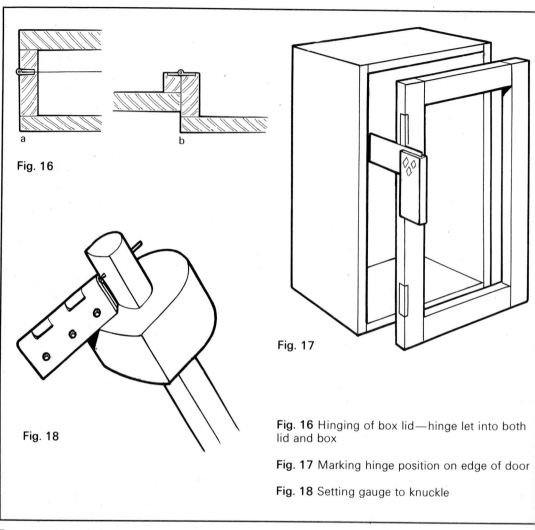

Fig. 16

a

b

Fig. 18

Fig. 17

Fig. 16 Hinging of box lid—hinge let into both lid and box

Fig. 17 Marking hinge position on edge of door

Fig. 18 Setting gauge to knuckle

Boxes are hinged similarly to doors, but as a rule the butts are let equally in lid and box as shown in Fig. 16, which shows the opening movement.

Rising butts. These, (I), Fig. 13, are used for room doors, their function being to raise the door clear of a centre carpet. They are made in sizes corresponding with ordinary butts, and can therefore be used to replace ordinary butts. One point to note is that they are right- and left-hand and the correct hand must be ordered. A framework intended for rising butts has its top rebate at an angle to allow for the slope. When the rebate is square, as when

simple butts are used, it is invariably necessary to take off the corner of the door when rising butts are fitted. This does not show when the door is closed because the rebate hides the corner. The hinges should be oiled periodically to give easy movement.

Hinging a door. Decide on the position of the hinges and square in across the edge as at Fig. 17. There is no rule about this but its own distance from the end is a general guide. To mark the width and depth set the gauge to the hinge itself as in Fig. 18. Do not over-run past the pencil lines. Saw

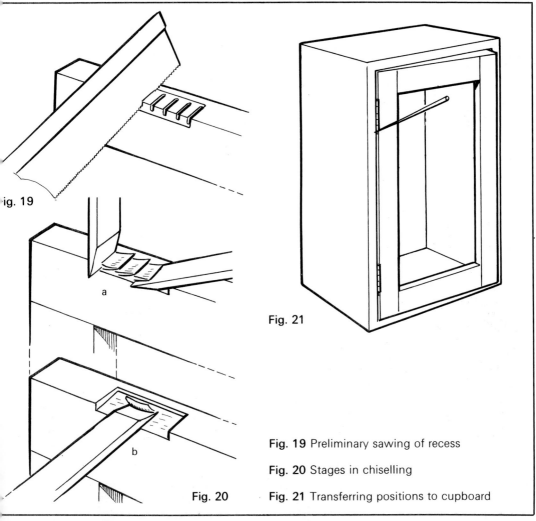

Fig. 19

a

b

Fig. 20

Fig. 21

Fig. 19 Preliminary sawing of recess

Fig. 20 Stages in chiselling

Fig. 21 Transferring positions to cupboard

ross down to just short of the diagonal as in Fig.
, the intermediate cuts serving to break up the
ain thus preventing a split from developing. With
keen chisel cut in the ends (a), Fig. 20, and
aste away the wood to be removed. Finally pare
e recess flat as at (b). Fix the butts with two
rews each only.

acing the door in position, transfer the butt
ositions to the cupboard as in Fig. 21, and mark
d cut the recesses similarly. Fix with a single
rew to each hinge, and try the movement. Carry
t any adjustment before adding the remaining

screws. The closing edge of the door needs to be
taken off at a slight angle at the inside, otherwise it
will tend to bind as it is opened.

Reversible screen hinges. These, (k), Fig. 13
enable a screen to open in both directions. They
have knuckles at both edges, and it is important
that the thickness of the wood equals the distance
between the pins. If the wood is thicker than this
the screen will bind as it opens. If it is thinner there
will be a gap down the joint as it opens. This is the
lesser evil of the two, but in the case of a draught
screen it means that it is not wholly effective.

127

Nails and Screws

Nails. Of the wide variety of nails made for special purposes, those shown in Fig. 22 are the most useful for general woodwork.

French nails (a) have a strong grip, and are used in positions where their large heads are not an objection. Thus they are used for carpentry, etc. A similar nail having a smaller head is known as the lost head (b). Not being so strong, but having a smaller head and not so liable to split the wood is the oval wire nail, (c). It is driven in with the long oval in line with the grain. Panel pins (e) are the general nails for cabinet work as they are thin and have small heads. They are thus not so unsightly, and are not liable to split the wood. A smaller variation is the veneer pin (f). Apart from its use in veneering it is handy for small mouldings, etc.

Cut nails (d) are for carpentry generally. Similar but rather heavier is the floor brad. Both kinds have the advantage of not being liable to split the grain. Tacks (g) are used generally for upholstery. The improved tack has a rather larger head. Clout nails (h) are used to a limited extent in upholstery for webbing, but are more generally used for fixing roofing felt, etc. The cut clasp nail (i) is an extrem strong carpentry nail.

Whatever the nail used, always endeavour to n from the thin wood to the thick. It is an advanta too, to dovetail the nails; that is, to drive them askew at a slight angle in alternate directions. the case of outdoor work use galvanized nails.

Screws. The main types are given in Fig. 2 which also shows where the length is taken fro The gauge is the diameter of the shank and regardless of length. Thus a No. 8 50mm. (2i screw has the same diameter as a No. 8 75m (3in.) screw. The clearance hole should be an ea fit as shown in Fig. 23e, and the thread hole shou be bored to the diameter of the central rod withc the thread. It is purely the hold of the thread whi gives the grip.

Phillips screws, (d), Fig. 23, are mostly used industry. There is a cross recess in the head ratl than a slot, the advantage being that there is danger of the screwdriver slipping out and causi a scratch.

Nailing the mitred corners of a picture frame.

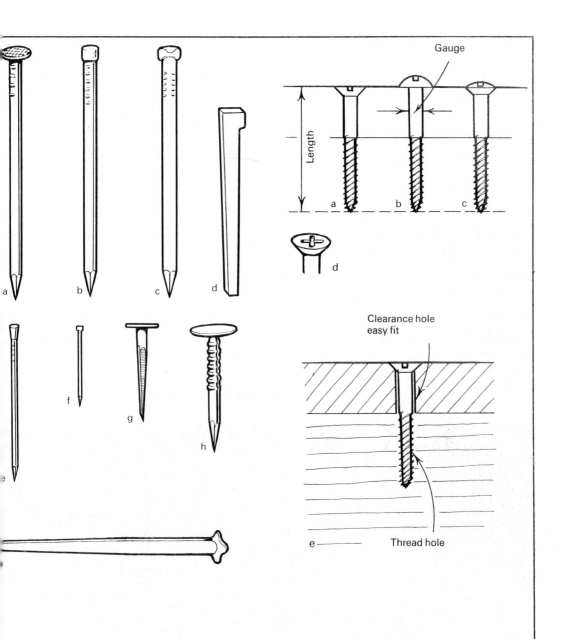

Fig. 22 Types of nails in everyday use: **a** French or wire nail; **b** lost head; **c** oval wire nail; **d** cut nail; **e** panel pin; **f** veneer pin; **g** tack; **h** clout nail; **i** cut-clasp nail

Fig. 23 Common types of screws and where size is taken from: **a** countersunk; **b** round head; **c** raised head; **d** Phillips head; **e** details of screw holes

Chapter ten

Veneering

This is an entirely legitimate process providing that it is not used merely to cover up bad workmanship and poor materials. It enables certain decorative woods to be used which would be unreliable if cut in the solid, and makes possible many attractive effects such as quartering and built-up patterns which would be entirely impracticable in any other way. Furthermore it has to be accepted that economy in the use of many of the fine decorative hardwoods is essential, and by cutting them into veneers there is a minimum of waste.

Groundwork. So far as the home craftsman is concerned, there are two main methods of veneering; caul and hammer. When a press is available this offers the simplest means. Whichever is used, however, the groundwork and its preparation are the same. Various materials can be used.

Solid wood. Almost any straight-grained wood can be used, but it must be reliable and it should hold glue well. Mahogany is excellent but expensive. Obeche, Parana pine, etc., are widely used. Baltic pine, too, is used, but it must be as free of knots as possible, any small, unavoidable ones being chopped out and the holes filled in. It is also necessary to give softwood a coat of glue size after preparation before the glue proper is used, otherwise it soaks up more than its share. Oak is sometimes used, but it is not ideal because its coarse grain is liable eventually to show through to the surface owing to the glue contracting in the pores. In any case it is not the best of woods for holding glue.

The most reliable form of solid wood groundwork is made from strips glued together side by side with the heart sides alternately up and down as at (a), Fig. 1, the reason being that any twisting tendency in one piece is countered by that in those adjoining which would tend to twist the other way. Another good solid ground is that at (b) in which the wood is quarter-cut and is not liable to twist either way.

It will be realized that veneer tends to pull a panel hollow as it dries out, and for this reason it is always wise to veneer the ground-work on both sides so that the pull is equalized. By taking certain precautions this pull can be minimized or even eliminated altogether, but it is always safer to

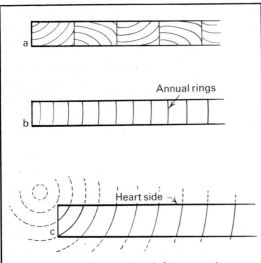

Fig. 1 Details of groundwork for veneering:
a solid ground made from solid strips with heart sides alternately up and down; b quarter cut board making good groundwork; c how to tell heart side of wood

eneer both sides, especially for such parts as oors which have no stiffening framework. When ingle side veneering is unavoidable it is advisable o lay the veneer on the heart side of the wood, (c), ig. 1. The reason is that the pull of the veneer is pposed to the natural twisting tendency of the vood.

lywood. This makes a good groundwork if of eliable make; the cheaper tea-chest variety is iseless. Gaboon ply is specially suitable. The eneer should always be laid with its grain at right ngles with that of the outer layer of the ply. The dges are sometimes a problem. Veneer does not old really well on the end grain, and generally the nly plan is to fit an edging as in Fig. 2. That at (a) i the usual trade method but, as the section is ather awkward to work with hand tools, that at (b) i simpler. The tongue on the ply is more easily vorked as there is more wood to grip. (c) is ltogether simpler, being just glued and pinned. It vould not be used in first-class work.

\ point to note in all these edgings is that if eneered first the edging affords considerable protection to the veneer which is always vulnerable at the edge. On the other hand the edging necessarily shows on the surface.

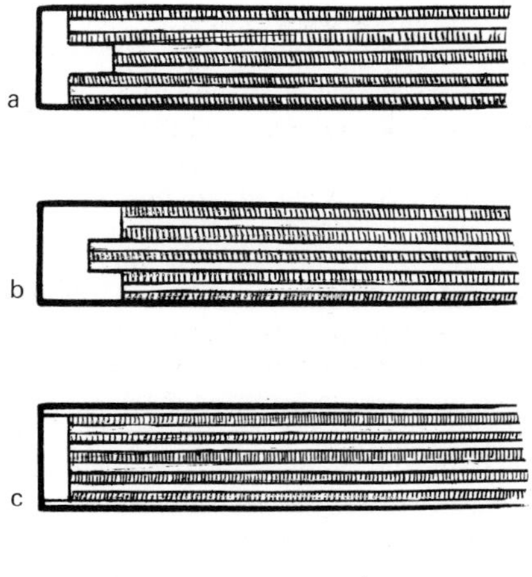

Laminboard, blockboard. These make good, reliable grounds. The former is the better since the narrow strips used in the core are less liable to movement. The notes about the direction of the grain given about plywood apply equally. The edgings in Fig. 2 can also be used.

Chipboard. This has come in for increasing use as a groundwork—much of it in fact can be obtained ready veneered. For panels and supported parts it is satisfactory, but it is not recommended for flush doors which have no stiffening framework. As an edging that at (a), Fig. 2, is the most suitable, with (c) as a cheaper alternative. (b) is unsuitable.

Hardboard. There are many varieties of these, some being more suitable than others. None is as durable as the materials already mentioned, and they would only be used for cheap work or less important parts.

Preparation of groundwork. As the veneer must be in close contact with the surface of the groundwork it is obvious that any inequality in the latter will show through the veneer. Solid wood if used must be planed dead true. Plywood and laminboard are already true enough. To roughen the surface so giving a key to the glue, and to take out marks left by the plane, a toothing plane, Fig. 3, is used, this being worked in all directions; along the grain, across, and diagonally. If the ground is softwood it should be given a coat of glue size and allowed to dry out. The inevitable roughness is removed by rubbing with coarse glasspaper held on a rubber.

Handling veneer. Most veneer nowadays is knife cut as it is produced with practically no waste. Occasionally saw cut veneer is found, and it is always thicker, and shows the marks of the circular saw on which it was cut. These marks on the side to be glued must be removed with a toothing plane, the veneer being held down on a flat board. The most convenient way of cutting knife-cut veneer is to place it on a flat board, press a batten with a straight edge on it, and cut with keen knife or chisel as in Fig. 4. The batten is essential as otherwise the veneer may cockle and split. When several strips of equal width have to be

Fig. 2 Edgings for multi-ply and laminated boards

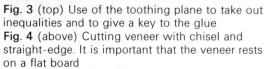

Fig. 3 (top) Use of the toothing plane to take out inequalities and to give a key to the glue

Fig. 4 (above) Cutting veneer with chisel and straight-edge. It is important that the veneer rests on a flat board

Fig. 5 (top) Cutting parallel strips with cutting gauge. The batten pressed down over the veneer prevents it from cockling

Fig. 6 (above) Trimming veneer on the shooting board. A batten prevents cockling

cut the cutting gauge may be used as in Fig. 5. Here again the veneer rests on a flat board, the edge overhanging about 3mm. ($\frac{1}{8}$in.), and a batten is pressed across it to stiffen it. A single cut will generally sever it, but thick veneer may need cutting from both sides. Saw-cut veneer has usually to be cut with a fine-toothed saw, the veneer held on a flat board and the saw drawn across it.

Sometimes it is necessary to trim the edge of the veneer, for example, when jointing. It is done on the shooting board, the veneer overhanging the upper platform by about 3mm. ($\frac{1}{8}$in.), and a batten is pressed down to prevent cockling. This is shown in Fig. 6.

Resin adhesive. This is described fully on page 163. It is widely used in the trade for veneering, and it is well adapted for use when presses are available. When there is no press the only plan is to use cauls. The hammer method (see under hammer veneering) is impracticable because the adhesive has not the tacky nature of animal glue and the veneer is liable to lift before adhesion takes place. To cheapen the cost the glue is often extended with rye flour. Resin is specially suitable for surfaces liable to wear as in the case of a table top, particularly as the adhesive is largely resistant to heat and damp. One advantage it has over animal glue is that it is used cold. There is thus ample time for assembling. Generally it is sufficient if the adhesive is applied to the groundwork only, but of course care must be taken that the joint is not glue-starved. In the trade a glue spreader is used which gives an even coat, but for home use the brush will have to be used, this being followed by a strip of wood with straight edge which will even the application. If a piece of work is wanted quickly, advantage can be taken of the fact that the resin sets rapidly with heat by using a heated caul. It needs rapid, deft handling, however, so that all the cramps are in position before setting takes place. For details of the method of applying cauls see page 134 where animal glue is dealt with.

P.V.A. glue. This is used similarly to resin glue but the even spread of glue is still more important because the glue tends to congeal quickly on exposure to air. The glue can be heat cured but this is not advisable unless a press is available because of the tendency to set rapidly before adjustment can take place. With some woods there may be a tendency to penetration.

Impact adhesives. These are useful on occasion, and a special type for veneering is marketed, being rather thinner and more easily spread than the normally-used type. It is scarcely suitable for really large areas because it might be difficult to obtain an even spread, free from lumpiness. The adhesive is applied to both groundwork and veneer, and a rather better result is obtained if two coats are given. The two are allowed to dry and the veneer is then pressed down when the bond is immediate. In fact care in positioning the veneer is essential because the two glued surfaces grab when brought into contact and it is almost impossible to shift the veneer when once in position. Many men use the slip-sheet method, a piece of flat brown paper being placed between veneer and groundwork and gradually withdrawn. The paper does not adhere as the impact glue on the one surface sticks only to that on the other surface after initial setting has taken place.

Another occasion on which impact adhesive is useful is when a small curved surface has to be veneered. It might be awkward to make a shaped caul, and if hammer veneering were used the veneer might be liable to spring up. With impact adhesive the grip is immediate. A further advantage of impact adhesive is that it is not liable to pull the groundwork hollow since there is no water used. Thus there is no swelling followed later by shrinkage, the cause of distortion when other adhesives are used.

Animal (Scotch) glue. The chief way in which the method of using this differs from other adhesives is that heat is necessary. Thus when a caul is used the latter must be thoroughly heated so that the glue is reliquified and can thus be pressed out all round. The same applies when a press is used. Another feature is that it is the only adhesive for which the hammer method of veneering can be used. The glue is prepared in a proper glue kettle (see page 163) and both groundwork and veneer coated. It does not matter if the glue chills because heat is applied later. There are jobs for which Scotch glue has its advantages over other adhesives. Thus when veneering a shaped edge the tacky nature of the glue enables the glue to be pressed down with a hammer without danger of its springing up. The application of a shaped caul might be difficult or impossible. Scotch glue is still widely used in the antique trade for repair work. The hammer method of laying is dealt with later.

Caul veneering. In this method the veneer is pressed down with a flat board of wood known as a caul. If any jointing in the veneer is needed this is done before laying. In a simple joint the edges are planed, the parts put together on a flat board, and a piece of gummed tape put over the joint. A pattern, other than the simplest kind, would need a drawing on which the veneer could be assembled.

The caul is a flat panel of wood slightly larger than the groundwork, and is cramped down over the veneer with a sheet of newspaper interposed to prevent squeezed-out glue causing it to adhere. For a small panel the cramps can be applied all round, but for a larger one it is necessary to use pairs of cross bearers with slightly curved edges as in Fig. 7. The idea is to drive the glue from the centre outwards, the curve ensuring that the pressure is felt in the centre first. Since the curvature in the pairs of bearers is opposed the work remains flat. Note too the order in which the battens are applied, the centre ones again being fitted first to drive the glue outwards. When both sides are being veneered, the operation is simultaneous, two cauls being used, one each side.

In the case of animal glue it is necessary to heat the caul because the glue has to be reliquified to enable it to be pressed out. The heating must be thorough, not merely on the surface, as the whole operation must be gone about speedily so that pressure is applied before the glue chills. When the veneer has to be positioned exactly as in the case of a built-up pattern, centre lines are drawn on both veneer and groundwork and these lines

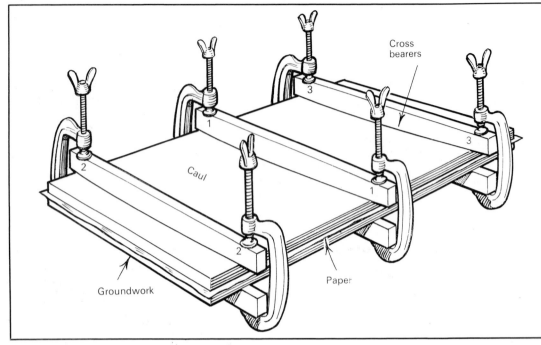

Fig. 7 (above) How caul is cramped down in caul veneering

Fig. 8 (below) How the veneer hammer is used

made to coincide. To prevent the veneer fro‌ floating out of position a couple of fine veneer pi‌ should be driven in in unnoticeable positions.

Hammer veneering. This method is used wit‌ Scotch glue only. The special tool shown at ‌ page 15, is used. It has a strip of brass about $1\frac{1}{2}$mr‌ ($\frac{1}{16}$in.) thick let into the edge, and it is used to pre‌ out the surplus glue. The groundwork bein‌ prepared and the veneer cut to size, both a‌ covered with glue and the veneer placed in positio‌ and smoothed down. The Scotch glue must ‌ free of lumps. If a light wood is being used a litt‌ flake white powder should be added to the glue ‌ this prevents dark glue lines from showing.

For a job of any size lightly damp about one ha‌ with a swab, and pass a warm flat iron across it ‌ liquefy the glue. Use only a minimum of dampnes‌ and do not have the iron hotter than is essenti‌ Work the veneering hammer with a zig-za‌ movement from the centre towards the end as ‌ Fig. 8, and try to avoid stretching the veneer in i‌ width. Most veneers will go down easily, b‌ woods with tricky grain may be inclined to lift, an‌ quite a lot of patience may be needed. It is som‌

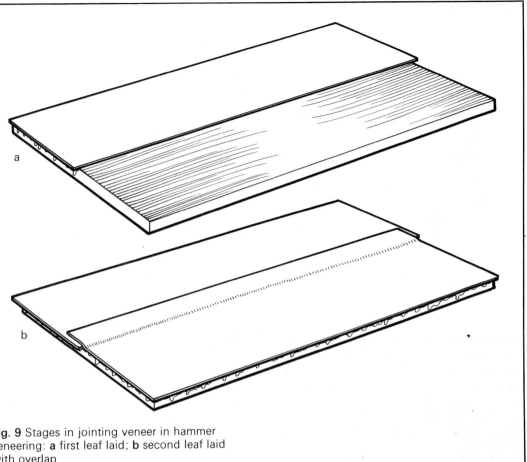

Fig. 9 Stages in jointing veneer in hammer veneering: **a** first leaf laid; **b** second leaf laid with overlap

...mes a help to place a block of metal (say an iron smoothing plane) on a part which is inclined to lift, as the cold metal will make the glue set more rapidly and hold the veneer. In extreme cases it may be necessary to cramp a wood block over the part with a piece of newspaper beneath to prevent it from adhering. To test whether the veneer is down tap it with the finger nails. A bubble (as it is called) will be apparent from the hollow feeling it gives.

One half being down correctly deal with the other in the same way. Any traces of glue on the surface should be wiped off with the damp swab straight away, but use as little moisture as possible because

it is chiefly this which causes the pull.

Jointing. This may be necessary simply because the veneer is not wide enough, or it may be needed in a halved panel in which two consecutive leaves of veneer are put down side by side, the grain matching. In this latter case the joint line must be drawn in pencil on the groundwork, and care taken in positioning the veneer to make sure that the grain is balanced.

For width jointing one piece of veneer is laid as at (a), Fig. 9. The next is laid similarly, overlapping the first as at (b). A straight-edge is laid along the overlap (in line with the pencil mark, if there is

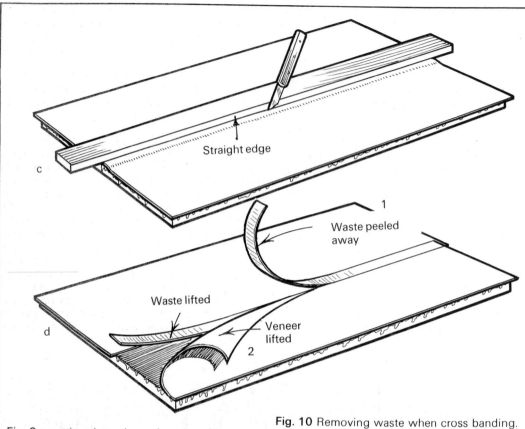

Straight edge

c

1

Waste peeled away

Waste lifted

d

Veneer lifted

2

Fig. 9 c cutting through overlap; **d** peeling away waste

Fig. 10 Removing waste when cross banding. The main sheet does not reach the edge and a cutting gauge is worked round the edge and the waste removed before the glue sets

Fig. 11 How joints in cross banding are taped. The tape is stuck over the joints immediately after laying

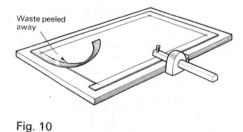

Waste peeled away

Fig. 10

Fig. 11

one), and a keen knife or chisel drawn along it as at (c). If the panel is large it is advisable to fix the straight-edge down with thumb-screws.

The one strip of waste can be peeled away straight away. The other is removed by lifting the veneer (d), so revealing it. It is necessary to replace the veneer at once and rub it down with the hammer. A piece of gummed tape stuck over the joint will prevent it from opening as the glue dries out. Some men prefer to shoot the joint in the veneer before laying and put the parts together with gummed tape, but some tricky veneers are liable to distort with the moisture and heat and may form either gaps in the joint or cause cockling.

Crossbanding. A detail sometimes needed in veneering is the crossbanding of a panel, especially in reproduction work. To do this the main panel is veneered normally except that the veneer is cut short all round. Immediately after laying a cutting gauge set to the banding width is run all round as in Fig. 10, and the waste peeled away.

The crossbanding is cut in cross-grain strips a trifle wider than the banding. The edge is trimmed on the shooting board and the strips cut with the cutting gauge (Fig. 5). In a panel of any great size it will be necessary to joint the strips, and this is done on the job itself, Fig. 11. Mitres are cut with a wide chisel and trimmed if necessary on the shooting board. The veneer is rubbed down with the cross-pene of the hammer, and pieces of gummed tape are stuck over the joints to prevent opening as the glue dries out.

Cleaning up. Leave the work for as long as possible before cleaning up. Any gummed tape on the surface should be lightly damped and peeled off, but avoid water as far as possible. Clean up the surface with a scraper. Often it is a help to hold the scraper at an angle so that it has a slicing cut. This is specially necessary on a crossbanded part as otherwise the grain may tear up. When satisfactory go over the whole with glasspaper wrapped around a cork rubber, first *Fine* 2, the No. 1. In the case of woods with intricate grain such as burr walnut, use only the finest glasspaper and use the rubber with a circular movement. This is necessary because the wood has no definite grain direction. Those who have an orbital sander will find it ideal for such work.

Fig. 12 Assembling cross banding around a sheet of veneer ready to be put down

Chapter eleven

Wood Carving

To get good results in wood carving it is essenti
that the tools are really sharp and are sharpened i
the right way. The method is different from tha
used in ordinary woodworking chisels in which th
bevel is on one side only. Carving gouges have th
main bevel at the outside, but a second bevel
formed inside, and this with repeated sharpenin
eventually becomes about one quarter or one thir
the length of the other.

There are several reasons for the inside bevel. On
is that when'the tool is used with the hollow sid
downwards it gives it a tendency to lift as the cu
is made. Without it the tool would tend to run int
the wood. Another point is that the inside beve
widens the clearance of the tool so that it passe
through a deep cut more easily. Lastly it conside
ably strengthens the edge.

Main sharpening is done with the oilstone an
oilstone slips, but a leather strop dressed with
fine abrasive is used to give a still finer edge and t
keep it in condition. The carver keeps these strop
handy, and rubs up the tools frequently. Th
guiding principle is little and often.

Range of tools. The chief kinds of tools ar
shown in Fig. 1, and of these the straight gouge (a
is used for all general carving. The curved gouge
(b) are for removing the waste when hollowing
say, a bowl. Similar in form but for much mor
acute hollows is the front bench gouge (c
The back bench gouge (d) has not many uses, an
should not be obtained until actually required.

There are two kinds of straight chisel, square (e
and corner (f). They are used mostly for setting i
the corner type being useful for reaching into acut
corners. For the cleaning up of recessed back
grounds the spoon bit (g) is invaluable. I
addition to the square type the L and R corne
are needed, again for acute corners.

The V or parting tool (h) is used chiefly for out
lining, lettering, and sometimes for leaf detail.

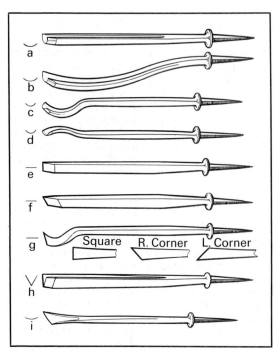

Fig. 1 Chief forms of gouges used in carving:
a straight gouge; b curved gouge; c front bent
gouge; d back bent gouge; e chisel; f corner
chisel; g bent chisel; h V tool; i spade gouge

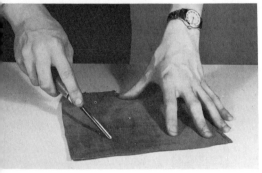

ig. 2 (top) Sharpening the main bevel of the ouge on the oilstone—it is given a twisting ovement so that the whole of the edge is narpened

ig. 4 (above) How gouge is stropped after harpening on the oilstone

ig. 3 (right) How inside of gouge is rubbed vith the oilstone slip

an be obtained with either 90 deg. or 60 deg. ngle. Spade gouges are available in almost all ne above forms, but it will be seen that the tool plays out at the ends and is of lighter form. It is sed chiefly for finishing off delicate carving.

All the tools are obtainable in varying degrees of urvature and in several widths. It can be rather onfusing, but the rule is that all tools of a certain umber have the same degree of curvature in elation to their width. As an example, the No 9 traight gouge is a half-round curve, whatever its vidth. Thus the 6mm. ($\frac{1}{4}$in.) No. 9 would be one alf of a circle struck from a 3mm. ($\frac{1}{8}$in.) radius. The lower the number the flatter the curve. Straight gouges run in numbers from 3 to 11. Curved and sent gouges, chisels, etc. have other numbers.

Sharpening the tools

Gouges. The main outer bevel is sharpened on the oilstone, the tool being held at right angles with the stone and turned with a twisting movement as it is moved back and forth as in Fig. 2. Now use an oilstone slip of curvature that approximates to the inside or is a trifle quicker, and rub it along the inside at a slight angle much as in Fig. 3. It takes many sharpenings to get the gouge into first-class working order, but it helps after the initial outer rubbing to sharpen chiefly inside.

Stropping follows, and for this a piece of soft leather is dressed with a mixture of oil and the finest crocus powder. The fine grade preparation sold for grinding in motor car valves can also be used. Place the leather on a flat board and draw the bevel of the gouge flat along it, as in Fig. 4, rocking it so that every part of the edge is stropped, and drawing it back slightly so that the edge is drawn away, not into the leather. For the inside either a piece of leather can be wrapped round the finger or bent on itself, as Fig. 5 shows, or the leather can be glued to a rounded rubber.

139

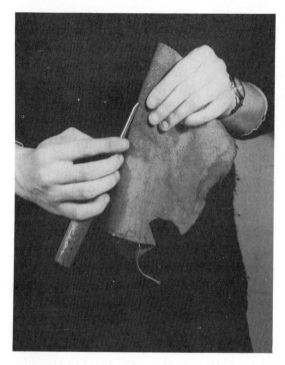

Fig. 5 Stropping the inside of the gouge

Chisels are sharpened in much the same way except that they are kept flat, not rocked. The bevels are equal on both sides. The V tool sometimes causes difficulty. Each outer bevel is rubbed on the stone, and a V shaped oilstone slip used at the inside, this being at an angle much as when the gouge is sharpened. When the slip becomes worn it frequently fails to reach into the corner, and instead of being sharp the angle becomes a slight hollow. This results in a point being formed, and will necessitate taking off the outer extreme corner.

Bench. The bench at which carving is done should be sturdy with a fairly thick top so that there is a solid feeling when the mallet is used. To hold the wood various methods can be used. Sometimes the ordinary joiners' G cramps are suitable, but it is always an advantage to avoid projecting parts. For this reason the carver's screw, Fig. 6, is useful, especially when the wood is fairly thick and when a hole in the back does not matter. The pointed

screw end is driven into the wood and tightened using the wing nut as a spanner. The end of th screw is passed through a hole in the bench and t nut tightened from beneath. When the wood thin the method in Fig. 7 can be followed. Roun head screws are passed through dogs or litt pieces of hardwood or metal into the bench. Th outer ends of the dogs rest on waste blocks about the same thickness as the work, and so ho the work firm. Some metal dogs are cranked ar have saw-like ends.

Lighting is important and should be from or direction only so that the undulations of th surface can be seen easily. An all-round lig eliminates the shadows caused by the varie surfaces and so robs the carving of form. F daylight a window at the back of the bench is ide At night time a single electric lamp which can b raised or lowered at will is the most satisfactor It should have a shade so that the work itself illuminated without glare to the eyes.

Using the Tools

When using the tools for the general run of wo the right hand provides the forward pressur whilst the left hand guides the tool and exercises certain restraining effect, so preventing the to from overshooting. Note also that the wrist an ball of the hand rest firmly on the work or the benc so steadying the tool, as shown in Fig. 8. We spea here of right and left hand, but in fact the goo carver is ambidextrous and can vary the hands will, this enabling awkward parts to be reache without having to shift the work.

Sometimes the mallet is used, especially for som setting-in operations, and the best type of mallet round in form. This enables the tool to be struc with any part of it, it being unnecessary to turn th mallet to bring the right face into use.

The tools should be laid out in a row at the back the bench, blades towards the carver. This enable the carver to grasp any tool with the hand in th position it will be held, so saving much unnece sary handling. A common practice is to have a the handles different, either in form, kind of woo or in colour, so that the right tool is quickl recognisable. In an elaborate piece of work ther

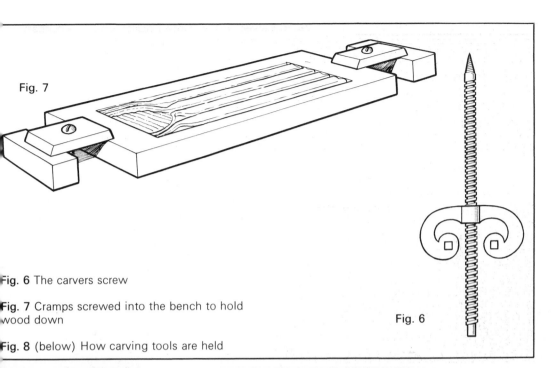

Fig. 7

Fig. 6 The carvers screw

Fig. 7 Cramps screwed into the bench to hold wood down

Fig. 8 (below) How carving tools are held

Fig. 6

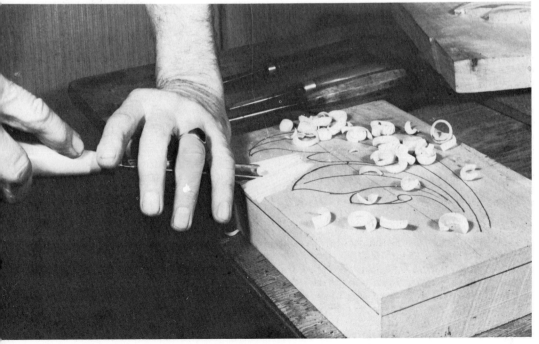

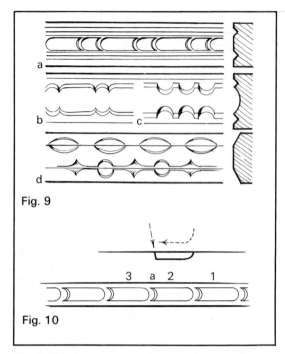

Fig. 9 Simple gouge cuts in a moulded section

Fig. 10 How gouge cuts are made and order of the work

may be as many as thirty or forty tools in a row, and much time is saved if the right tool can be spotted quickly. Sometimes a carver puts a ring of colour on the handle as a help. Handles are mostly octagonal as this prevents their rolling sideways on to the floor.

Carving may be divided into three main groups:

Incised work, in which the design is cut into the wood, generally with the V tool. The cut-away part forms the design.

Modelled work. Here the groundwork is recessed leaving the design standing up, and a certain amount of modelling is carried out. Thus the form of a leaf may be made to undulate, or one detail, such as a ribbon, made to appear to pass over another.

Carving in the round. The most difficult, all sides

being carved, without any background. The huma form, animals, etc., are examples of this.

The same general rules apply to all carving. Th whole thing is brought up to one stage before a further work is done. These stages, varied accordir to the job, are:

Setting-in. Here the main outline is cut in, eith with a gouge cut on the waste side, or by choppir down with gouges to suit the curves. Often bot are used as explained later.

Bosting in. In this stage the bulk of the unwante wood is removed, leaving main chunks where th detail will later be cut. The main undulations a worked without any attempt at detail.

Modelling. Here the detail takes shape, the for being worked, and the final surface chiselled.

In all carving, wood must always be cut, n scraped, torn, split, or levered away. The surfac too, must be left straight from the tool. Glasspap spoils it, and it is this that makes the work exactir No attempt is made to remove all the facets forme by the tool, and it is probably in this that the work the skilled man shows most to advantage. In h work the tool marks are purposeful and crisp, an their direction helps the flow of the design.

Sometimes the background can be given a spec texture by the use of a punch, but this must not t made an excuse for bad work with the gouge. I purpose is solely to show up the design itself t giving the background a completely differer appearance. Punches can either be bought read made, or they can be made from a 150mm (6in nail filed off square, and with indentations filed the end.

Gouge cuts. The best way of describing th process is to take actual examples, and for a sta the simple gouge cuts in Fig. 9 are good practic At (a) is a flat moulding formed with V cuts at ea side. A gouge rather narrower than the centr member is used to make a series of downward stat at the points (a), Fig. 10. Hold the gouge at a slig angle as shown by the dotted arrow in the section and use the mallet. There is an advantage in makir all the downward cuts first. The heavy work is rath hard on the tools, and, once this is done, it enabl

Fig. 11 Bed head with decorative carved corners

he edge to be kept in good condition for the ollowing process, that of scooping out the waste. urthermore the downward chopping may cause he short grain occasioned by the adjoining cut to plit out, though this difficulty can be avoided by aking the cuts in the order shown in Fig. 10.

Note that to preserve the parallel sides of the cuts he gouge must be taken downwards and the andle rapidly lowered as shown by the dotted line, ig. 10. As a rule a single cut is made first to remove he bulk of the waste, and a second cut to finish leanly to size. This work is mostly done by eye, part from the initial stepping of the stabs, though encil lines can be put in as a guide. They will have o be scraped out locally afterwards.

t (b), Fig. 9, a hollow section is worked first, and he position of the members either stepped in with ividers or marked from a slip of paper. A gouge is sed to cut downwards each side of the indenta- on, this being held at an angle so that the edge nishes in line with the outer sloping side of the '. The cuts must meet. A flat gouge can be used in ne with the side of the V to cut away small waste ieces.

A similar process is followed at (c), the gouge being used to cut the semi-circle. Again it is held at an angle so that the edge finishes in line with the outer slope of the V. This enables the little waste pieces to be cut out cleanly with a flat gouge or chisel. Some may find a skew chisel easier to use for this.

At (d) are similar devices worked at the corner of a chamfer. In both cases downward stabs are made, and the waste eased away with a flat gouge afterwards.

Modelled designs. In Fig. 11 are shown decorative corners carved at the top of a bed head, but the general idea could be used in other places. The designs could be varied, and alternatives are given in Figs. 12 and 13. The design could be drawn in on paper and transferred to the wood with carbon paper, or if preferred it could be drawn straight on to the wood from a preliminary sketch. The procedure is similar in both examples. The main shapes are outlined approximately with a V tool, and then set in with gouges which follow the final shape. This enables the background to be recessed, the waste being removed with narrower

143

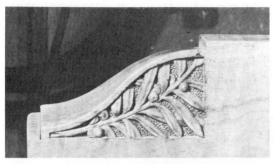

gouges or chisels, and finished with the spoon bit. It is for work of this kind that the R and L corner tools are invaluable. Care should be taken to make all the recesses even in depth. The slight modelling of the leaves and flowers follows. Where one leaf passes over the other, the curve should appear natural, not abruptly sloped at each side. Finally the background can be punched, though some prefer to omit this detail. Its advantage however is that it gives distinct texture which throws up the detail clearly.

Fig. 14 shows a swag partly completed. To the right is shown the background set back and the detail partly outlined. As the carving progresses the inner outlines are necessarily cut away, but it is as well to put them in because they show the places to be left full and those to be cut away. In

Fig. 12 (top left) Enlarged view of an alternative design for the bedhead in Fig. 11
Fig. 13 (middle left) Another alternative
Fig. 14 (below) A decorative swag carved in the solid in mahogany. The right hand side shows the early stage in carving

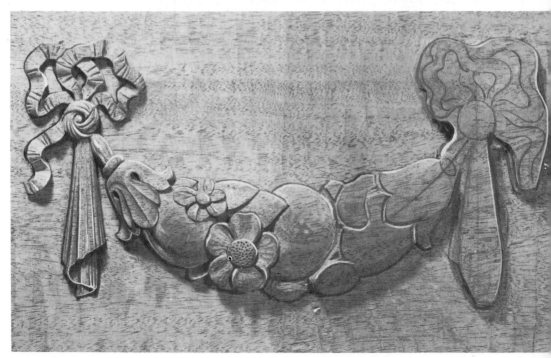

ig. 15 (above) Carved detail cut in thin wood etted to shape and stuck to a backboard

igs. 16, 17, 18 show stages in carving a andelabrum

ny case they are easily cut in afresh as the work roceeds.

nother piece of carved detail is that in Fig. 15. In is case it is intended to be applied rather than ut in the solid, and the wood is fretted to the utline and stuck down on to a flat board with ewspaper interposed to enable it to be lifted way on completion. It will be realised that without is backing it would be difficult to grip the wood, nd in any case the carving would be fragile. The wag given in Fig. 14 could be cut and applied in ie same way.

igs, 16, 17, and 18 are given as they show stages carving the arm of a candelabrum. Other items ould pass through similar stages. In Fig. 16 the iape has been fretted out and the detail pencilled . The next stage shows the work partly bosted in, iat is the main form is roughly carved. In Fig. 18 ie modelling is largely completed.

louldings are frequently carved, especially in production work. It is advisable to make a stencil oiled paper or thin foil showing one or more omplete repeat details. The shapes of the leaves tc. should be cut in the stencil with the same ouges used for the actual carving. It may in fact e a matter of adapting the actual detail to the urve of the gouges available. Work of this kind iould be done with as few cuts as possible. For

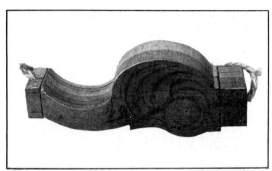

Fig. 16

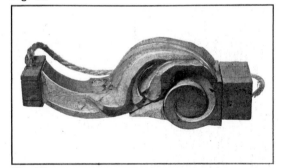

Fig. 17

Fig. 18

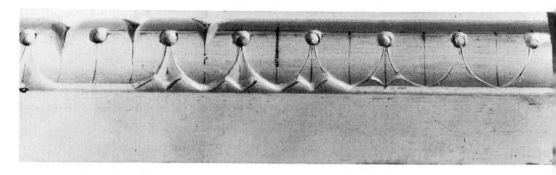

Fig. 19 Repeat detail carved in a moulding

instance in Fig. 19 the curve of the large leaves could be stabbed in with a single gouge. The lower ends separated by the darts are then deepened, also the sides of the darts cut in, and the triangle of wood between cut away with a chisel in a single

chip. This is not only to save time. It also gives clean crisp quality to the work. The modelling of the darts can also be done in two cuts, each sloping towards the leaves. At the top the small circular recesses are formed by revolving a small half-round gouge. If the latter is given a lateral flick after cutting the circle it will usually snap of the boss, leaving a clean finish. If not it may be necessary to make a punch from a French nail of suitable size, filing the end flat. Do not use this as a substitute for proper carving, however.

Chapter twelve

Turning

Wood turning is a big subject, and it is impossible in a single chapter to do more than outline one or two basic operations. For fuller details the reader should study a handbook on the subject.

It may be roughly divided into two classes: between-centres turning and face-plate turning. The former is used for all long items such as lamp columns, spindles, etc., and face-plate work for wide, shallow items, such as bowls, platters and so on. The actual turning operation is of two kinds: cutting and scraping. Each has its purposes and is essential for certain classes of work, though in some cases the methods are interchangeable. Cutting is generally much quicker than scraping, and is therefore often used for the preliminary roughing, even when scraping is necessary to finish off with. It is also essential for most soft-woods, which cannot be scraped cleanly. On the other hand, it is difficult to cut many really hard woods, as the tool edge is lost too quickly.

Between centres turning. The prong chuck is used at the driving end and the ring centre at the tailstock. The wood should be centred reasonably accurately by eye and then revolved by hand to see whether one corner stands out more than the others. This is easily tested by seeing whether the corners are the same distance from the tool rest. Incidentally, the wood at the tailstock end should be given a spot of oil to lubricate it. When running is satisfactory tighten the tailstock screw up hard then slacken off slightly. Too much pressure may bow the wood, causing excessive friction and consequent heating.

Gouge work. With a fairly large gouge run from end to end until all flats are taken out. Fig. 1 shows the operation. If working to an exact size set a pair of calipers to about 2mm. ($\frac{1}{16}$in.) full of the required diameter, and continue turning with the gouge until the calipers will just slip over, as in Fig. 2. Using the gouge will not produce an entirely flat, smooth surface, but large irregularities should be avoided.

Using the chisel. The long-cornered chisel is now substituted; this should be 30–40mm.

Fig. 1 Preliminary rough turning using the large gouge

($1\frac{1}{4}$–$1\frac{1}{2}$in.) wide. Hold it as shown in Fig. 3, using only the portion between the heel and the centre. The long point is never used for this work—if it should slip down it will dig into the wood with disastrous results. The chisel will enable a perfectly smooth and straight surface to be obtained. It cannot be started at the end, but must be placed in about 25mm. (1in.) and moved slowly along and right off at the other end. It can then be reversed and the process repeated in the other direction. Again test with the calipers until down to size. It will quickly be realised that the gouge removes the wood far more quickly than the chisel and it is for this reason that the wood should be brought down as close as possible to finished size with the gouge before the chisel is substituted.

The chisel is a tricky tool to use until mastery has been obtained. The secret is largely in letting the bevel of the tool rub the work. Unless this happens

Fig. 2 (left) Testing diameter with calipers

Fig. 3 (below) Using the long cornered chisel to smooth the cylinder

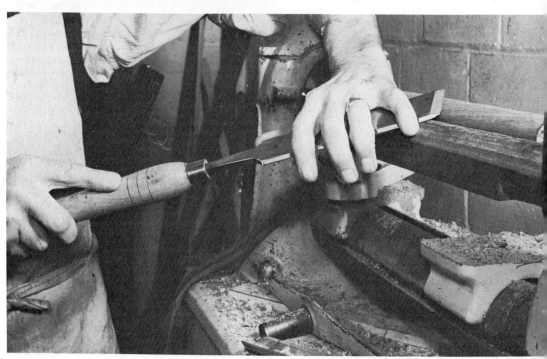

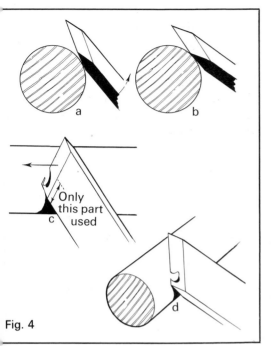

Fig. 4

the edge is liable to be carried in by the revolving wood so that the long corner digs in. The best way is to hold the tool so that only the bevel is on the wood as at Fig. 4a, they raise the handle until the edge begins to cut. The position is then maintained.

The chisel can be held in either of the two ways shown in Figs. 3 and 5. Fig. 5 is of special value when thin material is being turned. It supports the wood at the back, since the fingers bear lightly against it, so preventing bouncing of the wood and a trouble known as ribbing, which is a sort of spiral set up in the surface. Note that in both cases the edge of the chisel is at an angle to the wood, so that it has a slicing action.

Turning hollows. For the general run of hollows a small gouge is used, the edge being sharpened as in Fig. 6. The tool is taken in from each side of the hollow. Unless this is done it will leave a rough

Fig. 4 Using the chisel: a preliminary position; b handle raised to bring edge to wood; c and d side movement of chisel

Fig. 5 (below) Alternative way of holding chisel

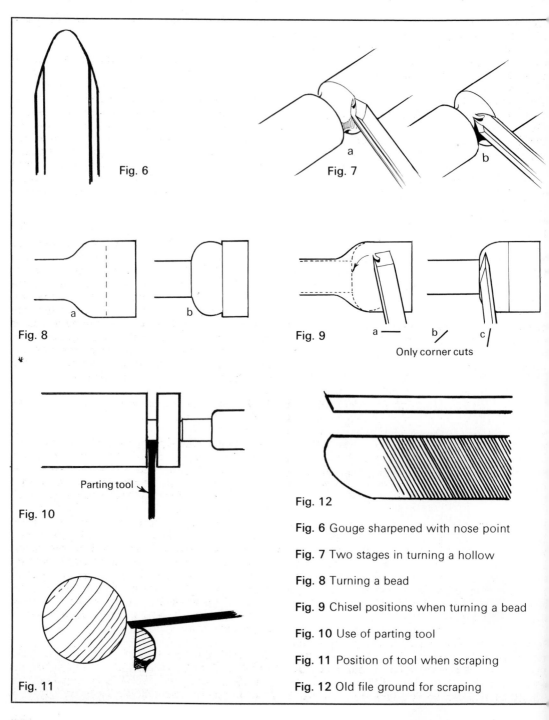

Fig. 6

Fig. 7

Fig. 8

a

b

Fig. 9

a —— b / c /

Only corner cuts

Parting tool

Fig. 10

Fig. 11

Fig. 12

Fig. 6 Gouge sharpened with nose point

Fig. 7 Two stages in turning a hollow

Fig. 8 Turning a bead

Fig. 9 Chisel positions when turning a bead

Fig. 10 Use of parting tool

Fig. 11 Position of tool when scraping

Fig. 12 Old file ground for scraping

nish. Dealing first with the right hand side of the hollow hold the gouge on its side, the bevel more or less at right angles to the wood, and by a combined movement move the handle to the right raising it at the same time and twisting it over so that it is on its back. The idea is shown in Fig. 7. In practice, the hollow is not taken down to full depth in one cut. What happens is that a cut is made as described at one side and the waste removed by a second cut from the other side. The hollow is then completed by further cuts from each side. The tricky part is in the initial entry of the tool, because it is liable to start over to the side and gash the wood, the reason being that, until a slight start has been made, the bevel has nothing to rub on. Once slightly into the wood the bevel prevents all side movement by rubbing on the wood.

The answer is in starting boldly because only a slight penetration is enough to give the bevel support. Equally important is starting with the gouge on its side so that the bevel is about at right angles with the wood, and straightway moving the handle to the side so that the bevel is pressed against the cut in the wood. The cut is in fact made by swivelling the handle rather than by pushing the tool forwards.

To turn beads and similar round parts the point of the square chisel is used. The work can be lightened by removing much of the waste first with the gouge. For instance, in Fig. 8 much of the preliminary wasting away can be done with the gouge as at (a), before finishing with the chisel. Remember that not only is the gouge an easier tool to use but it also removes wood more quickly.

Fig. 9 shows how the corner of the tool starts at the top of the bead and is turned over as it progresses down the curve. Only the point of the tool is used, and it is held at an angle as shown, passing from position (a) to (b), and on to (c). It is usual to use a square sharpened chisel so that each side of the bead can be formed without changing the tool.

Parting can be done either with a special parting tool or with the ordinary skew chisel. The latter gives a generally cleaner finish, but requires a greater length of wood in which to operate. Fig. 10 shows the parting tool. Note that it is slightly wider at the end so that it clears itself as it is pressed into the wood.

Scraping. Whereas chisels and gouges cut the wood, taking thick shavings like a coarsely set plane, scraping tools only scrape, removing little more than dust. Most softwoods cannot be scraped successfully but many hardwoods respond well, and in fact in some cases scraping is the only way. The tool is held as in Fig. 11 from which it will be seen that it droops slightly towards the wood. The idea is that if it should dig into the revolving wood it will immediately disengage, whereas if it were pointed upwards the movement would tend to draw it farther into the wood.

Sets of scraping tools can be bought, but usually they are ground from old files. These do perfectly well and can be ground to whatever section is needed. Fig. 12 shows how the serrations are ground away at an angle on the surface, and the edge ground at about 80deg. After a while one collects a number of such tools. When grinding always do the surface first and the edge last, as the latter sets up a burr which helps the cut. Some woods, such as elm and oak, scrape best with the tool direct from the grinding wheel. Others need the edge to be finished on the oilstone.

For boring holes through standards, etc., a special boring tool is used.

Face-plate turning. Items such as bowls are generally fixed to the face plate with screws, and it is as well to place a waste piece between the two, as this enables the turning to be completed without danger of the tool touching the face plate. Fig. 13 shows the idea. If the entire work is to be done in a single chucking the bottom of the wood must be planed flat so that it beds snugly on to the waste piece. The screws pass through the back plate and waste piece and engage only in the work (Fig. 13). Their length must be carefully calculated so that they do not project into the inside of the bowl. This must also be considered when boring the holes, because such holes would appear as a blemish.

Deal with the outside first, using a 6mm., (¼in.) or 9mm. (⅜in.) gouge. Hold it so that it cuts, not merely scrapes, and let the bevel of the tool rub the wood, so that any tendency to dig in is

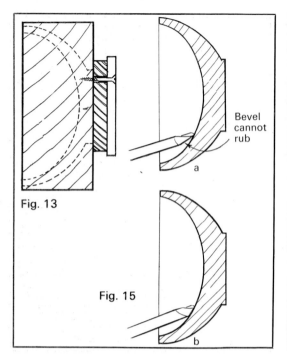

Fig. 13

Bevel cannot rub

Fig. 15

a

b

avoided. Fig. 14 shows the method. The inside can be dealt with in the same way to remove the bulk of the waste, but here it is vital to let the bevel rub. A point to remember here is that the angle of bevel affects the work. In fact, a long, thin bevel cannot be used for the inside, as it is impossible to let it rub as shown at (a) Fig. 15. Note how the less-acute bevel at (b) does enable it to rub.

To finish off cleanly the wood must be scraped as in Fig. 16. Again note that the tool is drooped slightly towards the point so that if it should dig in it will at once be thrown clear. Generally two tools are needed; a slightly curved one for the bottom (a), Fig. 17, and one of more acute curve, (b). Work the flat one across the bottom as far into the sides as it will go, then substitute the tool with the quicker curve. Work the tool sideways as this enables the sweetness of the curve to be judged. Fig. 17 shows the operation.

Get the shape right before using glasspaper and take out any tears. These last named can be troublesome to get rid of in a bowl which has the grain running crosswise as in Fig. 18. The

Fig. 13 Wood mounted on face-plate for bowl turning

Fig. 14 (top) Shaping outside of bowl using gouge

Fig. 15 Inside of bowl turned with gouge

Fig. 16 (above) Scraping inside of bowl

parts marked (a) and (b) have necessarily to b worked against the grain. The answer is shar tools and a fine cut. Any attempt to make heavy cut will cause the grain to tear out. possible, mount a grindstone on the other sid of the headstock and rub up the tool on it fre quently.

Finally, smooth with glasspaper, Middle 2 firs followed by No. 1½, and finally flour grade. A goo finish can be obtained by the use of Speedaneez The work is run at its slowest speed, and th rubber moved slowly across the surface. Leav for a few minutes, and repeat the process so that a medium gloss is built up. Allow as long as possible to harden, and polish with wax. With some wax polishes it is necessary to leave to harden after application before polishing; others can be polished straight away. The advantage of the preliminary french polish is that it builds up a foundation gloss, and helps to keep out dirt when the item is in use.

An attractive bowl with handles is shown in Fig. 19. In making this a wide rim has to be turned, the section of which approximates to that of the handles. The plan shape of the handles is then marked out on the top, and the unwanted part of the rim sawn away with the coping saw, and the surface cleaned up with file and spokeshave. Afterwards the scrolled effect is cut in with carving tools.

Fig. 17 Scrapers used for inside of bowl

Fig. 18 Parts of bowl liable to be rough

Fig. 19 (below) Turned bowl with carved handles

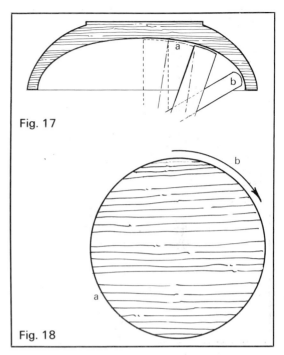

Fig. 17

Fig. 18

Chapter thirteen

Timber and Materials

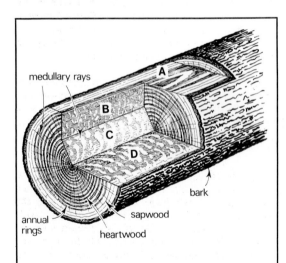

Oak log showing how figure is produced by different methods of cutting. **a** reveals no figure; **b** shows small figure; **c** and **d** show full figure

The range of timbers runs into thousands, and her we can deal with only the relatively few i common use.

To make a broad distinction timbers may b divided up under two headings: hardwoods an softwoods, the former referring to deciduou broad-leaved trees which shed their leaves i winter, and the latter to coniferous trees whic have needle-pointed leaves. The terms ar purely of convenience and frequently bear littl reference to actual hardness. The hardest of th softwoods are heavier and harder than th lightest of the hardwoods.

Hardwoods. For general cabinet-making oak i widely used. English oak when suitable board are available has a fine figure, but frequently it i unreliable owing to bad seasoning and is liabl to shakes and warping. An excellent alternative i Japanese oak, which, properly seasoned, i sound, well-figured, works well, and is availabl in good sizeable boards. Slavonic oak also is use(and is a fine timber.

Often oak is available only in squares of 37, 5(62, and 75mm. (1½, 2, 2½, and 3in.), suitabl only for legs, etc., but when wider pieces ai needed for such parts as rails these squares ca be sawn through when a circular saw is availabl and jointed together to give greater widtl

American oak is not often seen nowaday: presumably owing to exchange difficulties, bu when it is found it is in fine standard board: There are two kinds; red and white, the latt(being invariably of better quality.

Much of the attractiveness of oak is due to th figure derived from the rays which radiate fro the heart. A board cut parallel with these exhibit the largest figure and makes the most reliabl wood. The more the board departs from th parallel the smaller the figure until the rays pas through it at right angles and appear only a minute specks on the surface.

Silky oak, occasionally available, which deriv(from Australia is not a true oak at all, but gets i name from the pronounced figure it has. It worl well and is quite suitable for cabinet making as is capable of good finish and polishes well.

s a substitute for oak, chestnut is sometimes sed. It has no figure derived from the medullary ays, but resembles plain oak closely in both rain and colour. Beech is often available in quares and is thus suitable for turned legs, etc. has a good figure, though smaller than oak. wing to the shortage of walnut it is often used r turned parts, the rest of the job being walnut eneered.

Iahogany is an excellent cabinet wood, though ne finer wide boards are becoming difficult to otain. Practically the only true American ma-ogany available is the Honduras kind; Cuban is most unobtainable. African mahogany is fre-uently used, and, although it has not the same ne figure, is considerably cheaper. It varies idely in reliability and quality.

apele is sometimes referred to as a mahogany, nd has something of the colour and marking of ue mahogany. Its chief characteristic is the stripy e figuring consisting of narrow stripes of light nd dark wood. Both rauli and niangon have omething of the general appearance of mahogany, ut boards vary enormously. Some are entirely lain, whilst others have a most attractive figure. here are many substitutes for mahogany, of which aboon is quite common. It is not a true mahogany, ut is a useful secondary hardwood for drawer des, cabinet backs, etc. It is often used in the anufacture of multi-ply.

Valnut is a fine cabinet wood, but is generally ifficult to obtain. Both English and French alnut are occasionally seen but stocks of the ainer American or black walnut are seldom vailable. Australian walnut makes a good abinet wood, many of the boards being finely gured.

here are many other imported hardwoods, upplies of which fluctuate. Of these there is uli from Chile, a lightish-brown timber some-hat like beech but without ray markings. Iansonia has somewhat the colour of walnut nd is a useful cabinet wood. Afara from Nigeria as a light straw colour and is sometimes available. frormosia has a brownish yellow shade with terlocked grain which needs care in planing. All nese woods vary considerably in quality and the est plan is to consult a text book for their

characteristics, or to see whether the timber merchant has any information to offer.

Teak has become popular as a furniture wood and can be obtained in a good range of thicknesses and widths. It is not a good gluing wood owing to its greasy nature but the use of a degreaser helps. One of the modern P.V.A. adhesives with resin additives are the most successful.

Softwoods. Of the softwoods the chief timber for carpentry is the red Baltic pine. Quality varies widely, the chief drawback of the poorer grades being the presence of knots, but better boards can be reasonably free from larger knots. It is used widely for structural timber—roofs, flooring, doors, etc., but needs care in selection when used for joists, rafters, and similar purposes, as knots in bad positions can reduce the strength enormously. For back frames, concealed rails, etc., it is frequently used in furniture making, though the poorer grades should be avoided.

Yellow or white pine from North America is a delightful wood, but it is most difficult to obtain. If once-used timber is available it is excellent for veneer grounds, etc. Parana pine (South America) is in good supply and is a first-rate timber, often entirely free from knots, and is useful, though it often twists in drying and splits easily.

When Western red cedar can be obtained it makes an excellent joinery timber, wide, long boards free from knots being available. It is suitable for indoor and for outdoor use. For the latter no preservative is needed, and it is often used for roofing for this reason.

Plywood. Qualities vary enormously. The cheap tea chest is useless for work of quality; the layers have probably not been properly dried out, the gluing may be faulty, and there are most likely blemishes, such as gaps in the middle layer or even overlaps. A properly made ply by a reliable manufacturer, however, is quite sound and can be used for the carcase of a veneered job. Fuller information on this appears in the chapter on veneering. Thinner plies have three layers, the centre one often being thicker than the others and known as stout heart. When more than three layers are used it is termed multi-ply. Various woods are used in the manufacture—birch, alder,

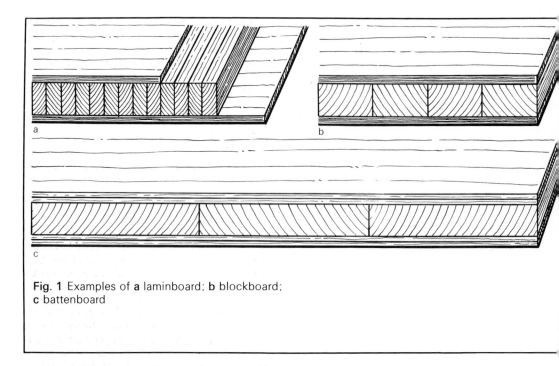

Fig. 1 Examples of **a** laminboard; **b** blockboard;
c battenboard

ash, pine, and gaboon. The latter when made up
as multi-ply makes a good ground for veneered
flush doors.

Laminated board, etc. These are built up as
shown in Fig. 1, there being an inner core with
thinner outer layers, the grain at right angles. Of
the three kinds shown the laminated board is the
least liable to move.

Chipboard. This is largely made from specially
prepared chips bound with resin glue and highly
compressed. It is frequently used for partitions,
backs, furniture parts, but is unsuitable for outdoor
use. In the best way the board is attached to a
framework, but when used structurally as distinct
from a filling, it should have a substantial lipping
around the edges, this being tongued in. Apart

from strengthening it, it provides a suitab
surface in which hinge recesses, etc., can be c

Veneering is quite successful, both sides bei
covered. Some chipboards are made by t
extruded process and are faced on both sid
with thick veneer. These boards are genera
reliable, but deep grooves which penetrate rig
through the veneers should be avoided becau
they are liable to snap through.

Wallboards. These cover a tremendously wi
range, from really hard, compressed boar
suitable for a caravan covering etc., to softboar
intended mainly for insulation. The better an
medium qualities are frequently used for back
drawer bottoms, and for panelling genera
which is to be painted.

Chapter fourteen

A wide range of material is available nowadays, and the choice depends on whether the item is to be used out-of-doors or inside, the wear it will have, the kind of wood it is made of, and personal preference. Some of the older materials have fallen by the wayside but others still remain popular for some work.

Paint

To give best results at least three coats should be applied; priming, undercoat, and finishing coat. It is advisable to obtain all three from the same manufacturer, as this ensures that they are safe to use together.

Wood Finishing

Priming. Having cleaned up the wood go over any knots with painter's knotting. Leave for half an hour and give a second application. Really bad knots should be cut out and plugged. Any nails should be punched in. Rub smooth with glasspaper, and give the coat of priming. This is usually of a grey or pink colour, though for a white or cream paint it is frequently white. It should be comparatively thin, and should be applied evenly, and brushed well into the wood. Work in the direction of the grain to finish off. Brush the paint into cracks, etc. Leave for 12–24 hours to harden.

Undercoating. All nail holes, cracks, etc., should be filled with putty, or one of the proprietary stoppings. This is pressed well in and the surface made smooth by drawing the flat of the knife across it. Incidentally, in the case of glazed windows, etc., the rebates should have a coat of priming before putty is used. Otherwise it will fail to adhere properly.

Rub down any roughness or unevenness with wet-dry glasspaper used over a cork rubber, damping the surface beforehand so that all dust is kept down. Any nibs or runs that may have formed should be smoothed, though they should be avoided altogether as far as possible.

The undercoating invariably approximates in colour to the finishing coat, though there is usually a slight difference so that it is easy to see which parts have been covered. The application is similar to that of the priming coat. Work well into awkward places first, avoiding the filling in of detail, and laying-off with long, even strokes in the direction of the grain. Again leave for 24 hours to harden.

Finishing coat. Once again rub down with abrasive paper as before, and brush away any dust. As gloss paints have the property of flowing out and eliminating brush marks no more re-crossing is necessary than that needed to give an even coat—in fact prolonged working is in-advisable because an initial set takes place early. Work towards edges as far as possible so that fat edges and runs are avoided. If there are any runs at adjoining edges work them out straight away.

All paint should be well stirred before use, and if a skin has formed on the surface cut it round with a knife and remove it. Oil paint which has stood for some time should be strained through old silk before use. Brushes which are to stand overnight for use next day can be placed in a jar of water. When finished with altogether they should be cleaned with turps, and finally in warm soapy water.

Furniture Finishes

Polyurethane Lacquer. This is based on synthetic resin and is generally known as P.U. lacquer. It is usually of the catalyst type, the lacquer remaining in good usable condition for an almost unlimited time if kept sealed. Only when the catalyst is mixed with it does hardening begin. As a rule a third container is supplied with the pack, this containing thinners which can also be used for brush cleaning. As a rule at least two coats are required for a good finish, and generally the best results are obtained by thinning out the lacquer and applying extra coats rather than using one thick coat. When hard the surface can be lightly smoothed with flour glasspaper or the finest grade steel wool. It can be brought to a brilliant gloss by burnishing with a fine abrasive cream after the lacquer is fully cured. The lacquer is brush-applied and does not call for great skill other than careful brush work. It may be necessary to use a grain filler if the wood is open-grained and this is used before the application of the lacquer. It is advisable to use the filler supplied by

the maker of the lacquer as other makes may not b compatible.

Cellulose. This is another finish frequently use today. According to type it can be either brush or spray-applied, the latter preferably. Whe the brush is used it calls for a deft touch when second coat is applied because the latter tends t soften that previously applied. In some cases th work can be left as it is from the brush or spray but a more brilliant effect can be obtained from what is known as 'pulling over'. A pad is made from cotton wool covered with wash leather, the fac brought to a smooth surface free from all crease It is dampened with a special 'pull-over' liqui which has a mild solvent action on the cellulos and is rubbed over the surface first with a circula movement and afterwards with straight stroke in the direction of the grain. This not only take out inequalities in the cellulose but also has th effect of forcing the cellulose into the open grain If this is too bright for taste it can be dulled dow by rubbing over the surface with steel woo lubricated with wax polish.

Teak oil. The present-day use of teak as furniture wood, plus the liking for a semi-glos finish, has led to the popularity of teak oil as finish. Apart from teak it can also be used o other hardwoods. It gives a soft lustrous finis and is one of the simplest finishes to apply. It ha merely to be rubbed on with a rag. New wood need several applications, but a dull shine gradually built up. Teak oil largely replaces th older oil polish in which linseed oil with tereben driers was used. It dries more quickly and give better adhesion.

French polish. Although not used as widely a formerly this is still preferred by some worker especially in the antique restoration trade. It capable of giving a most attractive finish but ha the drawback of not being resistant to hea water, spirit, and other markings. Furthermore calls for a considerable degree of skill if a real clean finish is to be obtained. For home us most workers prefer the more modern and simple finishes.

To describe the stages briefly the wood is staine (if required), the grain filled in (again if required and the polishing proper begun, this consisting o our stages; fadding, colouring, (if needed), bodying, and finishing. French polish is made in various types; garnet, a dark brown shade; button, a yellowish colour; orange, a medium polish; white, a creamy shade; and transparent, an almost colourless liquid. The light polishes are for light woods, and the garnet to deepen the colour of wood. Orange is the most generally used.

A polishing rubber is made as in Fig. 1, and the polish applied to the cotton wool pad, the covering cloth having been removed. In the preliminary fadding stage the rubber is moved along the work in straight strokes as at (a), Fig. 2, the rubber being fairly generously charged with polish. This is followed by the bodying process in which a good body of polish is built up. In this the polish is applied with a circular movement as at (b), Fig. 2, followed by the figure-of-eight (c), this being varied by an oval movement (d).

Finally straight strokes are used. A spot of linseed oil on the rubber face is necessary to lubricate the rubber, but no more than is essential should be used. Several applications with drying intervals are necessary.

The work can be finished by stiffing or spiriting off. In the former the rubber is charged with half-polish and half-spirit and is glided on to the surface in straight strokes along the length of the grain as at (f). Lightness of touch is essential.

For the spiriting off method a fresh rubber is made, and the cotton wool pad given a couple of drops of spirit only. Apply to the surface in large circles or figures-of-eight, changing gradually to straight strokes. As the rubber dries out the pressure can be increased until it acts as a burnisher in removing the oil. The face of the rubber will become greasy as the oil is lifted and the cover should be changed to a fresh face.

Wax polish. This is simple to use, and can be renewed at any time. If an oil stain has previously been used it is essential that it is first fixed with at least two coats of French polish. Otherwise it may be lifted unevenly in patches. In any case it is a good plan to body up the wood, using white French polish for a job to be in natural colour or lacquer. It not only helps to keep out dirt, but builds up a preliminary shine.

You can use any good proprietary wax polish, or you can make your own from beeswax shredded into turps. Best American turps is the most satisfactory but a good grade substitute (white spirit) is cheaper and may have to be used. The absorbing process is quickened by heating the mixture in a can of hot water (do not use a naked flame). To harden the polish add a small proportion of rosin whilst molten and stir in well. When cold the polish should be the consistency of butter in summer time.

Apply freely with a brush (boot brush type) and leave to harden for 12–24 hours. Polish with a similar brush and finish with a rubber. No shine can be built up until the turps has evaporated.

Table top polish. This finish is considerably more resistant to heat, water, and spirit marking than ordinary French polish. It is applied in practically the same way but no oil is used.

Varnish. This is not widely used nowadays having been largely replaced by finishes based on cellulose and catalysed lacquers. There are many varieties of these, many of them setting to an extremely hard surface which is resistant to heat, spirit and water marking. However, varnish is still used to an extent, the two kinds being oil varnish, sometimes used over paint or on bare wood to be exposed to the atmosphere, and spirit varnish which includes the various french polishes, and is not so durable for outside work and is more generally used for finishing indoor items either by themselves or in combination with french polishing. It is sometimes known as transparent lacquer.

Stains. Although the tendency nowadays is to use wood in its natural colour, stains are still preferred in some circumstances. It should be realized at the outset, however, that some modern finishes are not compatible with all stains as a reaction may set in, causing various troubles. The instructions supplied with the finishes should therefore be consulted. There are many proprietary stains, water, oil, and spirit based, which are available in a wide range of shades. Apart from this however there are certain materials which are invaluable for darkening, lightening, or colouring woods.

For oak a most useful basic stain is made from

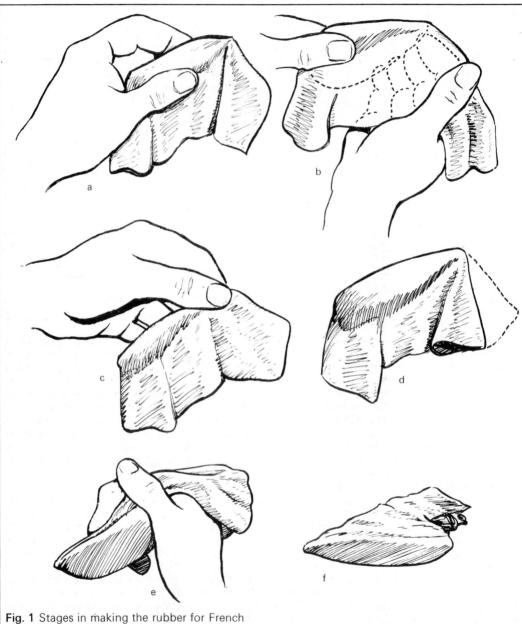

Fig. 1 Stages in making the rubber for French polishing. Unbleached cotton wool is used for the body of the rubber, this being moulded into a pear shape. After charging with polish this is wrapped in a piece of fine linen

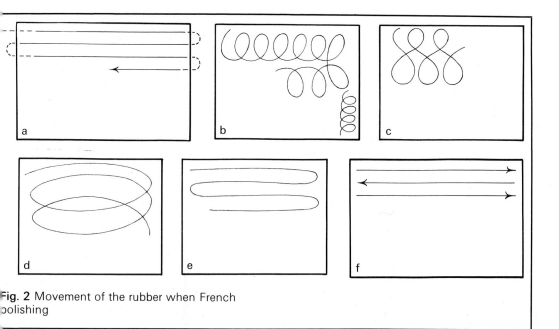

Fig. 2 Movement of the rubber when French polishing

ndyke crystals dissolved in warm water, the quantity depending on the depth of colour required. Stir thoroughly and strain through muslin. The usual plan is to make a concentrated solution and dilute as required. Immediately before use add a little ·880 ammonia as this helps to drive it into the grain.

ahogany crystals can also be obtained, these having a much redder shade. The two can be mixed together (after making up separately) to obtain any special shade. Another material useful for warming up is eosin powder which, dissolved in water, gives a bright red stain. It is seldom used as a stain by itself but is handy for adding to others. Be careful not to overdo its use.

To darken mahogany bichromate of potash is generally used. The crystals are steeped in water which becomes bright orange in colour. Its effect on the wood is chemical, however, and turns the mahogany a brown shade, the depth depending on the strength. It is widely used in the reproduction trade. It can also be used on oak which it turns a slightly greenish brown. By adding it to vandyke crystals and ammonia a variety of shades can be obtained.

Sulphate of iron, or green copperas, dissolved in water will turn oak a bluish grey tone (avoid using it too strong or you will end with a bright Air Force blue colour). It is sometimes used to make mahogany match up to walnut. As its effect becomes noticeable chiefly when it dries out it should be used with care. It should be practically water-clear, and the effect should be tried on spare wood and allowed to dry out. Sycamore is often treated with it to turn it a grey colour.

Ammonia has a darkening effect on oak. In the best way the liquid is not applied to the wood, but the latter is exposed to its fumes. The whole is placed in an air-tight container, all glue and grease being removed from the surface, and all doors, drawers, etc., opened. The liquid is poured into a couple of saucers, and the container sealed. If an inspection glass is not practicable, a hole should be bored and a piece of the same oak inserted. The time taken may range for ten minutes to several hours in accordance with the depth of colour required, and the size of the container. As some varieties of oak are more readily affected than others, the same kind should be used in any one job.

161

Take care not to bend over the fumes as they are powerful, and may have unpleasant results. Do not directly handle ammonia as it can be painful to the fingers and turn them yellow.

Oil stains. These are usually bought ready made. They have the advantage of not raising the grain, but are not so transparent as water stains, and their effect is different in that they leave a dark deposit in the open grain. After drying they should be given two coats of french polish before any wax polish is applied, as otherwise the stain may be lifted unevenly in patches.

Spirit stains. These again do not raise the grain, but, owing to the rapid evaporation, they require deft and confident handling. On larger surfaces it is difficult to keep the edge alive. They are obtained ready made, or in powder form mixing with spirit.

Aniline dyes. Owing to the colours being bright and somewhat unorthodox from the woodwork angle, the anilines should be used with care. Frequently they are used to add to other stains for toning purposes. Generally the most useful are vandyke brown, a somewhat cold brown used chiefly for oak, black for ebonising, and Bismarck brown, a powerful red used chiefly to tone brown stains. A wide range of colours is available, green, blue, yellow, etc., and they can often be used in finishing toys, etc.

Aniline dye is in powder form and can be obtained soluble in either water or oil. The former can be dissolved in either water or spirits, and if a binder is necessary add a little glue size to the water, or white French polish to the spirits. This spirit-soluble type is often useful to add to french polish to make colour polish. Oil-soluble aniline is dissolved in turps substitute, and in the event of a binder being required a little gold size can be added.

Application of stain. Either a brush or a rag can be used. In all cases keep the edge alive to avoid unsightly joining marks, and finish off along the grain. Before water stain is used the surface of the wood should be damped with warm water, allowed to dry, and glasspapered flat.

Then when stain is applied the grain will not rise unduly. As end grain soaks up the stain more readily and is inclined to turn darker in consequence, the stain should be diluted for these parts. When it has dried go over the surface twice with french polish. This serves to fix the stain.

Filler. Oak is usually polished just as it is, but hardwoods such as mahogany and walnut generally have the grain filled. Various proprietary paste fillers are available. Fillers can be obtained natural (grey) or in various tones to suit the wood. In any case it can always be toned with an oil stain. If too thick, thin out with turpentine. Keep the lid well pressed down as the filler will otherwise harden. It can be applied with a brush or rag, but the latter is used after the initial set has taken place to force the filler into the grain. It is applied across the grain.

For softwoods the usual plan is to use glue size. This can be ordinary glue thinned down until it no longer feels tacky. Thick size remains on the surface, whilst a thin size soaks into the grain and seals the pores. When thoroughly dry it is glasspapered smooth, and the work is ready for polishing. Incidentally, the size cannot be applied over work which has been oil stained. In this case the paste filler must be used.

Chapter fifteen

Adhesives

There is a wide range of adhesives available to the woodworker today. The modern types have largely ousted the older animal or Scotch glue because they are more convenient in use and in most cases are more damp resistant. On the other hand they are generally more expensive. Scotch glue is still widely used in the antique repair trade, and providing that the item is not exposed to damp is an excellent glue if properly used.

Synthetic resin. The UF (*urea formaldehyde*) is widely used in the trade and almost exclusively in the home workshop. It is used cold, is highly damp resistant and is non-staining. Various types are available. One is of syrup form with separate water-like hardener and having only a limited shelf life. More convenient for the small user is the powder form requiring only to be mixed with water when it becomes the same adhesive as the syrup form. Its shelf life is considerably longer. Another powder form of adhesive has the hardener already incorporated and again requires only to be mixed with water. It is an extremely strong, all-round adhesive.

PVA (*polyvinyl acetate*) is a white emulsion ready for use as it is. Several makes are available many of them having resin additives. It is used cold as a general adhesive and has good strength though its resistance to damp is low. It is free from staining though some brands are liable to turn brown on contact with certain woods such as oak.

Casein. This is not used so much as formerly, but is a strong glue in powder form for mixing with water. One drawback is its liability to stain some hardwoods such as oak, mahogany, walnut, etc. It has good damp resistance.

Epoxy resin. This is used mainly for bonding metal to wood. It is in two parts which have to be mixed before setting begins. It has limited use in the woodworking shop, being expensive. For special jobs it is useful and is highly damp resistant.

Animal glue *(Scotch).* A general-purpose strong glue, though it has no damp resistance and cannot be used for outdoor work. It needs to be used hot which entails joints being heated before assembly. Proprietary makes are available which require no heat except in winter time. Animal glue is non-staining and is the only glue that can be used for veneering by the hammer method.

It is obtained in pearl or cake form, the latter requiring to be broken up in sacking. It is placed in the container of a glue kettle, covered with water, and left overnight. The kettle is then heated and the glue stirred. When hot it should run freely from the brush without lumpiness yet without breaking up into drops. Never heat the glue directly over a flame, and avoid boiling it.

Impact. The chief use of this is in fixing plastic laminates to timber, though it can be used in some instances for special veneering jobs. It is applied to both joining parts, allowed to stand a short while and the two brought together when the grip is immediate. It is useful in some repair work of awkward shapes which would be difficult to cramp. It cannot be used for framing joints of any kind because the grab is immediate and such joints as tenons or dovetails could not be pushed home.

Chapter sixteen

Designs

Tea Trolley with Loose Tray

This is a handy item that could be used in the garden as well as in the house. The loose tray enables items to be carried from the kitchen, and is an advantage when steps have to be negotiated. The tray could also be used independently of the trolley. Practically any sound hardwood could be used for the framework though it should match up if possible with the plywood tray. Alternatively the tray could be covered with plastic laminate.

It will be seen that the legs are tapered both upwards from the shelf slats, and downwards to the bottom. The inner edges from shelf to top however, are parallel. Apart from appearance this has the advantage that the shoulders of the rails are square. A simple fixing for the slats is shown in Fig. 2, two thin rails being notched to the legs and the slats sandwiched between.

The legs are shaped and mortised at the top for the

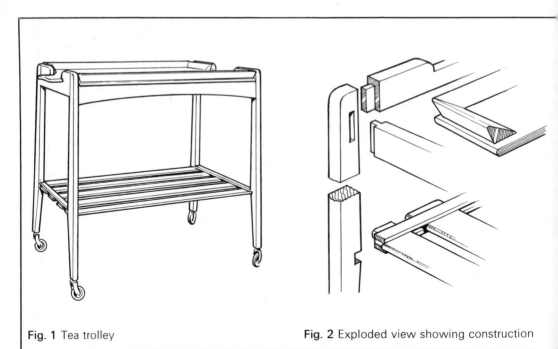

Fig. 1 Tea trolley

Fig. 2 Exploded view showing construction

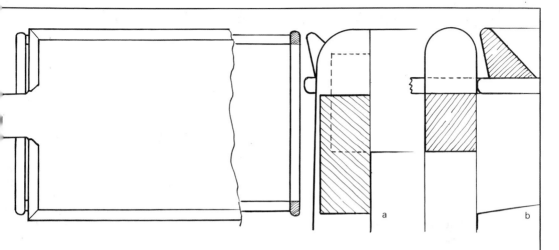

Fig. 3 (above) Plan of top

Fig. 4 (above) Top and tray sections

Fig. 5 (below) Front and end elevations with main sizes

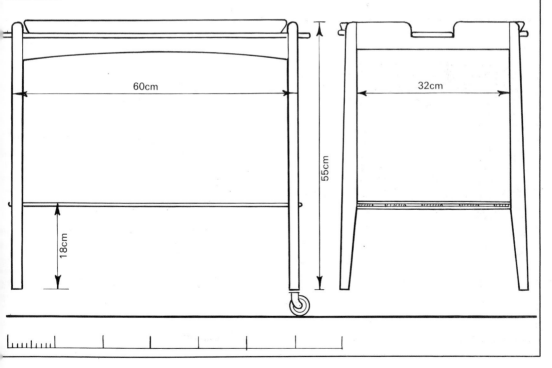

60cm

18cm

55cm

32cm

rails. The end rails are cut away centrally for the tray handles to pass over, Fig. 5. The legs are notched for the twin stretchers carrying the slats, the notches being stopped near the outside face and not carried through. Side rails may be shaped as shown in Fig. 5. They are tenoned to the legs. For additional strength the inside corners could be braced below the tray bottom.

The slats have rounded edges and ends and are held by the two stretchers at each end, the slats projecting slightly. Glue and pin from below. When complete the slatted shelf is housed and glued into the legs, and good stout panel pins driven in diagonally from below into the legs.

An alternative for the shelf is to use a piece of 9·5mm. (⅜in.) plywood, this fitting between the stretchers. In some ways this is an advantage in that cups, glasses, etc. are not liable to fall off. The real purpose of the shelf, however, it to hold a spare tray. It is advisable to use 9·5mm. (⅜in.) thick plywood for the tray, the edges being rounded. If solid wood is used it should be sound and dry.

The rim mouldings are bevelled from a wide piece and sawn down. If the bevelled faces are held temporarily together with pins the opposite edges can be bevelled off with the plane. Attach the mouldings by screwing up through the tray bottom, mitring the corners and slightly rounding off from outside.

Cutting list

Cutting list	Long	Wide	Thick
	cm.	cm.	mm.
4 legs	58	4·5	22
2 rails	36	6	22
1 tray moulding	100	6	22
2 rails	60	5·5	19
1 tray	66	42	9·5
4 stretchers	40	2·5	6·5
5 slats	63	5·5	6·5

Garden Lights

The light can either be made single as in Fig. 1, or a two-frame light can be arranged as in Fig. 2. Sizes can be adapted within a little, but it is wise to keep to the 308mm. (12⅛in.) between the

rebates as this enables the standard 12in. width of glass to be used. At the time of going to press glass is still being made to imperial sizes. Sometimes the glasses are arranged two or three to an opening, in which case an overlap should be allowed.

Body portion. Construction is given in Fig. 2 sizes being made to suit the frame. Tongued-and-grooved boarding is used, and it is as well to arrange the height so that an even number of boards is used front and back, allowing for the unwanted tongues or grooves to be planed away. Put the front and back together independently screwing corner posts flush with the ends and (in the case of the double light) cross pieces in the centre. It is advisable to paint all joining edges before fixing.

The ends are added to these, the two bottom complete boards being fixed first. Place the two top boards in position above them, mark a line across with a straight-edge to give the slope, and cut away the unwanted parts. Screw the sides through the posts at the back, and add the guide pieces. The last named stiffen the whole, though centre uprights can be added if there appears to be any weakness. It is advisable to cut draining grooves along the top sloping edges of the sides. For the two-light frame an inverted T section is made by nailing or screwing two pieces together as in Fig. 2. Notches are cut in front and back to receive it. Punch in all nails as the work proceeds. The holes are not stopped, however, until after the priming coat has been given.

Frame. Sizes are given in Fig. 3. If preferred standard section timber can be used, especially in the case of the bars. If this is done it may be necessary to adapt the sizes to suit. Joints of the main frame are given in Fig. 4, and it will be seen that the bottom rail is thinner than the other since the glass has to lie over it. Consequently a bare-faced tenon is needed. A haunch is cut at the lower end as shown. Note that in all the joints mitres are cut and the wood cut away locally opposite the mortise level with the rebate. The advantage of this is that it enables level shoulders to be cut. In all cases the tenons are taken right through and are wedged from outside.

Fig. 5 shows how the bars are joined to the frame.

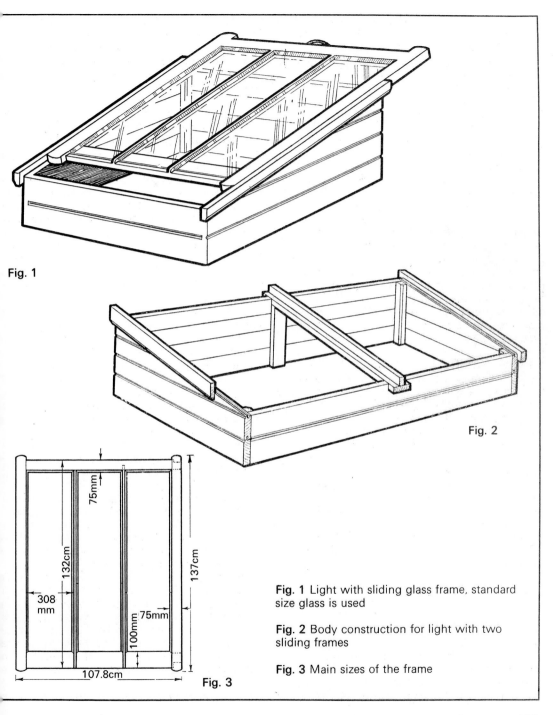

Fig. 1

Fig. 2

Fig. 3

Fig. 1 Light with sliding glass frame, standard size glass is used

Fig. 2 Body construction for light with two sliding frames

Fig. 3 Main sizes of the frame

75mm

132cm

308 mm

137cm

75mm

100mm

107.8cm

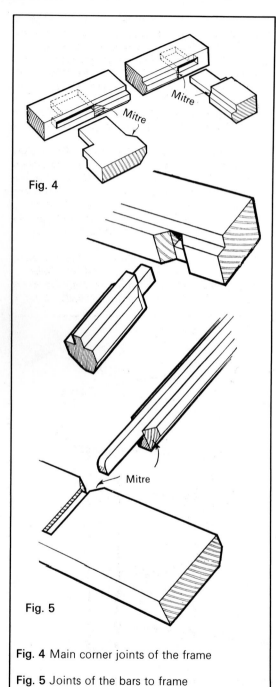

Fig. 4

Fig. 5

Fig. 4 Main corner joints of the frame

Fig. 5 Joints of the bars to frame

At the lower end a notch is cut in the rail to receive the projecting portion, and mitres are cut as before. It is advisable to work a drip groove along the underside of the upper rail to prevent moisture from running down inside. Assemble the whole thing with resin glue. The main tenons of the frame are wedged from outside.

Having levelled the joints go over any knots with knotting. Give the whole a coat of priming including all rebates, and when dry fill in all nail holes, cracks, etc., with putty and carry on with the glazing. Thumb a fillet of putty into the rebate and press in the glass so that it beds evenly, and work an even filling of putty all round. Finish with an undercoat followed by a finishing coat, and keep well painted, paying special attention to end grain, corners, etc. It increases the life of the light if it rests upon a row of bricks all round, or a fillet of cement.

Cutting lists   Single light

Body	Long cm.	Wide cm.	Thick mm.	
6 pieces	107	15	22	T & G
8 pieces	137	15	22	,,
2 posts	64	5	50	,,
2 posts	33	5	50	,,
2 guides	140	10	23	,,
Frame				
2 stiles	140	7·5	50	,,
1 rail	110	7·5	50	,,
1 rail	110	10	38	,,
2 bars	137	4·4	50	,,

Double light

Body				
6 pieces	220	15	22	T & G
8 pieces	137	15	22	,,
2 posts	64	5	50	,,
2 posts	33	5	50	,,
2 guides	140	10	22	,,
1 T piece	140	7·5	22	,,
1 T piece	140	5·5	22	,,

Frames
As single light but double quantities.

ench

ssential requirements of a bench are that it is igid, has a top which is straight and as thick as ossible and which can be completely flush when ecessary, and is provided with strong vice and laning stop. Size is largely decided by the space vailable, but the rule is to make it as large as the vorkshop will allow.

Details. In the bench in Fig. 1 rigidity is ensured by he wide top front rail (apron rail) which is notched ver the legs. The top is dependent upon the naterial available, but assuming that only 25mm. 1in.) stuff is used its freedom from bending is gain helped by the wide front rail. If a thicker top s available it would certainly be better, and the izes in Fig. 2 could be adapted accordingly.

A well is provided, as this enables everyday tools o be kept on top without fouling wide wood

placed on the bench. In addition is a wide shelf for larger tools and appliances, and a tool rack at the back. The bench stop is a block of wood which can be tapped in flush. To help in cutting wood at the rear end of the bench an end stop is provided, this again folding down flush. To support long work when held in the vice a series of 12·5mm. ($\frac{1}{2}$in.) holes is bored in the right hand leg, a dowel placed in one of these affording a useful resting place.

Framework. For the legs 75mm. by 50mm. (3in. by 2in.) stuff is used. Hardwood such as beech, birch or ash is preferable, but softwood is frequently used with success. Square to section and mark out the joints. The back legs are shorter than those at the front to allow for the tool well, and the top end rails are notched accordingly (Fig. 2).

Side rails are tenoned in, those at the top being haunched as in Fig. 2. Bottom and back rails are also tenoned, and to avoid weakening the wood unduly the bottom rails are staggered, those at

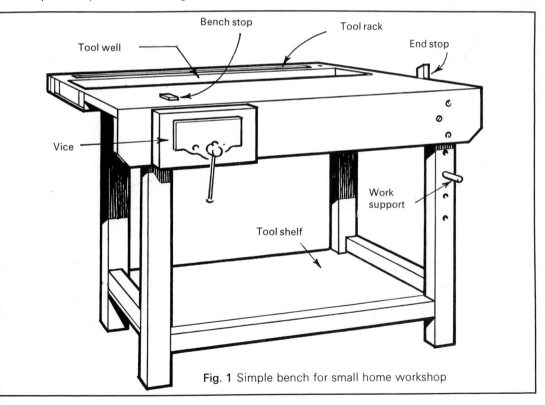

Fig. 1 Simple bench for small home workshop

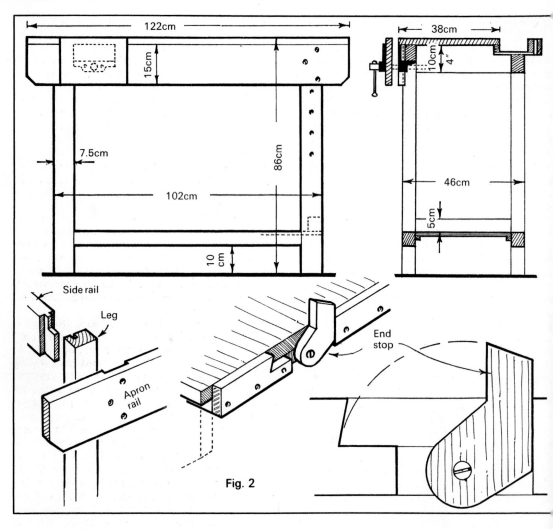

Fig. 2

front and back being immediately below those at the ends. Top front or apron rail (Fig. 2) is not tenoned but is grooved to fit over the face of the legs. A close-fitting joint is essential here as the chief function of this wide rail is to prevent racking.

Glue the two end frames together independently. It is a good plan to draw-bore them. This not only saves having many cramps, but helps to keep the joints tight. The peg hole is bored through the mortise, the tenon cramped in position, and marked by passing the bit into the hole. The parts are

separated and the tenon bored about $1\frac{1}{2}$mm ($\frac{1}{16}$in.) near the shoulder. The pegs should be slightly pointed to enable them to enter easily. The parts are glued when assembling, of course.

The glue having set the front and back rails are added, these again being preferably draw-bored. Finally glue and screw on the apron rail.

Top. If possible use a hardwood such as beech for this. A thickness of 22mm. ($\frac{7}{8}$in.) the minimum; if possible it should be 50mm. (2in.), in which case the top end and back rails would be cut and ositioned to suit. Fix it with screws driven downards into the front rail, recessing the screws and ugging the holes. At the sides pocket screwing is e simplest method, but the holes should be enerous in size to allow for possible movement aused by shrinkage.

he tool tray is like a simple shallow box with dgings nailed or screwed together with a plywood ottom screwed beneath. It is screwed in position, d a tool rack added at the back, this being mply a batten screwed at the back with three stance pieces interposed to enable tools to pass rough.

tops. To receive the bench stop a rectangular ole is cut through the top. The stop itself (of ardwood) is made a tight friction fit in the hole. g. 2 shows how the pivoted end stop can be dded. It is shaped so that it folds down flush when ot in use. Hardwood should be used for it, and an dging should be screwed to the end of the bench s shown. It is not an essential feature and can be mitted if preferred, the bench hook being used r all cross cutting.

ice. This will certainly require a packing block eneath the top, the thickness depending upon the asting of the vice and the thickness of the top. uite possibly too the apron rail will have to be cessed to take it, and slots may have to be cut— ertainly holes to receive the screw and guide bars ill be needed. It is impossible to give exact etails since the vice casting varies in different akes. A strong rigid fixing is essential, and the ce of the vice must be in line with the edge of e bench. In some cases it may be better to fix the asting to the back of the apron rail rather than in ont. A wood check is screwed to the movable w.

he addition of a tool shelf completes the bench. It screwed beneath the side rails, and fillets are dded inside front and back rails to support it as in e side section in Fig. 2.

utting list

	Long	Wide	Thick
	cm.	mm.	mm.
legs	86	75	50
legs	84	75	50
1 apron rail	123	160	25
1 rail	102	75	50
2 rails	102	50	50
2 rails	46	—	50 sq.
2 rails	46	100	50
1 top	123	390	25
1 shelf	103	370	12.5 ply
1 well bottom	123	160	6.5 ply
1 well rail	123	30	22
1 well rail	123	50	25
2 well rails	12	50	25
1 tool rack	123	60	12.5

Coffee Table

This is a simple item to make, consisting of a plywood top with two screwed-on rails beneath into which the legs are tenoned. If preferred the top could have a facing of plastic laminate either in colour or in natural wood finish. Its light weight enables the table to be lifted easily to the chair side.

Cut out the top first. It is in 12·5mm. (½in.) plywood and should preferably be veneered both sides so that it does not tend to pull hollow. If, however, plastic laminate is used there is no bother providing it is put down with contact adhesive. In the latter case two coats of adhesive are advisable on the plywood to give good adhesion. First, however, cut out the top to shape. The curves can be marked out with a lath bent to shape, a pencil being drawn around the edge. A chamfer is worked around the underside as shown in the section in Fig. 1, and the upper corner is rounded. When plastic laminate is to be used the ideal way of cutting is on the bandsaw fitted with a metal-cutting saw. The edge can afterwards be trimmed to a sweet curve, and the lower chamfer worked. Finally the upper corner is rounded.

The two rails are chamfered on their outer edges and ends, and through mortises chopped to take the legs. As the last named slope, the mortises must be cut at a corresponding angle. They must also be wider at the top than at the bottom to allow the wedges to be effective. Fig 3 shows the tenon cut at the top of the leg. Note that the shoulders must be at an angle to give the slope. The ends of the tenon are parallel with the outer line of the leg.

171

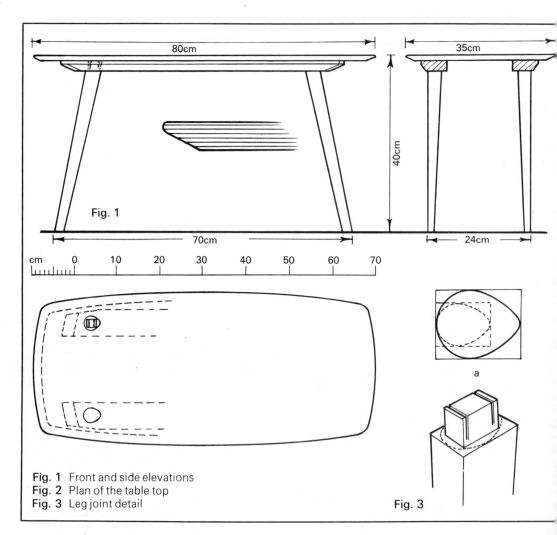

Fig. 1
40cm
80cm
35cm
70cm
24cm

cm 0 10 20 30 40 50 60 70

a

Fig. 1 Front and side elevations
Fig. 2 Plan of the table top
Fig. 3 Leg joint detail

Fig. 3

Fig. 3 shows at A the section shape of the legs. Having cut the joints taper the legs from top to bottom in both width and thickness. In width all the taper takes place at the inside. The same thing applies to the thickness. The rounded oval section is now planed as at A Fig. 3. It is advisable to work all four legs progressively, passing from one to the other in stages. Thus tapered chamfers should be worked first on all followed by the rounding over.

Finally glue the legs to the rails, testing for the correct angle and driving in the wedges. When one leg has been glued the others can be tested against it. Lastly the rails are glued and screwed beneath the top. An excellent finish for all wood parts is plastic lacquer diluted to half strength followed by wax polish.

Cutting list

	Long cm.	Wide cm.	Thick mm.
1 top	81	36	12·5
2 rails	67	6·5	25
4 legs	41	4·5	32

172

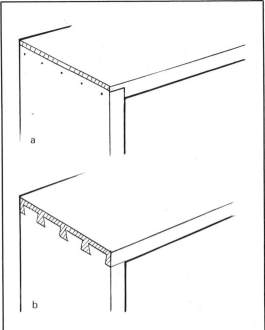

Fig. 1 (left) Room divider with good display space

Fig. 3 (above) Alternative construction of boxes

Cabinet construction. The various parts of the three boxes should be cut to size and veneered on their inner faces. They are then trimmed and the corner joints cut. For a simple job the plain rebated joint can be cut as at (a), Fig. 3. For a better job lap-dovetails can be cut (b). These illustrations show solid wood being used and this may be preferred. For blockboard the dovetails should be fairly large as otherwise the grain is liable to crumble. In the case of the bottom box a centre division is fitted, and this should be housed in. After assembling the carcases the outer surfaces should be veneered. When the glue has set the overhanging veneer should be trimmed, and the front lippings added.

The fronts of the bottom box could either take the form of doors hinged at the sides, or they could be falls hinged at the bottom and fitted with stays to limit the movement. Both sides are veneered, and at the front the veneer should be about 10mm. bare

Room Divider

his would look well with solid parts of mansonia nd Australian walnut veneers, or African mahoany solid members and Honduras mahogany eneers. Veneered parts have a groundwork of lockboard, and it should be noted that the grain f the outer layers of this should be at right ngles with that of the facing veneers.

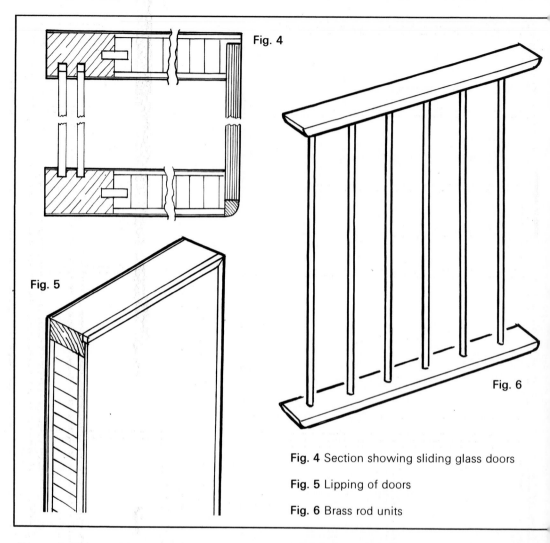

Fig. 4 Section showing sliding glass doors

Fig. 5 Lipping of doors

Fig. 6 Brass rod units

all round. This enables a cutting gauge to be worked round the edges for cross-banding. The waste veneer should be trimmed away before the glue hardens.

In the case of the middle box which has sliding glass doors it is necessary to work grooves near the front edges, and it should be noted that those at the top are double the depth of those at the bottom as shown in Fig. 4, this enabling the doors to be passed upwards and dropped into the bottom grooves. Note that when block-board is used it is

necessary to tongue on facings of solid wood a block board does not lend itself to grooving. Fig. also shows alternative ways of fixing the plywoo backs. At the top is a rebate, but a simple alternative is that at the bottom where the plywoo back is fixed straight on and a quarter-round moul added all round.

Stand. This is a separate construction. It is pu together with mortise and tenon joints. The leg are tapered, and if the tapering is taken righ through as in Fig. 2 the shoulders of the rails mus

174

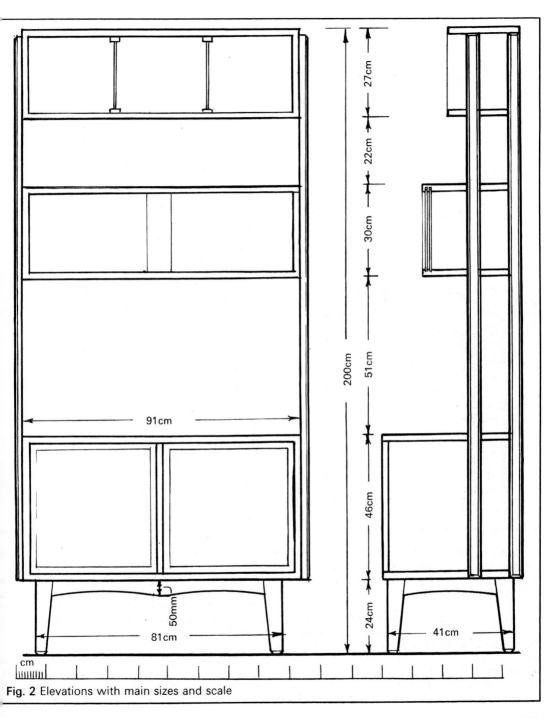

Fig. 2 Elevations with main sizes and scale

175

be at a corresponding angle. Alternatively the shoulders can be square, in which case the tapering must be started below the rails.

Fitting up. The three boxes are held together with two main uprights at each side. They are fixed with screws driven through the box sides into the uprights. Having bored the holes in the boxes, the uprights should be held with cramps whilst the screws are being driven in. It looks neat if the uprights are either chamfered all round or have their edges pencil rounded. The stand is fixed by screwing up from beneath into the bottom box. In the top box two brass rod units are fixed. They are shown in Fig. 6.

Finish. The whole thing should be dismantled as far as possible as this simplifies the finishing. An excellent finish is plastic coating which is brush applied. Several coats are needed, and it can be brought to a brilliant gloss with burnishing cream, or it can be given a semi-matt finish by rubbing over with the finest grade steel wool lubricated with wax polish. Alternatively french polish can be used.

Cutting list

	Long		Wide	Thick
	cm.	mm.	mm.	mm.
2 top and bottom	91	5	235	19
2 ends	27	5	235	19
2 top and bottom	91	5	325	19
2 ends	30	5	325	19
2 top and bottom	91	5	465	19
2 ends	46	5	465	19
1 division	44	—	465	19
1 back	91	—	460	6·5
1 back	91	—	300	6·5
1 back	91	—	270	6·5
2 doors	44	—	450	19
4 uprights	177	—	55	25
4 legs	27	—	—	63 sq.
2 rails	81	—	55	25
2 rails	41	—	55	25

Portable Bird House

There is frequently an advantage in a house that can be moved from place to place. That shown in Fig. 1 is preferably in oak or possibly chestnut. Well made in the first place, and given an occasional coat of preservative, it will last for years.

Post. The main post is made from a 5cm. (2in.) square, and is 147cm. (58in.) long, including the tenons at both ends. Plane it straight, and mark out the joints. Both tenons pass right through, that at the bottom being square in plan (Fig. 3) whereas the top one is in alignment with the grain of the cross-piece in which it fits (Fig. 4). The taper starts just above the struts.

For the feet use 7·5cm. (3in.) by 25mm. (1in.) stuff, halving them together. Blocks 10cm. (4in.) square are screwed on beneath at the ends. Cu

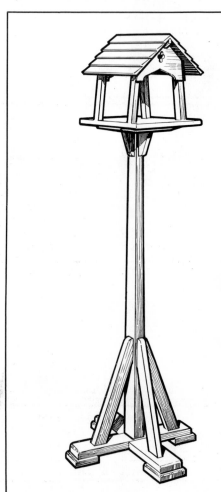

Fig. 1 Portable bird house

e mortise right through the halving, splaying
it in one direction beneath so that wedges can
knocked in. The struts are also tenoned to the
et, but join the post itself with a form of sloping
tch joint as in Fig. 3. Assemble the whole
ing in one operation, fixing the struts on the post,
d adding the base. Resin glue, which is water
sistant, can be used, but it is advisable to peg
e top strut joints.

the top fit the cross-piece, enlarging the mortise
the top so that there is room for expansion when
the wedges are knocked in. Fig. 4 shows how the
brackets fit in sloping notches. If cut as shown they
can be added after the cross-piece is in position.

House. This is made up complete in itself.
Notches are cut in the edges of the floor to receive
the uprights which are screwed in. Remember
that the inner surfaces must be at a slight angle.
Shallow notches at the top receive the gables.
The top slope is not cut until later, when it is made
to agree with the gable slope. A halved joint is
used where the ridge joins the gables. Details

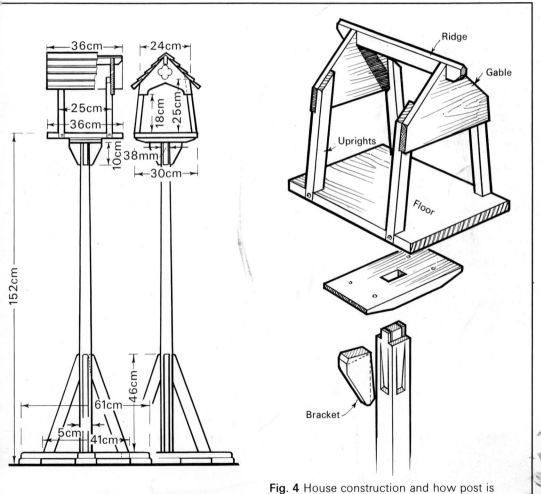

Fig. 2 Elevations with main sizes

Fig. 4 House construction and how post is
joined to it

OW—12**

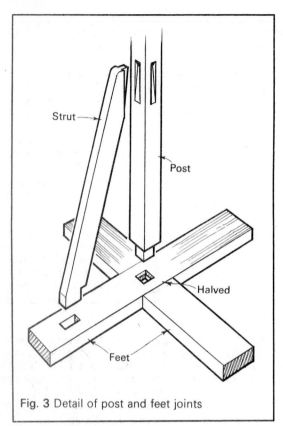

Fig. 3 Detail of post and feet joints

of the shaping and decorative holes in the last named appear in Fig. 2.

Put the parts together with resin glue, screwing or nailing where required. Screws through the cross-piece hold it in position. For the roofing use either plain tapered boarding or the rebated kind.

Assuming that the house is to be natural colour, give a coat of clear preservative and leave to weather naturally. If preferred, a combined stain and preservative can be used.

Cutting list

	Long cm.	Wide mm.	Thick mm.
1 post	150	—	50 sq.
2 feet	62	90	25
4 struts	55	60	25
4 blocks	11	110	25

1 table	37	310	25
4 brackets	12	90	25
1 cross piece	31	170	25
4 uprights	32	—	25 sq.
2 gables	26	190	12·5
1 ridge	37	60	20
10 weather boards	37	75	12·5

Jardiniere

Indoor plants have become extremely popula and this has brought about a revival of th jardiniere, though in revised form to suit mode taste. That shown in Fig. 1 will hold five to s pot plants in the main container at the top, ar several on the bottom rack. The sloping sides the box are the natural outcome of the shape the usual earthenware pots, but if any speci or unusual pots have to be accommodated th size or shape should be altered accordingly.

The box is made up as a separate unit, the leg being fixed to it with screws. Cross-rails t each pair of end legs together, and the slats whic form the rack stiffen the whole. Note that th splay of the legs is desirable to give stability.

Box. This is put together with simple groove joints. Those who have a machine router will fir it a simple matter to work the stopped groove Otherwise they will have to be cut by har methods. A circular saw could be used to part cut them from the bottoms or open end, but would have to be stopped well short of the to stop and finished by hand. Theoretically th groove should be cut slightly out of right angle since both sides and ends slope, forming a con pound angle, but the slope is slight and the ang can scarcely be measured. It can therefore be right angles.

The tongue is easily cut either on the router, th circular saw or with the tenon saw. The tongu is bare-faced, and the first cut should be mad across the grain. Use a fine-toothed saw. Th thickness of the tongue should be gauged at th end, but the cut should not be made at this stag because when the moulding of the main surfac is carried out the shoulders may otherwise b damaged. Lastly, the bottom edges are rebated

Fig. 1 Jardiniere in African mahogany

up with glasspaper wrapped around a block. Begin with Middle 2 grade and finish with No. $1\frac{1}{2}$ or No. 1.

The ends are shaped at the top, this being cut on either the bandsaw or the jigsaw, or by hand with the coping saw. It is cleaned up afterwards with a file, followed by scraper and glasspaper held around a rubber.

It will be seen from Fig. 1 that an inlaid panel is fitted at the front. This is not essential, and can be omitted if preferred. Alternatively, it can be a plain panel with a face veneer of an attractive wood. It is fitted in a recess cut at the front.

When assembling wood blocks should be placed beneath the cramp shoes, with paper beneath to prevent damage to the surface. If not enough cramps are available, cord will have to be tied around and tightened tourniquet fashion. In this case corner blocks are essential. The bottom is screwed in finally.

Stand. Legs are prepared first in square-edged form and are tapered. Stub rails are fitted at the top with the rather special mortise-and-tenon joint shown in Fig. 4. Note that the back edge of each leg is taken off at an angle at the top, this enabling square shoulders to be cut on the stub rails. As the leg has to be planed to an oval section, it is necessary to plane the sides of the rail towards the bottom. The simplest way is to fit the joint whilst the wood is still square-edged and to plane the leg to the oval section. When the joint is put together dry, a sharp pencil can be run around at the shoulder showing clearly the extent to which the rail has to be planed away.

After cleaning up, the legs can be fixed with screws driven downwards through the bottom. By planing the top edge of the rail and leg the latter can be set at any required slope. Short cross-rails are fitted at the ends, and the simplest construction is to cut small flats in the legs in which mortises can be cut. Shoulder length is obtained by direct measurement.

The woodwork is completed by the addition of the bottom slats, which are fixed with brass screws fitted into screw cups. As they must bed down flat, the top edge of the end cross rails must be at a slight angle, and this, of course, must be done

receive the bottom. The rebate will of course have to be stopped on the ends, and this again calls for the use of the router or chopping out by hand methods. The only other alternative is to take the rebate right through and fill in the ends after assembling.

Moulded surface. This takes the form of a stepped effect rather like the appearance of a venetian blind. There are various ways in which it can be worked, but, whichever way it is done, the main idea is first to cut a series of narrow grooves nearly down to the full depth and work the sloping grooves afterwards. The idea is shown in Figs. 2 and 3. The preliminary grooves are worked either on the circular saw, the router, or with the hand plough.

Lastly, the sloping surface is worked with the rebate plane. Finally, the surfaces are scraped to get rid of tears in the grain, and finally it is cleaned

179

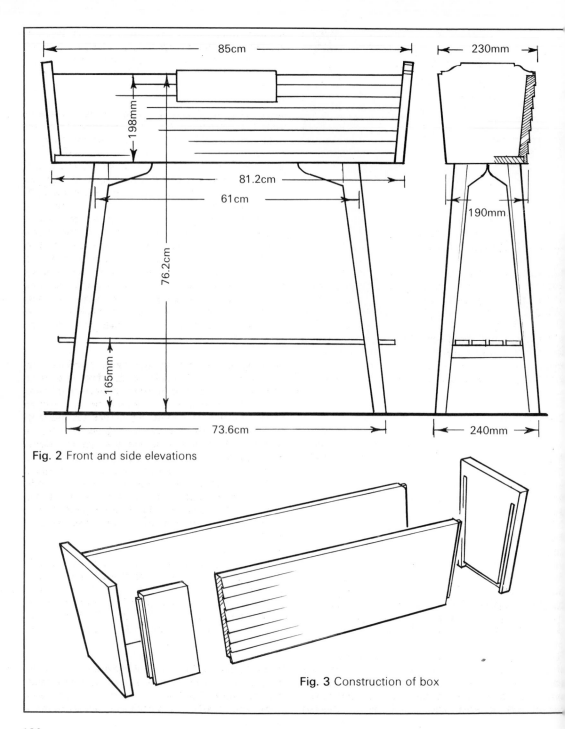

85cm

230mm

198mm

81.2cm

61cm

76.2cm

190mm

165mm

73.6cm

240mm

Fig. 2 Front and side elevations

Fig. 3 Construction of box

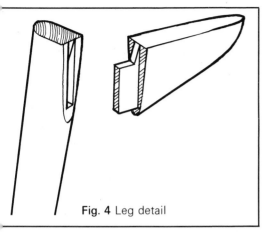

Fig. 4 Leg detail

efore the tenons are glued into their mortises. The nds of the slats are cut off at an angle, so that vhen the four are screwed down they end in a urve.

\ desirable addition to the interior is a metal liner, o that any moisture that may leak out as a esult of watering does not affect the woodwork. t should have a turned-up edging, but this need ot be more than about 25mm. (1in.) deep.

utting list

	Long		Wide	Thick
	cm.	mm.	mm.	mm.
sides	85	0	205	19
ends	—	232	232	19
bottom	81	2	190	12
legs	58	5	55	32
stub rails	16	5	55	32
rails	22	8	32	25
slats	77	5	38	10

ommodious Sideboard n Teak or Mahogany

his has been designed to enable veneered hipboard to be used for the main structure. The dvantage of this material is that it is readily vailable, faced with either teak or mahogany eneer, whereas solid wood in suitable thicknesses is more difficult. The only solid parts in fact are the legs and narrow rails. Sizes can be adjusted to suit individual requirements, though the standard sizes of the material should be kept in mind.

Ideally chipboard should be worked with machine tools, especially if tungsten steel cutters are fitted. This enables parts to be cut off dead to size and with complete accuracy so that only a rub with glasspaper is needed to finish off. Furthermore rebates and grooves, etc. can be easily worked. With purely hand methods it is rather more difficult, though it can be done. First the veneer has to be cut through on both sides with chisel or knife, and the saw cut made immediately to the waste side. It is then a matter of trimming with shaper or plane right down to the line. Chipboard is not a pleasant material to plane because only dust can be removed, not shavings, and the edge of the cutter is soon blunted owing to the abrasive nature of the resin adhesive with which the particles are assembled.

Ordinary joints such as dovetails, mortises and tenons, etc. are scarcely practicable, and it is simpler to use butt joints with dowels as shown in Fig. 3. For this it is an economy in the long run to make a dowelling jig, either for marking out the positions or actually to guide the bit or drill. An alternative is to use the special 'Conti join' fittings made for the purpose. These are screwed inside the carcase and hold the parts together with bolts. The only point to note in this case is that for such parts as drawers, etc. there must be clearance for the fittings, and it will probably mean setting down the drawers accordingly.

The main edges of the chipboard are veneered, but where saw cuts have been made it is necessary to veneer afresh. This is usually best done after the joints have been made. For such parts as drawer sides and backs 9·5mm. (⅜in.) plywood is used, though the fronts are in veneered chipboard.

Main carcase. Cut out all the parts for the main carcase first. Note that although the top rests upon the ends, the bottom is contained between them. Since the back fits against fillets set in from

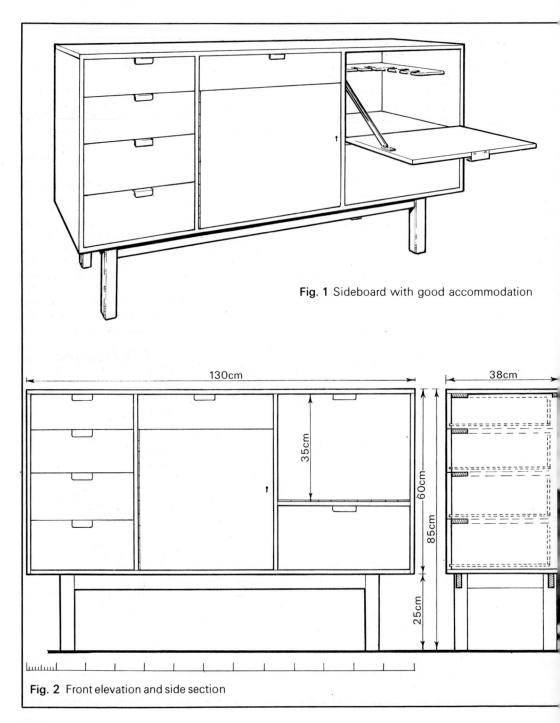

Fig. 1 Sideboard with good accommodation

130cm

35cm

60cm

85cm

25cm

38cm

Fig. 2 Front elevation and side section

he back edges, the ends and top are of the same width. The bottom, divisions, and shelf, however, re narrower by the thickness of the back because he back is fixed directly to their back edges. It vill be found convenient to mark the positions of he drawer runners, shelves, etc. before assembling he whole thing—in fact the runners could be lued and screwed in position at this stage.

Vhen gluing up, cramp the two inner divisions o the bottom, slipping in the centre drawer rail vhilst doing so. If there is a shortage of cramps he work can be then left for the glue to set, roviding that the whole is tested for truth. The nain ends are now added, the drawer rails to the eft and the shelf to the right being put in at the ame time, and the work again set aside. Finally he top is glued down. It will be seen from Fig. 3 hat square fillets are fixed inside the top corners, hese being glued and screwed. They add considerably to the strength. They are set in at the ront by the thickness of the chipboard drawer ronts and flap. The addition of the plywood

back screwed to fillets glued and pinned to the top and ends completes the main carcase.

Stand. At this stage the stand can be made. Solid wood is used throughout. The rails are tenoned to the legs, and there are two intermediate cross rails either dowelled or slot-dovetailed in. Glue the front and back rails to their legs and put aside for the glue to set before adding the end and intermediate rails. Pocket screws are used to fix the stand beneath the main carcase.

Drawers, etc. The most suitable construction is shown in Fig. 4. The plywood sides are fitted into rebates in the fronts. If these rebates are taken right across it is necessary to glue in blocks at the top corners because the sides stand down by the thickness of the drawer rails. It makes a neater job, however, if the rebates are stopped as at A, but it takes rather longer to cut the rebates. At the back through dovetails are used in the best way, though some may prefer the simpler alternative of the grooved joint at B.

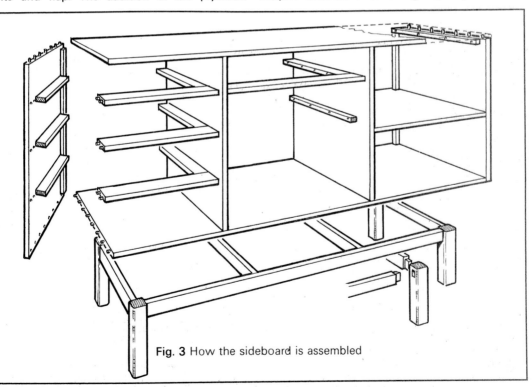

Fig. 3 How the sideboard is assembled

183

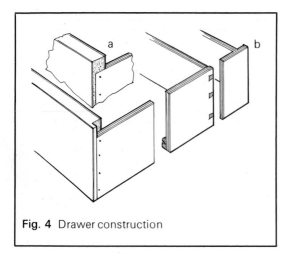

Fig. 4 Drawer construction

The bottom fits in a groove in the front, and in grooved drawer bottom moulding at the sides.

It will probably be necessary to joint two pieces of veneered chipboard for the main door. If the joining edges are veneered the veneer should preferably be removed first. When a close joint has been made four or five dowels should be used to strengthen it. A strip hinge is used to the left and fillets fixed beneath the drawer rail above and to the side of the partition to act as a stop.

For either mahogany or teak plastic coating can be used, or for a dull finish teak oil may be preferred.

Cutting list

	Long cm.	Wide cm.	Thick mm.
			Veneered chipboard
1 top	131	38	17
1 bottom	128	38	17
2 ends	61	38	17
2 divisions	58	38	17
1 shelf	45	38	17
1 door	47	47	17
1 flap	47	36	17
1 drawer front	36	12	17
1 drawer front	36	15	17
1 drawer front	36	17	17
1 drawer front	36	18	17
1 drawer front	46	12	17
1 drawer front	46	22	17
			Ply
1 back	130	60	6·5
1 back	36	10	9·5
1 back	36	13	9·5
1 back	36	15	9·5
1 back	36	16	9·5
1 back	46	10	9·5
1 back	46	20	9·5
2 sides	36	12	9·5
2 sides	36	15	9·5
2 sides	36	17	9·5
2 sides	36	18	9·5
2 sides	36	12	9·5
2 sides	36	22	9·5
4 drawer bottoms	35	35	5
2 drawer bottoms	45	35	5
			Solid
3 rails	36	5·5	22
1 rail	46	5·5	22
4 legs	27	5 sq.	—
2 rails	107	5·5	22
2 rails	35	5·5	22
2 rails	31	5·5	22

Garden Workshop

The shed in Fig. 1 is made in sections to be bolted together. The sizes are given in Fig. 2, but these could be adapted within a little to suit any special requirements.

Framework. For the main framework 50mm. by 38mm. (2in. by 1½in.) stuff is used, though 50mm. (2in.) squares would make a more rigid structure. Cut off the various members to length, and fit the uprights into the horizontals with notched joints. This is stronger than plain butted joints since the notches resist side thrust. Test for squareness with a diagonal rod, and fit the sloping struts.

Covering. The boarding should be from 16mm. (⅝in.) to 22mm. (⅞in.) thick. For thin stuff the rebated joint shown in Fig. 4 is effective. Thicker boards should be tongued and grooved. Cut off the boards full to allow a plane to be run along after fixing. The boarding of the short gable ends finishes flush at the ends, but that of the long sections projects by an amount equal to the thickness of the framing (see enlarged section in ig. 2). The fixing of the boarding to finish flush is obvious, but for the long sides it is advisable to have an odd piece of framing material handy to use as a guide for the projection at the end. Nail to the framework and punch the nails in straight away.

At the window openings the boarding at the sides finishes at the middle of the upright framework member (see Fig. 4). This enables the square fillet (B) to be nailed in afterwards. At top and bottom of the window opening the boarding finishes flush, and it may be necessary to trim the boards back locally. At the bottom a sill with sloping edge and drip groove is cut in and nailed on (Fig. 4), and at top a similar member is fixed. Finally the fillets (A) are nailed all round to make the windows weather-proof. They are set back by the thickness of the window frames.

At the door aperture the boarding finishes at the middle of the uprights similarly to the windows. This allows finishing fillets to be nailed on. To make the door weather-proof fillets are nailed around the opening. The boarding of the door stands in front of the bottom rail of the framework.

Floor. The side frames having been put together the floor should be made. Tongued and grooved 19mm. (¾in.) or 22mm. (⅞in.) boards are desirable. They are nailed down on to four joists at least 50mm. (2in.) square in section. It would make a stronger job to have 75mm. (3in.) by 50mm. (2in.) stuff. If a concrete base is to be laid the floor can rest directly on it. Otherwise a number of brick piers should be used to keep the timber away from the ground. Every joist should be supported at both ends, and preferably at the centre also.

Dig holes for the bricks and consolidate by ramping. Make all as level as possible, using a long straight-edge and spirit level. Lay the floor in position, and erect the sides. Later it may be necessary to carry out some adjustment of the level, and a convenient method is to make pairs of folding wedges in oak and drive these between the joists and bricks at any point where the floor sags. If you stoop down level with the floor and look along, any sag will be at once obvious.

Erecting. Put two adjacent sections together, knock in a couple of temporary nails, and bore two holes right through to receive the bolts. These

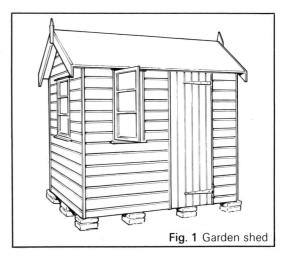

Fig. 1 Garden shed

should be 8mm. ($\frac{5}{16}$in) or 9½mm. (⅜in.) round-heads with square shoulders. Oil the threads, and put washers beneath the nuts.

When all four sections are together the top boarding end of the long sides can be bevelled to align with the slope of the ends. Note also that blocks (X) in Fig. 2 are nailed in on the sloping ends. They serve to strengthen the gable end. The outer corners of the shed are filled with fillets nailed in. Fix them to one side or the other, not both.

Roof. One section of this is shown in Fig. 3. It consists of a series of 16mm. (⅝in.) tongued boards nailed to two purlins. Cut all the boards to length and nail the whole together. The ridge edge is planed at an angle so that a mitre is formed when the two sections are in position. To receive the upper purlin a notch has to be cut in both gable ends. This is essential because, apart from making a close fit, the notch serves to hold the purlin rigidly. The two roof sections should just drop into position.

To hold the roof down screws can be driven upwards through the sloping framing rails of the gable ends into the purlins. Two battens are also fixed to the lower side of the roof with screws driven from the outside. These battens should be level with the inside of the framework. Screws driven through them into the latter hold the roof firmly. When it is not intended that the shed shall

185

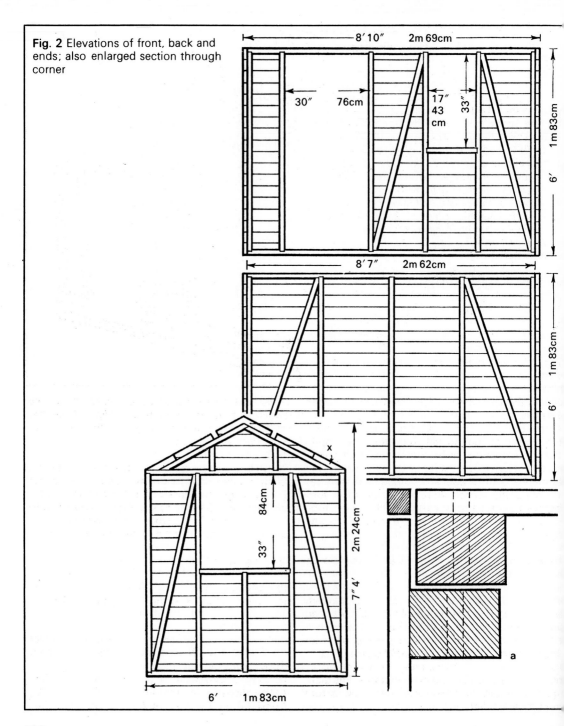

Fig. 2 Elevations of front, back and ends; also enlarged section through corner

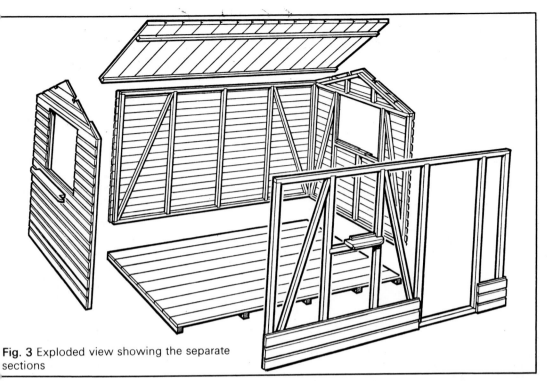

Fig. 3 Exploded view showing the separate sections

ver be dismantled the whole roof can be nailed own.

hree strips of roofing felt run along the length. llow overlap for it to be turned under all round, nd fix the two lower strips first. Hold in position emporarily with a couple of tacks each, and lay e centre strip which will lie right over the apex nd overlap those below by several inches. Tack long the bottom edge using galvanised roofing ails.

he addition of barge boards nailed on at the ends ompletes the roof.

Vindows. These are best made from standard ash material put together with the usual wedged nortise and tenon joint as in Fig. 5. The double vindows can both be hinged, or one can be made close fit and nailed in position. The centre join is nade weather-proof by rebating the joining edges nd inserting a bead in the moving frame. The glass puttied in, but the rebate must be primed before e putty is applied.

Door. In the simplest way this can be the simple ledged and braced type shown in Fig. 5. Note that the ledges stand in at the edges so that they clear the framework.

Painting. Three coats of paint are needed, priming, undercoat, and gloss coat. The former should be given before any of the nail holes, etc., are filled with putty. The first step, however, is to go over all knots with two coats of knotting with a drying period of at least half an hour between.

Cutting list

The covering boards will have to be varied in accordance with the width of material available.

	Long Metres	cm.	Wide mm.	Thick mm.
Gable ends				
12 uprights, struts	1	83	50	38
4 horizontals	1	88	50	38
2 uprights	—	97	50	38

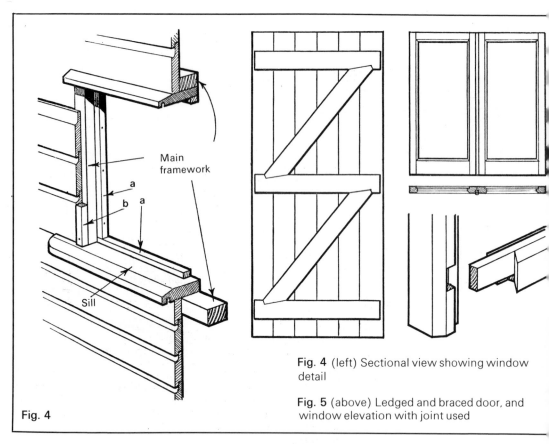

Fig. 4 (left) Sectional view showing window detail

Fig. 5 (above) Ledged and braced door, and window elevation with joint used

Fig. 4

4 roof rails	—	97	50	38
4 uprights	—	31	50	38
2 window rails	—	86	50	38

Long sides

15 uprights, struts	1	83	50	38
4 horizontals	2	70	50	38
1 window rail	—	48	50	38

About 150 metre run of 100mm. (sight) by 16mm. to 22mm. T & G Boarding for covering all four sides. This should be in lengths which will cut economically into 2·70 metres and 1·83 metres lengths.

Door

6 pieces	1	86	150 (sight)	22
3 ledges	—	76	100	22
2 braces	1	10	100	22

Windows

4 sills, drips	—	92	120	22
2 sills, drips	—	56	120	22
8 stiles	—	92 sash mould		
8 rails	—	46 sash mould		

Floor

9 boards	2	70	200	22
5 joists	1	83	50 or 75	50

Roof

32 pieces	1	10	180	16
4 purlins	2	80	50	38

Lengths allow for cutting. Widths and thicknesses are nominal. If the board widths vary the metre run will have to be corrected accordingly.

188

Index